THE MAKING OF THE SECOND WORLD WAR

THE MAKING
OF THE
SECOND WORLD WAR

Anthony P. Adamthwaite
Professor of History, Loughborough University

*Of the uncertainties of our present age the most dreadful
and alarming is the uncertain continuance of reason.*
Samuel Johnson, *Rasselas*

London
GEORGE ALLEN & UNWIN
Boston   Sydney

First published in 1977
Second edition 1979
Third impression 1985

GEORGE ALLEN & UNWIN LTD
40 Museum Street, London WC1A 1LU

© George Allen & Unwin (Publishers) Ltd, 1977, 1979

British Library Cataloguing in Publication Data

Adamthwaite, Anthony
   The making of the Second World War. - 2nd ed. -
   (Historical problems, studies and documents; no. 28)
   1. World War, 1939-1945 - Causes - Sources
   I. Title   II. Series
   940.53'11'08   D741   79-40245

   ISBN 0-04-940057-6

Printed in Great Britain
in 10 on 11 point Plantin
by Hollen Street Press Ltd.,
Slough, Berks.

For my parents

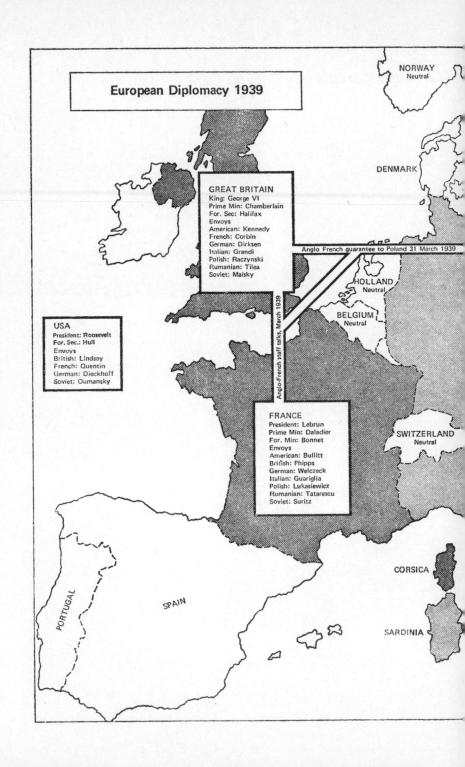

European Diplomacy 1939

NORWAY
Neutral

DENMARK

GREAT BRITAIN
King: George VI
Prime Min: Chamberlain
For. Sec: Halifax
Envoys
American: Kennedy
French: Corbin
German: Dirksen
Italian: Grandi
Polish: Raczynski
Rumanian: Tilea
Soviet: Maisky

Anglo French guarantee to Poland 31 March 1939

HOLLAND
Neutral

BELGIUM
Neutral

Anglo-French staff talks, March 1939

USA
President: Roosevelt
For. Sec.: Hull
Envoys
British: Lindsay
French: Quentin
German: Dieckhoff
Soviet: Oumansky

FRANCE
President: Lebrun
Prime Min: Daladier
For. Min: Bonnet
Envoys
American: Bullitt
British: Phipps
German: Welczeck
Italian: Guariglia
Polish: Lukasiewicz
Rumanian: Tatarescu
Soviet: Suritz

SWITZERLAND
Neutral

CORSICA

PORTUGAL

SPAIN

SARDINIA

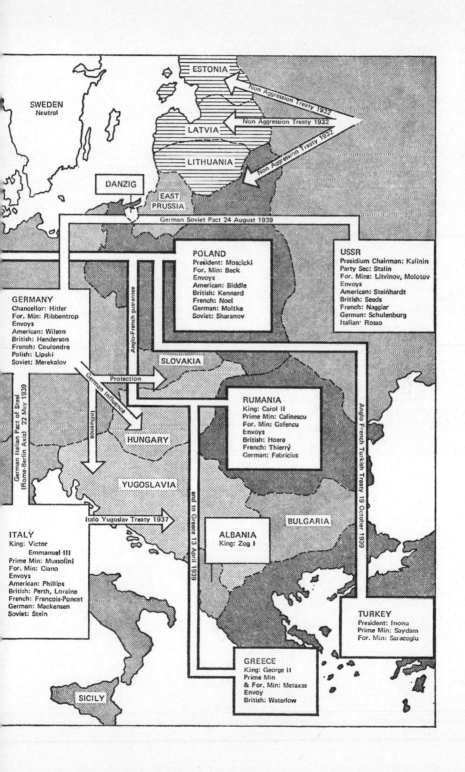

SWEDEN
Neutral

ESTONIA

Non Aggression Treaty 1932

LATVIA

Non Aggression Treaty 1932

LITHUANIA

Non Aggression Treaty 1932

DANZIG

EAST PRUSSIA

German Soviet Pact 24 August 1939

POLAND
President: Moscicki
For. Min: Beck
Envoys
American: Biddle
British: Kennard
French: Noel
German: Moltke
Soviet: Sharanov

USSR
Presidium Chairman: Kalinin
Party Sec: Stalin
For. Mins: Litvinov, Molotov
Envoys
American: Steinhardt
British: Seeds
French: Naggiar
German: Schulenburg
Italian: Rosso

GERMANY
Chancellor: Hitler
For. Min: Ribbentrop
Envoys
American: Wilson
British: Henderson
French: Coulondre
Polish: Lipski
Soviet: Merekalov

Anglo-French guarantee

SLOVAKIA

German Influence

Protection

German Italian Pact of Steel
(Rome-Berlin Axis) 22 May 1939

Influence

HUNGARY

RUMANIA
King: Carol II
Prime Min: Calinescu
For. Min: Gafencu
Envoys
British: Hoare
French: Thierry
German: Fabricius

YUGOSLAVIA

BULGARIA

Anglo French Turkish Treaty 19 October 1939

and to Greece 13 April 1939

Italo Yugoslav Treaty 1937

ITALY
King: Victor
Emmanuel III
Prime Min: Mussolini
For. Min: Ciano
Envoys
American: Phillips
British: Perth, Loraine
French: François-Poncet
German: Mackensen
Soviet: Stein

ALBANIA
King: Zog I

TURKEY
President: Inonu
Prime Min: Saydam
For. Min: Saracoglu

SICILY

GREECE
King: George II
Prime Min
& For. Min: Metaxas
Envoy
British: Waterlow

PREFACE

Though books on the origins of the Second World War are numerous, selections of documents are few. Moreover the chronological limits of specialist studies are often narrow. This selection spans the years 1932-9, with the emphasis in distribution on the late 1930s. In selecting material, I have given preference to French sources because the series *Documents on German Foreign Policy, 1918-1945* is complete for the 1930s whereas the collection *Documents diplomatiques français, 1932-1939* is still in progress. And, alas, many students have little or no French. Constraints of space compelled a choice between an analysis of the causes of the European conflict which began the war and the global conflagration of 1941. I have concentrated on the origins of the European conflict. Again, for reasons of space, rather than offer a relatively superficial treatment of a wide range of topics it seemed preferable to investigate in some depth the unfolding of the international crises that led to war in 1939. I am fully conscious of the consequent omissions, notably of American and Japanese foreign policies. However, my purpose in writing will be served if the introductory essay and documents whet the reader's appetite for the original documents and monographs.

I am grateful to the Controller of HM Stationery Office for permission to quote from Crown copyright records, and also to the Directeur des Archives Diplomatiques for allowing me to use French diplomatic papers. I am grateful also to other owners of copyright material for permission to use it. I have been helped by many librarians and archivists – especially in the Archives Nationales, Paris, and in the Fondation Nationale des Sciences Politiques, Paris, and by the staffs of Birmingham, Bradford and Leeds university libraries.

I have incurred debts to the British Academy for financial assistance; to Professor Arthur Marwick for his kind encouragement; to Mr Maurice Cowling for allowing me to read the typescript of his book *The Impact of Hitler: British Politics and British Policy, 1933-1940* (Cambridge, 1975); to Dr Esmonde M. Robertson for generously supplying me with the texts of Italian documents and for letting me see the typescript of his book *Mussolini as Empire-Builder: Europe and Africa 1932-1936* (London, 1977); to Mr Michael Moorey for kindly translating documents. I am deeply grateful to Professor G. R. Elton and to the publishers for their understanding and patience. My over-riding debt is to Professor W. V. Wallace, whose lectures on this subject I heard as an undergraduate, and who encouraged my research. Lastly, for my wife 'all my thanks, which my heart can conceive' for her 'many travails and Care taken for me'.

ACKNOWLEDGEMENTS

Grateful acknowledgement is made to the following sources of material used in this book.

Jonathan Cape Ltd and A. D. Peters & Co Ltd for *Documents on Nazism, 1919–1945*, eds Jeremy Noakes and Geoffrey Pridham; Chicago Sun-Times for *Ciano's Diary, 1939–1943*; André Deutsch Ltd and Houghton Mifflin Company for *For the President: Personal and Secret: Correspondence between Franklin D. Roosevelt and William C. Bullitt*, ed. Orville H. Bullitt (1973); Ministry of Foreign Affairs of the USSR for material from *Soviet Peace Efforts on the Eve of World War II: Documents and Records*, ed. V. M. Falin *et al.*, parts 1 and 2 (1973); Librairie Arthème Fayard for Georges Bonnet, *Dans la Tourmente, 1938–1948* (1971); Fondation Nationale des Sciences Politiques for extracts from the Léon Blum and Edouard Daladier Papers; Franco Angeli Editore for G. Rochat, *Militari e politici nella preparazione della campagna d'Etiopia: Studio e documenti, 1932–1936* (1971); Cassell & Co Ltd, and David Higham Associates Ltd for *The Diaries of Sir Alexander Cadogan, 1938–1945*, ed. David Dilks (1971); Hutchinson Publishing Group Ltd for Adolf Hitler, *Mein Kampf*, trans. Ralph Mannheim (1969); Macmillan London and Basingstoke for Sir Keith Feiling, *The Life of Neville Chamberlain* (1946); Oxford University Press for the extract from *Soviet Documents on Foreign Policy*, vol. III, 1933–1941, selected and edited by Jane Degras (1953) (published for the Royal Institute of International Affairs); Librairie Plon for extracts from General M. G. Gamelin, *Servir*, vol. II (1946) and from Hubert Lagardelle, *Mission à Rome, Mussolini* (1955); Madame Paul Reynaud for permission to use a letter from the Reynaud Papers; the University of Birmingham for material from the Austen Chamberlain Papers; Harvard University Press for *The Moffat Papers: Selections from the Diplomatic Journals of Jay Pierrepont Moffat, 1919–1943*, ed. Nancy Harvison Hooker (1956); Weidenfeld & Nicolson Ltd, Martin Gilbert, André Deutsch Ltd and Sidney Aster for the map 'European Diplomacy 1939' from Gilbert, *Recent Historical Atlas* and Aster, *1939: The Making of the Second World War*.

CONTENTS

INTRODUCTION: THE MAKING OF THE SECOND WORLD WAR

I

Introduction : Sources and Historiography

The Reformation, the French Revolution, the First World War were episodes so explosive and cataclysmic that the discussion of their origins exercises a perennial fascination. The Second World War is in a similar category. There are several reasons for the attraction it exerts: fashionable nostalgia; the background of intense ideological struggle between fascism, communism and democracy; the decisive contribution of the war to the decline of western Europe from the political pre-eminence enjoyed for four hundred years; the mass of public and private papers – never before have historians been able to write so close to events with the benefit of archives; lastly the fact that it was a peoples' war, involving all the machinery and resources of the modern state.

The Second World War, far more than the First, was vital in the making of the modern world. With its intense ideological character the war was *sui generis*. Although a narrow nationalism and jingoism poisoned the Europe of 1914, nazism was a new phenomenon, posing a more deadly and direct threat to liberal values than the *Weltpolitik* of Wilhelmine Germany. The death camps which reduced the number of European Jewry from a prewar total of $9 \cdot 2$ million to $3 \cdot 8$ million had no parallel in the previous conflict. The war was fought on both sides with a satanic savagery and barbarism, a direct result of ideological frenzy and of the application of technology to war. Physically the fighting was more destructive than in 1914–18. It is estimated that the dead in Europe 'approximated 30 million – a toll half again as great as that of the First World War'.[1] By far the most important military legacy of 1939–45 was the invention of atomic weapons. With the dropping of the atomic bomb on the cities of Hiroshima and Nagasaki in August 1945 a new age began. Man acquired the power to put an end to civilised life.

Politically the results of the 1939–45 struggle were more far-reaching than those of 1914–18. Austria–Hungary and Turkey apart, the First World War left the constellation of European powers almost intact. Germany and Russia were defeated but their restoration as great powers was not in doubt. Europe after 1945 was vastly changed. Of the world's five leading powers in 1919 – Britain, France, Italy, Japan and the United States – the United States alone counted, now transformed into a super power. The key changes were the destruction of Germany and Japan as military powers. Above all Europe was eclipsed, dependent on the two great flanking powers: the Soviet Union and the United States. The effects of the Far Eastern conflict were equally decisive. Japanese conquests irreparably damaged European power in the Far East and prepared the way for post-1945 decolonisation.

The effects of the Second World War on individual countries were cataclysmic. Two examples may be cited. In Britain the war created the centre coalition of May 1940 – in terms of radical reform the most important administration since 1906.[2] Its political and social legacy dominated British politics until the early 1970s. In Germany Hitler's Third Reich and the defeat of 1945 finally modernised German society and broke the hold of the old Prussian ruling class which even under the Weimar Republic had continued to preserve its power and privileges.[3]

The student of the origins of the Second World War faces two major barriers. The first concerns the sources – a mountainous mass of material on many issues, extremely fragmentary on others.[4] The second problem is partly inherent in the subject, partly historiographical. The origins of the war have generated so much controversy that it is difficult for even the most impartial observer to survey the issues with detachment. Let us consider these two problems in order. The serried rows on library shelves of the collections of American, British, Belgian, French, German and Italian diplomatic documents are only the tip of an iceberg. Compounding the challenge of published sources are governmental and private archives as well as archive film.[5] Even if the bulk of the contemporary political and economic record is disregarded, the student of international history is faced with an *embarras de richesse*. The 1967 Public Records Act reduced the traditional rule limiting access from fifty years to thirty.[6] The sheer quantity of material is overwhelming. In 1913 the number of dispatches and papers received at the British Foreign Office was 68,000; in 1938 the figure was 224,000. The French foreign ministry holds more documents for the post-1914 period than for the whole of French diplomacy from the seventeenth century to 1914.

Happily all hope need not be abandoned: *panta rei*, all things move. Historians are themselves a part of history and different historians select and present their material in different ways. 'History', as the Dutch historian Pieter Geyl wrote, 'is an argument without end'.[7] No agreed and final version of events is possible. Seventeenth-century English history remains a minefield of argument.[8] The causes of the First World War still arouse lively debate. It is as well to realise that to many interesting questions there are not and never will be any genuine answers. The

contingencies that shape the unfolding of events will always be a source
of unending inquiry, but they are far too complicated to be totally un-
ravelled.

The sources are also fragmentary. For the late 1930s we have only
incomplete Italian and Japanese documentation, the German archives
were partly destroyed during the war,[9] and many secret French papers
were lost or destroyed. The French record is particularly impoverished
because the governments of the Third Republic did not keep official
minutes of their deliberations. Thus there is nothing to parallel the British
collections of Cabinet papers dating from 1916. Yet even the British papers
have alarming gaps. At the Dominions office 'all significant papers on
foreign affairs have been destroyed under statute' and Foreign Office
decisions on the dominions cannot be fully assessed because 'the dominions
intelligence files for 1938 have been destroyed'.[10]

The record is incomplete in another respect. The papers open to inspec-
tion do not include the 'missing dimension' of international history –
intelligence reports.[11] Only recently has it been revealed that, thanks to
the possession of a copy of the German army's coding machine 'Enigma',
allied leaders in 1939–45 were able to intercept lop-level German operational signals.[12] The record discloses only tantalising glimpses of pre-1939
intelligence activity. Under present policy all intelligence files are closed,
even after the normal thirty years have elapsed.

'Beware of documents,' counselled Clemenceau. Mesmerised by the
official memoranda, the forager in the Public Record Office may end up
writing official history, perpetuating the Establishment's own reading of
its problems and policies. There are other pitfalls for the unwary. The
German, Italian and Soviet documents have built-in limitations. The
intensely personal, idiosyncratic style of the totalitarian regimes has left
few traces in the diplomatic record. Hitler distrusted his diplomats. In
the late 1930s he did not keep a diary and wrote few private letters or
memoranda. The process of decision making in the democracies is often
no clearer. The British and French papers, while indicating what decisions
were reached, are sometimes silent about the way in which they were
reached. In 1938 the outcome of two Anglo–French conferences was
decided in private conversations between the British and French prime
ministers.

This barrier to understanding is supplemented by another – concealment. The evidence is rarely doctored or deliberately misleading. The
French foreign minister in 1938–9 was accused of having doctored certain
telegrams from the French legation in Prague during the Czechoslovak
crisis. But his accuser, the former French envoy to Czechoslovakia, could
not produce any written evidence to corroborate the charge. The truth
will probably never be known because the texts in the French archives
are based on copies supplied by the French foreign minister.[13] Often the

reasons given for a particular decision may not be the most important. When an action has to be taken for an unavowable reason a specious statement may be supplied for the record. In December 1937 a new post of chief diplomatic adviser was established for Sir Robert Vansittart, permanent under secretary since 1930. Sir Maurice Hankey, secretary to the Cabinet, sent two letters to the ambassador in Paris. One was a 'discreet' typewritten explanation which could be shown to the prime minister. The other was a 'more informative' handwritten letter, giving the real reasons for the change.[14]

Pressures towards concealment increased between the two world wars. Before 1914 ministers and their servants assumed that, excepting the occasional publication of government Blue Books, secrets could be locked away indefinitely. After 1918 the new internationalism, with its call for open covenants and support for the League of Nations, forced a break with tradition. Moreover the former belligerents continued the propaganda war by publishing collections of documents on the origins of the conflict. Consequently ministers and functionaries became much more wary about putting pen to paper. In the 1930s the editors of the *Survey of International Affairs* found that 'information was harder and harder to get because governments were all becoming much more cagey about their activities'.[15] Civil servants could not trust their political masters. Sir Eric Phipps, ambassador in Berlin, sent home caustic vignettes of Field Marshal Hermann Göring. The first dispatch of 13 June 1934 was circulated to the Cabinet and was believed to have leaked in Berlin. An equally caustic dispatch of 22 March 1935 was kept in the Foreign Office in order to prevent further leakages.[16]

The diplomatic record is also deficient for another reason. The British and French foreign offices were much less important in shaping policy than they had been before 1914. The emphasis on personal meetings between heads of government undermined the influence of foreign ministers and career diplomats. The common opinion that secret diplomacy had been a prime cause of conflict in 1914 engendered a distrust of the professionals. In Anglo–German relations, for example, economic and defence issues came increasingly to the fore after 1931, with the result that 'the first and often the last word . . . was spoken by the Treasury or the Bank of England or the service departments rather than by the Foreign Office'.[17]

The memoirs of the period rarely compensate for documentary inadequacies. They are always tendentious and frequently mendacious.[18] Prime movers of events usually remember only what they wish to remember. Memory quickly fades. When writing *The World Crisis* (4 vols, 1923–9), Winston Churchill found that a number of major events in which he was personally involved had completely passed from his mind.[19] For the 1930s the best-known memoirs are those of Sir Anthony Eden

(Lord Avon).[20] Contrary, however, to the argument of the memoirs, Eden, who was foreign secretary from 1935 to 1938, was not a consistent opponent of the German and Italian dictators. It can be argued that he raised no fundamental objection of principle to the Hoare–Laval Plan until its terms became public knowledge. In November 1936 Eden agreed to the opening of Anglo–Italian conversations which led to the 'Gentleman's Agreement' of January 1937. Again, it was the foreign secretary, not the prime minister Neville Chamberlain, who in July 1937 urged that a new approach be made to Italy. In the memoirs Eden presented the Nyon Conference of September 1937 as an alternative to appeasement. At Nyon, Britain, France and the Soviet Union agreed to joint naval action in the Mediterranean in order to put a stop to Italian attacks on ships trading with Republican Spain. Eden implied that Nyon might have been the foundation of an anti-fascist front. At the time, however, an anti-fascist front was the very last thing Eden wanted. He fought hard to exclude the Soviet Union from the conference.

As important as the documentary *lacunae* are the unspoken assumptions that guided European policy makers. Two key ideas were taken for granted. First, a sense of superiority and self-sufficiency. Witness the Four Power Pact of 1933 and the Munich Agreement of 1938. Even such a sharp critic of contemporary society as the historian R. H. Tawney shared this assumption of superiority: 'He found the Russian revolution interesting; toward America he was . . . vaguely curious, open-minded and a shade condescending. But neither country impinged upon Tawney's Britain, which he saw as a fixed "Middle Kingdom".'[21] The second idea taken for granted was the belief that war still 'retained a national function as well as some rational purpose . . . it still brought adventure to everyday lives when it occurred; and by demanding great sacrifices it still generated or regenerated social unity.'[22] So much has been said about the pacifist temper of the time that it is easy to forget the preoccupation with war. The 'expectation of a coming war became an insistent part of the consciousness of the 'thirties . . . It enters into . . . some of the best work of the decade's best writers, as a central image.'[23] In 1939 some men eagerly enlisted – the 50-year-old publisher and historian Guy Chapman, a survivor of 1914, volunteered in 1939 because 'my fear was that I might not be given the chance to relive years when I was contented and sensuously alive at a deeper level than it had seemed possible I could ever be again'.[24]

The popular stereotype of the origins of the Second World War was that of a wicked Hitler plotting a war of conquest, opposed at the eleventh hour by the timorous democracies who had whetted his appetite by shameful surrenders. The classic statement of this view was the book *Guilty Men*, published in July 1940.[25] In historical writing the morality-play theme was enshrined in Sir John Wheeler-Bennett's *Munich:*

Prologue to Tragedy (1948) and in the writings of Sir Lewis Namier.[26] As late as 1963 Martin Gilbert and Richard Gott in *The Appeasers* echoed the sententiousness of their elders.

Why did this interpretation prove so enduring? One reason was that the 'facts' seemed to support it. Such was the gigantic scale and destructiveness of the war and its devastating aftermath that it was readily assumed that the war was the result of premeditated aggression. In retrospect, therefore, the failure to defend Austria and Czechoslovakia against Germany in 1938 seemed a betrayal of western interests. Another reason was the durability of wartime myth. The war created new regimes in Britain and France. Churchill's centre coalition of May 1940 marked a watershed in British politics, the collapse of interwar conservatism and the ascendancy of the Labour Party. The need for national and political survival led to denigration of the Baldwin and Chamberlain Cabinets. *Guilty Men* was prefaced by Churchill's words: 'the use of recriminating about the past is to enforce effective action at the present'. The coalition survived and claimed to have won the war. Victory against the Axis and the promise of postwar social and economic reconstruction was contrasted with prewar domestic and foreign failures. People were persuaded by the propaganda of the time that this was 'their finest hour', an age of virtue after years of class conflict and economic misery.

In France the Third Republic which fell in July 1940 was anathema to both the Vichy regime of Marshal Pétain and the Free French movement of General de Gaulle. After the liberation of France in 1944 national regeneration seemed conditional upon assigning the responsibilities for war, occupation and collaboration. Wounded national pride found its heroic legend in the *Maquis*. The strength of this legend was shown in 1971 when the film *Le Chagrin et la pitié*, depicting the acquiescence of many Frenchmen in the occupation and even their collaboration, was banned from French television.[27]

Finally, the ideological conflict between liberal capitalism and communism which preceded the Second World War continued to influence assessments of the 1930s. In Stalinist eyes appeasement was a capitalist conspiracy aimed at turning Germany against the Soviet Union: 'As far back as 1937 it became perfectly clear that a great war was being hatched by Hitler with the direct connivance of Great Britain and France.'[28] Western cold-war warriors were determined to avoid the surrenders of the 1930s. On four major issues – postwar planning, the Truman doctrine, the decisions to intervene in Korea and in Vietnam – American policy makers were crucially influenced by the received wisdom about British and French foreign policies in the 1930s. Sir Anthony Eden described the theme of his memoirs as 'the lessons of the thirties and their application to the fifties'. His efforts as prime minister to apply 'the lessons' contributed to the disastrous Suez Crisis of 1956.[29] Thus from the 1940s to the 1960s appeasement and Munich were political smear words, signifying a policy of retreat, surrender and betrayal.

Revision began in the late 1950s. A. J. P. Taylor's *The Origins of the Second World War* (1961) was a frontal assault on the orthodox version. The war had 'little to do with Hitler' and the 'vital question' was why Britain and France failed to resist Germany before 1939.[30] With the massive release of public and private archives in the late 1960s a new picture emerged. Appeasement, it was stressed, far from being a policy of fear and cowardice, was a realistic search for European *détente*, propelled by a deep detestation of war and the conviction that Germany had genuine grievances. Military and economic weaknesses combined with worldwide threats to British and French power left the statesmen with no choice but to conciliate the dictators. Above all, the policy met with wide public sympathy.[31] Reinterpretation readily becomes rehabilitation. Maurice Cowling's impressively documented *The Impact of Hitler: British Politics and British Policy, 1933–1940* (1975) gives a much more sympathetic portrait of Neville Chamberlain than previous studies.

The reassessment of German foreign policy also began in the 1950s. Controversy centred on Hitler's ultimate aims. In 1939 Hermann Rauschning, a former nazi who claimed to have been one of the Führer's familiars, had warned that Hitler was the 'beast from the abyss', an anti-Christ rather than an anti-Bolshevik, aiming at world domination.[32] At the Nuremberg Trials the defendants were charged with a 'conspiracy' against peace, but the judges admitted their inability to decide 'whether a single master conspiracy . . . had been established by the evidence'. Professor H. R. Trevor-Roper argued that Hitler's primary purpose was *Lebensraum* in the east, not conflict with the west.[33] According to A. J. P. Taylor, 'Hitler did not make plans – for world conquest or for anything else. He assumed that others would provide opportunities and that he would seize them.'[34]

The version which emerges is that of a Hitler driven forward by a mixture of power politics and ideology, aiming at continental hegemony and world-power status and ultimately at world domination. However, *Weltherrschaft* was reserved for the dim, distant future. Mastery of Europe, however, implied much more than a *Drang nach Osten*. It meant the defeat of the western democracies, colonies in Africa, and a powerful navy with bases in the Atlantic. But Hitler never planned a great war to achieve his ambitions. On the contrary he was determined not to repeat the Kaiser's mistake of taking on a worldwide coalition. Opponents would be isolated and tackled separately. Flexibility and improvisation marked Hitler's pursuit of his aims. None the less the long-range vision of world-power status leading ultimately to world domination remained unchanged.

This essay has two main themes: first, the need to avoid what F. W. Maitland called 'after-mindedness'[35] – there was nothing foreordained about the Second World War. The war in the way that it came about was an avoidable one. Second, there is the theme of the interplay and interdependence of internal and external conflict. The war was in part a European civil war, reflecting a general breakdown in European society which had its origins in the years before 1914. The defects of the 1919 peace settlement exacerbated the First World War's legacy of international instability, but the international system remained remarkably resilient until the end of the 1920s. Though the world economic crisis of 1929–33 hastened the political and diplomatic dissolution of Europe, the process need not have ended in war. There were turning-points on the road to 1939. The disintegration of the European security system was a cumulative, self-reinforcing process. Each major explosion generated the heat required to ignite the next. The Abyssinian crisis of 1935–6 was crucial in this respect. But the appeasement pursued until March 1939 proved fatal because it was a policy of meeting German and Italian demands without insisting on firm reciprocal advantages.[36] It rested on the false premise that Hitler's aims were limited – limited to preponderance in central and eastern Europe, with some economic and colonial satisfactions. The alternative was the creation of a solid Anglo–French military alliance. Such an alliance would have deterred Mussolini in 1935, and probably Hitler in 1938.

Aftermath, 1919–29

International instability was a permanent feature of the interwar years. The balance of power which had broken down in 1914 was completely shattered in 1918. The war showed that Germany, with only modest help from Austria, could defy a coalition of four leading European powers – Britain, France, Russia and Italy. Only the intervention of the United States in 1917 saved the Entente powers from defeat or deadlock in the west.

Though vanquished in the west, Germany was victorious in the east. By the armistice of 11 November 1918 the allies acknowledged the survival of German power. The armistice provisions were designed to prevent Germany from continuing the war. *Ipso facto* the allies tied their own hands, because the armistice was concluded with representatives of the new Weimar Republic, and the preservation of that government against Bolshevism became a major allied interest.[1] Only a moderate and stable German government could be relied upon to honour the armistice conditions. But Germany remained a great power and sooner or later she would contest the verdict of 1918.

Of the five treaties which together made up the Peace of Paris, the Treaty of Versailles signed with Germany on 28 June 1919 was by far the most important.[2] Germany lost Alsace and Lorraine to France, Eupen and Malmédy to Belgium, Posen and West Prussia to Poland, the ports of Memel and Danzig to the allies (Danzig was made a free state under League of Nations administration). Plebiscites were to decide the future of Upper Silesia, Schleswig and the Saar. The Saar was placed for fifteen years under international administration. Germany lost all her colonies and was disarmed, her army was limited to 100,000 men and the east bank of the Rhine was demilitarised to a depth of 50 miles. The Rhineland was placed under allied administration for fifteen years. Occupation costs were to be borne by Germany. Of the economic clauses the most contentious was Article 231, the War Guilt clause, covering the payment of reparations. Germany had to accept 'responsibility . . . for causing all the loss and damage . . . as a consequence of the war imposed . . . by the aggression of Germany and her allies'. The use of the word 'aggression', the source of so much international misunderstanding between the wars, reflected the practical convenience of the drafter, not a deliberate moral indictment.[3]

The peace settlement confirmed the existing instability because it lacked moral force. Almost to a man Germans denounced the *Diktat* of Versailles. More important though were the dissensions and doubts of the peacemakers. The best-known critic of the settlement was John Maynard Keynes, a member of the British delegation to the peace conference. His devastatingly destructive treatise, *Economic Consequences of the Peace*, was published in December 1919 and translated into nine languages within a year. Keynes argued that the financial and economic chapters of Versailles were unjust and unworkable. Reparations would be a millstone hung about Germany's neck, preventing not only her recovery but also the recovery of Europe as a whole. In truth, however, 'Keynes's demonstration of Germany's incapacity to pay a sum of more than £2,000 million . . . rested on a completely static and neoclassical concept of economics, and was fallacious. It did untold harm in supporting the Germans' contention that they were unable to pay.'[4]

One reason for German resentment was the fact that they had been encouraged to expect a treaty inspired by President Woodrow Wilson's Fourteen Points. In fact the principle of self-determination was applied only when it worked against Germany, for example in the creation of the Polish Corridor. It was ignored when it would have worked in Germany's favour. The peace treaty with Austria prohibited an *Anschluss* with Germany. The War Guilt clause was also resented. Yet at the heart of the matter was *amour propre*. Germany would not accept her defeat and would almost certainly have resented any peace treaty however mild.

So much was said at the time and afterwards about the Carthaginian peace that it is easy to overlook the crucial fact that Versailles was a defeat for France. 'This is not peace, it is an armistice for twenty years,' pronounced Marshal Foch, allied generalissimo. He pleaded in vain for his country to be given the left bank of the Rhine. Instead of territorial pledges France accepted an Anglo–American treaty of guarantee which fell through in October 1919 when the United States Senate refused to ratify Versailles. To say that the treaty of guarantee offered only a 'paper security', since American and British forces could not have landed in time to prevent a German invasion, is to ignore the vital element of confidence.[5] France's failure to maintain her primacy after 1919 was due in part to the erosion of political will. An Anglo–American treaty would have buttressed French morale. In the event the treaties weakened France's position in Europe. The re-creation of an independent Poland destroyed much of the usefulness of a Franco–Russian alliance since Germany had now no common frontier with Russia and Russia was unable to put direct pressure on Germany. Moreover the establishment of Poland out of German and Russian territory gave both powers a common interest, a possible prize.

Much more can be said for the peace settlement than was conceded at the time. In the perspective of more recent history Versailles was a brave attempt to deal with intractable, perhaps insoluble, problems. Peace-making went on for five years after the armistice of 1918, but after 1945 the process went on in Europe for nine years, with Japan for eleven years, and no peace treaty has been concluded with Germany. The Paris peace conference has been compared unfavourably with the Congress of Vienna. The comparison is not a fair one. The collapse of four empires in Europe and the Middle East confronted the Paris statesmen with problems on a scale which no previous peace congress had encountered. The pressures were enormous. The conference met against a background of bloodshed, violence and economic disruption which had not been experienced since 1848.[6] The Vienna statesmen safely ignored the incipient nationalism of their world; allied leaders in 1919 were presented with a *fait accompli* – self-determination in central and eastern Europe was a reality. The Europe of 1815 was a self-contained system; in 1919 the old balance of power had gone for ever. Russia, a central link in the pre-1914 balance, was torn by civil war and absent from the conference. The United States disavowed Wilson's work and withdrew from Europe.

What augured ill for the future was the territorial settlement in central and eastern Europe. The collapse of Austria–Hungary left a vacuum. The confirmation of national self-determination created new sources of tension. Ethnic minorities were included in the Succession states in order to give them political and economic viability – Sudeten Germans and Poles under Czechoslovak rule, Germans under Poland. The remnant of Austria seemed too small to survive. The new states of Czechoslovakia and Poland were at daggers drawn. In 1919–20 Poland had to fight for her existence against Bolshevik Russia. The little *Entente* states of Czechoslovakia, Romania and Yugoslavia were menaced by Hungary, embittered by territory lost at the peace conference.

The moral consensus underpinning the pre-1914 balance of power was destroyed. The peace settlement was perforce an uneasy compromise between old-fashioned power politics and the internationalism enshrined in the Covenant of the newly established League of Nations. But the new dispensation was flawed by the fact that the Covenant was part of the peace treaty with Germany. In German eyes, therefore, the League was seen as a weapon for enforcing the territorial settlement.

Versailles left unsolved the problem of Germany. The withdrawal of the United States and the exclusion of Russia left Britain and France to shoulder the burden of peacekeeping. Italy, disappointed in her hopes of spoils from the dissolution of the Ottoman and Habsburg empires, had no loyalty to the settlement. Japan had profited from alliance with the *Entente* but was too remote to be able to contribute to European security. Neither Britain nor France had the power or the will to uphold the settlement. The foreign policies of both countries were sharply circumscribed by the consequences of the war. They were not powers by virtue of their intrinsic strength, as the United States and the Soviet Union were fast becoming between the wars. With Germany disarmed and Britain rapidly disarming, France was the leading military power in Europe. But her military primacy masked an underlying weakness. Bled white by the carnage, deprived of the Russian alliance and Anglo–American guarantee, overwhelmed by the cost of paying for the war and restoring the devastated regions, France was preoccupied with her own security. The determination to avoid a repetition of the holocaust was one of the main influences shaping French policy. Edouard Daladier, French prime minister, justified his Munich policy on the grounds that France must 'not sacrifice another million or two million peasants'.[7]

British and American condemnation of France's insistence on reparations has coloured historical writing.[8] For example, the figure for the German reparations debt widely cited in general histories of the period is 132 milliard gold marks. In fact the debt established in May 1921 was put at a nominal value of 50 milliard gold marks. What is also little known is that Germany had offered to pay a much larger amount less than a fortnight before. German propaganda, assisted by western critics, made the most of the burden of reparations, but the settlement was perhaps not unfair or unpayable. Arguably the key to the reparations problem lay not in Berlin or Paris but in Washington. By withdrawing into political and economic isolation and insisting on allied repayment of war debts the United States made European recovery extremely difficult.

The limits of French power were illustrated in 1923 when France, assisted by Belgium, occupied the Ruhr to enforce payment of reparations.[9] In 1924 the French government accepted the Dawes plan which settled the question for the next five years. But the modest financial gains of the Ruhr action were greatly outweighed by the blow to France's international standing. Anglo–American goodwill was forfeited and British suspicions that France wanted to keep Germany down indefinitely were confirmed. The military occupation increased the internal stresses in German democracy. Germany recovered her prosperity, but the memory of the 1923 episode – hyperinflation, middle-class impoverishment, the humiliation of having French colonial troops on German soil – contributed to the collapse of Weimar after 1929. 'Having been robbed, the Germans became a nation of robbers,' wrote Thomas Mann.[10]

French weaknesses would have mattered less if Britain had been a strong and sure partner. But for reasons of geography, natural resources and population the position of world dominance which Britain held before 1914 could not survive the rise of the United States, Japan and the Soviet Union. British strength had always been overextended even at its zenith in the 1880s and 1890s. The *Pax Britannica* was upheld by what has been aptly termed a 'mirage of power'.[11] The First World War eroded British power and created a new sense of insecurity. Sea power was no longer sufficient. The development of air power placed Britain's frontiers on the Rhine. Britain's dethronement as the supreme naval power was formalised by the Washington Naval Treaty of 1922. The old two-power standard of prewar days – the principle that the Royal Navy should be as strong as the next two most powerful navies in the world combined – was sacrificed. Japan stepped into Germany's shoes as a leading naval power. In effect Britain and the United States handed over to Japan strategic command of the western Pacific. The implications of the Washington Treaty became clear in the Far Eastern crisis of 1931-3. Under American pressure Britain abandoned in 1921 the Anglo-Japanese alliance of 1902.[12] Rearmament was not considered until the early 1930s. The Ten Year Rule, introduced in 1919, assumed that at any given date no major war need be expected within ten years. In 1928 Winston Churchill, chancellor of the exchequer, established the rule as permanent. It effectively lapsed in 1933-4.[13] Economic changes contributed to Britain's loss of power. By 1914 British industries lagged behind those of Germany and the United States. After 1918 the cushion afforded by inherited wealth gradually disappeared. Correlli Barnett's thesis that the British governing classes were emasculated by public school Christianity, liberalism and imperial pretensions is not without some truth.[14]

Imperial responsibilities imposed new constraints on British and French policy makers. Participation in the war imbued the dominions with a confidence and taste for full independence, demonstrated in their demand for separate delegations to the Paris peace conference. The Chanak episode of September 1922, which brought Britain to the verge of war with Turkey, exemplified the trend towards full sovereignty. When dominion governments were invited to send contingents to help Britain against Turkey their replies were Laodicean, to say the least. Only New Zealand expressed mild interest. By the Balfour resolutions of the Imperial Conference of 1926 and the Statute of Westminster of 1931, Australia, Canada, New Zealand and South Africa were authorised to conduct their own internal and external policies.

The First World War speeded the winds of nationalist revolt against European colonial rule. France, the second greatest colonial power, faced challenges in her North African territories, in Mandated Syria and in Indo-China. There were insurrections in Syria in 1925 and 1936. A joint Franco-Spanish expedition was required in 1926 to crush the rebellion of the Moroccan leader, Abd-el-Krim. France had to transfer abroad a third of her military strength.[15] Britain's main anxieties were Egypt and India. After 1929 unrest in India tied down substantial forces. In the same year an Arab revolt against Jewish immigrants broke out in Palestine, then under British Mandate. The bulk of the regular army was posted to

Palestine. In the late 1930s Italian propaganda was active in the Middle East, inciting Arab nationalism against British and French rule.

This running fight against nationalist revolt was a constant drain on the energies and resources of the two leading colonial powers. The expenditure of so much blood, sweat and tears produced a determination to hang on to the empire at almost any cost. The consequences were caution and compromise in Europe. In 1938 a senior Foreign Office official defended Munich on the grounds that the risks of war were so much greater for Britain and France than for Germany: 'If we lose, the whole Empire goes, if Germany loses, she can recover.'[16]

Would different decisions in the 1920s have arrested the decline in British power ? It is argued that Britain should have pressed the dominions to accept closer imperial links and written off the empire if such support was not forthcoming.[17] It is also suggested that the Anglo–Japanese alliance of 1902 should have been renewed in 1921, even at the cost of a worsening in Anglo–American relations.[18] But closer political ties with the dominions were not feasible at the time. The whole temper of dominion feeling was inimical to such a development. Besides, British governments were not in fact free to divest themselves of empire. Sentiment and great-power status demanded its preservation, while writing it off would have meant greater reliance on the United States. Renewing the Anglo–Japanese pact would not have compensated for a breakdown in Anglo–American relations. Japan was a valuable ally in the Far East but only the United States was capable of offering effective aid in both Europe and the Far East.

The problem of peacekeeping in a changed and changing environment might have been mastered if Britain and France had joined forces. Working in close harness the two allies might have contained the expansionist energies of Germany and Italy. In the event the *mésentente cordiale* which prevailed greatly helped Germany's resurgence. German leaders exploited Anglo–French differences. France's efforts to resurrect the wartime military alliance were rebuffed. Between 1921 and 1923 relations were at their lowest point since the Fashoda crisis of 1898.

The upshot of Britain's political and economic preoccupations was that she assumed a mediatory role, promoting a European *détente* but avoiding hard and fast commitments. Arguing that neither Britain nor France was strong enough to control the Continent, the British Foreign Office, seconded by the Treasury, sought to speed the political and economic recovery of Germany. Only German acceptance of the status quo, it was said, could in the long term safeguard the peace. France was warned that she could not 'count in perpetuity on a combination of powers to hold Germany down in a position of abject inferiority'.[19]

Beggars could not be choosers and France accepted the international guarantees offered her in the Locarno Agreements of October 1925

Germany, France and Belgium agreed to recognise their existing frontiers as permanent, including the demilitarised Rhineland zone; Britain and Italy guaranteed this arrangement and the treaty provided for the settlement of all disputes through the League of Nations. The treaty was a mixed blessing for France. Though Germany freely recognised the territorial settlement in western Europe she did not abandon her opposition to the settlement in the east. Thus Locarno confirmed the 'deadlock' of French policy.[20] France was guaranteed but her eastern allies, Poland and Czechoslovakia, were not. Consequently offensive action against Germany in support of these allies would jeopardise the Locarno guarantees. This 'deadlock' could only have been ended in one of three ways: by a British decision to underwrite the settlement in the east; by a French decision to act offensively on the assumption that Britain would be bound to follow her; by French disengagement from eastern Europe. It was this third path that France slowly and reluctantly followed after Locarno.

Locarno fostered an illusion of *détente*, an illusion nourished as much by the economic prosperity of the mid-1920s as by the treaty itself. Germany's admission to the League in 1926 encouraged hopes of amity. The conversation between the French and German foreign ministers at Thoiry in September 1926 seemed at the time to contain the seed of great things, but bore no fruit.[21] By the end of the decade the Locarno spirit had evaporated. It had meant different things to different statesmen. As one French diplomat quipped: '*Il y a trois choses, le Locarno spirit, l'esprit de Locarno, et le Locarnogeist.*'[22] For the German foreign minister, Gustav Stresemann, Locarno was the first step towards treaty revision; for the French minister, Aristide Briand, it was the first step on the road to compliance; for the British foreign secretary, Austen Chamberlain, it was an assertion of British detachment. By guaranteeing the Franco–German frontier Britain implicitly repudiated responsibility for any other European frontier. Munich was the logical sequel of this policy.

'All of them distrust Germany to the point of regarding it as almost an insult to suggest that they should make a pact with her,' remarked Austen Chamberlain after meeting French leaders in March 1925.[23] French suspicions were well founded. The long-range aim of Weimar's political and military leadership was the overturning of Versailles. What is not clear is how far Stresemann envisaged the use of force to achieve this aim. He could hardly have expected France to abdicate without a struggle. The Weimar Republic, in collusion with the Soviet Union, evaded the disarmament clauses of Versailles. The Treaty of Rapallo in April 1922 normalised German–Soviet relations. Reichswehr leaders advocated a German–Soviet military alliance with the aim of partitioning Poland. The German archives make it plain that Stresemann knew all about the military connection with the Red Army and made no attempt to sever it, in spite of Locarno.[24]

Breakdown, 1929–35

The *dies irae* of the interwar world was Tuesday 29 October 1929. It was the day of the Wall Street crash, the collapse of the American stock market. United States' investors recalled short-term loans from Europe. Neither Britain nor the United States was able or willing to stop the Gadarene rush which followed, with one country after another leaving the gold standard and setting up tariff barriers. The trough of the depression was 1932. This was the worst year for industrial output in all the major manufacturing countries. By 1932 unemployment in Germany totalled 6 million, in Britain 3 million, in the United States 13 million.

The world economic crisis, by causing deep social fissures within states and by disrupting the international economy, contributed to the destruction of the territorial settlement. The trauma of depression scarred the foreign policies of Britain and France almost as deeply as the recent war. Economic breakdown led to political upheaval which in turn destroyed the international status quo. Germany was the most striking example of this complex interaction. Without the depression Hitler would not have gained power. Mass unemployment reinforced all the resentments against Versailles and the Weimar democracy that had been smouldering since 1919. Overnight the National Socialists were transformed into a major political party; their representation in the Reichstag rose from 12 deputies in 1928 to 107 in 1930. The deflationary policies of the Weimar leaders sealed the fate of the Republic. Chancellor Brüning, who took office in March 1930, saw in deflation a device to free Germany from reparations.[1] For two years Weimar economic policy deliberately kept unemployment high and thereby stoked the fires of political extremism.

Equally significant for the causation of the Second World War was the fact that the economic blizzard hit France later than her neighbours.[2] 1929 was France's *annus mirabilis*. The economy reached a peak which it was not to equal again until the early 1950s. In 1931 the bubble burst, though the worst effects were delayed until 1932–3. While the British, German and American economies convalesced in the mid-1930s the French economy was in the doldrums. Between 1929 and 1938 industrial production increased by 20 per cent in Britain and by 16 per cent in

Germany, whereas in France it fell by 24 per cent. Unlike Hitler and President Roosevelt of the United States, who were prepared to break with economic orthodoxy, French statesmen were adamant in their support of the gold standard and a balanced budget. Only in the winter of 1938-9 did the French economy show some signs of recovery. This time lag before the onset of depression had three consequences: it widened the gap between French and German industrial strength and so increased France's sense of inferiority; French rearmament was delayed; and France's internal quarrels were intensified.

After 1933 the depression tailed away like a hurricane, leaving a track of ruin. The most serious damage manifested itself as economic nationalism. Protectionism and beggar-my-neighbour policies wrecked international understanding. The European debtors of the United States insisted that allied war debts and reparations were linked. France maintained that she could not pay war debts to the United States unless Germany paid reparations. Brüning said it was impossible for Germany to continue payments and reparations were virtually cancelled at the Lausanne conference in 1932. In June 1933 Germany stopped payment of all foreign debts. France's refusal to pay war debts reinforced American isolationism. The Johnson Act of 1934 denied the right of countries which defaulted on war debts to borrow on the United States money market. In August 1935, as Mussolini prepared to invade Abyssinia, Congress passed the Neutrality Act, forbidding the shipment of arms to either aggressor or victim. The international initiatives taken – President Hoover's moratorium of 1931 suspending repayments for one year, the world economic conference of 1933, the Stresa conference of 1932 – were swamped by a tide of nationalism and self-interest. Japanese and Polish requests for support for an international public works programme were answered by the United States: 'We would oppose without any ambiguity a proposal that we finance someone else's programme.'[3]

The economic blizzard provided compelling reasons for conciliating the fascist dictators. War, it was feared, would destroy the prospects of economic recovery. Though Keynes's *General Theory of Employment, Interest and Money* was published in 1936, there was no Keynesian revolution until after 1945. Accordingly governments sought to nurse sick economies back to health by prescribing the orthodox medicine of the period – deflation, retrenchment, balanced budgets. Hence rearmament was delayed because massive spending on arms was seen as the short road to ruin. Statesmen feared that even the modest scale of rearmament started in 1936-7 would prove 'unbearable'.[4] By the mid-1930s Britain and the United States were recuperating, but recovery was only partial. Apprehensions of a relapse were revived by the Roosevelt recession which engulfed the United States in August 1937. Unemployment, which stood at 6 million in early 1937, jumped to 11 million in the autumn. European bourses registered the recession in the winter of 1937–8. This economic downturn spurred forward the search for agreement with Germany and Italy in 1938.

In the wake of depression came class conflict. Though the worst of the storm was over by 1933 the propertied classes lived in fear of a general social collapse. Unemployment and low wages fuelled the ideological conflict between left and right in Europe. Economic misery divided society in Britain and France and prevented national unity when it was most needed. The anxiety and uncertainty which pervaded the political climate furnished a powerful argument for some accommodation with the dictators. A European war seemed certain to end in Bolshevism. 'You see, whether we win or lose, it will be the end of everything we stand for,' declared one British minister in 1938.[5] 'Any war, whether we win or not, would destroy the rich idle classes and so they are for peace at any price,' reasoned another observer.[6] The inability of governments to cure economic ills bred a growing impatience and exasperation with parliamentary democracy. Anger and disillusionment were common to the left and right. The left believed that capitalism was on its last legs and would soon expire. In the interim firm rule was needed. In 1934 Sir Stafford Cripps's Socialist League called for virtual dictatorship in the first days of a Labour government. In France right-wing fury, especially that of ex-servicemen, vented itself in the ultra-nationalist leagues. Anti-parliamentary feelings exploded in the riots of 6 February 1934.

Internal preoccupations determined the reactions of the powers in the Far Eastern crisis of 1931–3. 'There has scarcely been a period in the world's history when war seemed less likely than it does at the present,' the League Assembly was told on 10 September 1931.[7] Within a week Japanese forces seized key points in Manchuria from Chinese garrisons. In May 1933 Japanese armies swept southwards menacing Peking and the North China plain. At this point the Japanese stopped and concluded a truce with the Chinese. The truce lasted until July 1937 when a full-scale Sino–Japanese war began.

In the light of the Second World War the Manchurian affair was widely believed to have been the beginning of the slide to disaster. For a long time a conspiracy theory held sway, according to which British ministers and City interests, indifferent to the League and jealous of American economic and naval power, cynically disregarded Chinese interests and favoured Japan. Hitler and Mussolini were thus encouraged to try their luck in Europe and Africa. The United States, it was said, was ready to resist aggression, but her initiatives were rejected.

There is no evidence to support the conspiracy theory. The myth that the Far Eastern crisis was the detonator of later crises has been effectively demolished. Inevitably the Manchurian affair was linked to later events but it did not 'cause' them. Neither Mussolini's invasion of Abyssinia in

1935 nor Hitler's march into the Rhineland in 1936 can be related to Manchuria. That the League and collective security suffered a grievous blow is undeniable. Chinese appeals to the League were answered by the dispatch of a commission of inquiry, the Lytton Commission. Meanwhile the Japanese conquest proceeded unhindered. The League voted against recognition of the Japanese puppet state of Manchukuo. The sanctions imposed were derisory – refusal to recognise Manchukuo passports, currency and postage. Japan replied by leaving the League in March 1933. Yet the blow to the League was not a mortal one and the decisive test came two years later in the Abyssinian crisis.

Manchuria demonstrated that the League was toothless. Collective security depended on the readiness of the great powers to defend the status quo. Although Britain, France and the United States had much to lose in the Far East, Japanese expansion was not yet seen as a direct threat to western commercial and colonial interests. Indeed, France was inclined to see Japan as a bastion of order against anarchy and Bolshevism. In fact there was no chance of collective action against Japan. Western governments were engrossed in problems of economic recovery and disarmament negotiations. 'We have all been so distracted by day to day troubles that we have never had a chance of surveying the whole situation and hammering out a policy,'[8] the British prime minister, Ramsay MacDonald, wrote. In the United States elections were in the offing and the Hoover administration had no thought of diplomatic and economic sanctions, let alone war. Nor is it certain that sanctions would have sufficed to stop Japan. The Japanese Kwantung army in Manchuria might well have ignored directives from Tokyo. Even assuming that Manchuria had been restored to China by force of arms it does not follow that the European dictators would have been deterred; on the contrary they might have seen in western involvement in the Far East an opportunity to act in Africa and Europe.

Though Manchuria, by discrediting the League, contributed to the breakdown of the peace settlement, the fate of the settlement hinged primarily on relations between the European powers. Accounts of the 1930s frequently convey the impression of a steady slide towards war. If distinctions are drawn, the Rhineland crisis is usually seen as the turning-point in the run-up to war. In fact there were two quite distinct periods. In the first, from 1933 to 1935, the fascist dictators followed separate paths. On the whole their diplomacy was cautious and conciliatory. The second period from 1935 marks the prewar period proper. If there was a turning-point on the road to war it was the Abyssinian crisis of 1935-6.

The first major test for the European security system came in 1932-4. Germany's demand in 1932 for equality of rights in the Geneva disarmament talks gave France her first serious challenge. By 1934 France had lost the diplomatic leadership in Europe and Britain became the senior partner in the *Entente*. A mixture of economic crisis and political upheaval enfeebled France. The 6 February 1934 riots which followed the exposure of the financial swindler Stavisky convinced many observers that the Third Republic was on the brink of civil war. Ministerial instability did not help. In the four months from Germany's departure from the League in October 1933 to the riots of 6 February France had four changes of prime minister.

But the main reason for France's loss of the initiative was the fact that the revival of Germany under Hitler presented her with an apparently insoluble problem. A preventive war was not practical politics. At the time it was rumoured that Marshal Pilsudski of Poland had suggested to Paris a war against Germany but there is no hard evidence that such a proposal was ever made (Doc. 5).[9] Probably the Poles deliberately spread the rumours in order to prepare the way for a *rapprochement* with Germany. It was a Polish initiative that led to the 1934 German–Polish non-aggression pact. France's hands were tied. A repetition of the Ruhr adventure of 1923 would have deprived her of the Locarno guarantee and allied support. The domestic constraints were also powerful. The elections of May 1932 returned a solidly left-wing Chamber, and pacifist sentiment excluded the use of force.

Disarmament offered no solution. Since Germany was determined to rearm it was plain that any disarmament pact would have to legalise some measure of German rearmament. This might have been acceptable provided France retained military superiority. However, German demands from 1932 were for 'equality of rights', which meant reducing French armaments until parity was achieved. Disarmament talks required France to surrender her lead without any guarantee that Germany would keep her word. As a gesture of goodwill French military expenditure was reduced in 1932–3; all to no purpose. Germany walked out of the disarmament conference in October 1933 and France rejected further disarmament negotiations in a note of 17 April 1934. The logical result was rearmament: 'We are initiating . . . a policy of force,' affirmed one French minister (Doc. 9). Nothing happened: French rearmament did not begin until the autumn of 1936.

Co-operation with Mussolini found favour in Britain and France. Sir John Simon, foreign secretary, saw Italy as 'the key to peace' (Doc. 7). In March 1933 Mussolini proposed that Britain, France, Germany and Italy should conclude a Four Power Pact, calling on other countries to adopt a policy of peace. This was innocuous enough. But the pact also affirmed 'the principle of the revision of the peace treaties'. France's eastern allies protested because revision directly threatened their existence. The pact was signed in July 1933 but never ratified. However the notion of a European directory was realised in the Munich Agreement of 1938. Edouard Daladier, French prime minister in 1938, returned from Munich saying: 'It's my policy, it's the Four Power Pact.'[10]

France's eclipse was inevitable since Britain would not underwrite the settlement in the east and Weimar governments had made clear their resolve to undo Versailles. Yet German demands need not have resulted in war. It was Hitler's coming to power in January 1933 that focused and fuelled German discontents. His ideas and personality were paramount in the making of the Second World War. Historians have tackled nazism in two ways. The first, and by far the most popular approach, is the biographical.[11] The second is the analysis of the conditions and forces which sustained the nazi dictatorship. Both approaches have their limitations. In discussing the forces that brought Hitler to power it is easy to see Hitler as a pawn in the hands of monopoly capitalism, as Marxist writers have tended to do. The weakness of the biographers, especially the psycho-historians, is that their obsession with the minutiae of the man – his sexual habits, medical health, childhood – brings us no nearer to understanding his place in history.[12] Hitler's success stemmed not so much from possession of a demonic force as from the fact that he was a sounding board for German society. Much more remains to be discovered, not about Hitler the man, but about the workings of his government, at local, regional and national levels. The German economy still awaits an authoritative analysis.

Three points are worth making. First, the ambiguities and ambivalences that are to be found in Hitler have to be accepted, not explained away or ignored. Hitler was a blend of fanatic and opportunist, mad visionary and shrewd politician. His personality and policy cannot be encapsulated in a neat either/or categorisation. Second, Hitler's role in the origins of the Second World War is not simply a jigsaw puzzle from which some of the pieces are still missing. Certainly many interesting questions about the Third Reich remain unanswered but in the last analysis Hitler and nazism can be understood, interpreted or used as each generation wishes. To every man his own Hitler. Third, the dictator's personality and policy must be seen as a whole. Ideological, military and economic factors were much too closely interlocked to allow of a clinical separation. Narrow concentration on specific issues may obscure two truths. First, the 'singleness of purpose and consistency of aim of Hitler's policies and beliefs . . . the continuity he established between persuasion, propaganda, threats of terror and terror itself'.[13] Second, 'the continuity, so utterly bewildering to his English and French negotiating partners, between "Peace" and "War" on which his foreign policy was based, where subversion, propaganda, diplomatic and economic pressure, war of nerves, threat of war, localised war and general war itself all merged into a single spectrum'.[14]

Much of the driving force of Hitler's foreign policy came from the ideology of national socialism. Some writers have dismissed it as mere window dressing. In fact it was as important as traditional power politics. Though nazism borrowed from pre-1914 pan-Germanism, its force lay in the fusion of familiar cliches into an official doctrine, animating a mass movement and nation. Nazism, as Hitler insisted in 1936, was a 'doctrine of conflict'. Violence was of its essence, starting with the early street fights, through the mass meetings policed by storm troopers, to the labour camps and foreign conquests. The party prided itself on being a movement. Movement was the word because the momentum of the myth had to be sustained. Like Frankenstein, Hitler was destroyed by his own creation.

Discussion of Hitler's aims has been dominated by the debate as to whether he was a planner or an opportunist. The argument that Hitler was an opportunist runs as follows. Hitler had no deep-laid plans. *Mein Kampf* embodies the daydreams of a political thinker, not a programme for conquest. There were no detailed advance plans for the destruction of Austria, Czechoslovakia or Poland. Hitler never intended to fight a world war and became involved in war in 1939 through a miscalculation.[15] It is argued that since Hitler did not create large-scale armaments or stockpile raw materials he could not have wanted a European war. Several comments may be made. It is simplistic to discuss Hitler's policy in either/or terms. His temperament was many-sided, and a satisfying interpretation must take account of different and often conflicting traits. The contention that Hitler was an opportunist rests on a confusion between policy and plans. The fact that Hitler did not plan a European war in the sense of issuing precise military directives does not mean that he did not have a warlike policy. The general principles of his diplomacy – the need for German expansion, the readiness to use force – were bound sooner or later to involve him in war with his neighbours. Finally, it is not true that Hitler had no military plans for the destruction of Czechoslovakia and Poland. Intensive military preparations for the invasion of Czechoslovakia were initiated on 30 May 1938 (Doc. 50).

The debate about Hitler's foreign policy is in part an artificial one because it posits a misleading distinction between planning and opportunism. The evidence reveals a consistent commitment to aggression inherent in the Third Reich. In Alan Bullock's words, Hitler displayed 'consistency of aim with complete opportunism in method and tactics'.[16] *Mein Kampf* was not a programme for world conquest but its ideas were central to Hitler's thinking.[17] History, according to Hitler, was a story of racial struggles (Doc. 3). Germans were called on to rule the world, but they were hemmed in and infiltrated by inferior races, notably Jews and Slavs. In order to survive and preserve her racial identity Germany needed more territory. Living space was to be conquered in eastern Europe at the expense of Russia and other east European states. These countries would be colonised by force. In the west France was the hereditary enemy. Britain and Italy were potential allies. In June 1941 Hitler invaded the Soviet Union and the creation of a slave empire in the east began in earnest. Nor did he waver in his antagonism to France.

Ample documentary evidence exists showing the consistency of purpose which informed Hitler's policy after 1933 (Docs 4, 37). Hitler's emphasis on the rapid expansion of the *Wehrmacht* alarmed even the generals. His determination to give priority to military requirements and to increase German self-sufficiency in strategic materials led him to encourage expensive domestic production of low-grade iron ore, synthetic rubber and petroleum at the expense of foreign trade. Despite serious shortages of foreign exchange and rising import costs Hitler did not swerve from his purpose. In a memorandum of August 1936 he firmly rejected any reduction in the rearmament programme and denied the value of stockpiling raw materials (Doc. 37). He was quite willing to embark on hostilities provided the immediate requirements of the army were met.

In what sense, if any, was Hitler offering a new prospectus of policy? Or was it the old business under new management? During the First World War the Kaiser and his generals had coveted extensive territories in eastern Europe. Plans were well advanced for an economic *Mitteleuropa*. By the Treaty of Brest–Litovsk in March 1918 Germany swallowed Poland, Lithuania, Latvia, Estonia, the Ukraine and Transcaucasia. Hitler's style was new – utilising fifth columns, exploiting the competing and overlapping influences of party and state, an ideological vocabulary, contempt for traditional diplomacy. But his aims were largely those of the old governing class, namely, the destruction of Versailles and the re-establishment of Germany as the leading power in Europe. Disagreement between Hitler and his professional advisers turned on questions of timing and method, not objectives. For example, Ernst von Weizsäcker, state secretary in the German foreign ministry, who claimed in his trial before the Nuremberg war crimes court to have tried to oppose the aggressive plans of Hitler, advocated the 'chemical dissolution' of Czechoslovakia and threatened in August 1939 to have Poland 'eradicated'.[18]

What was new, though, was the ultimate aim of world domination based on the rule of a master race. This master race would form a new elite supplanting the conservative elites in German society. Also new was Hitler's systematic subjugation of other races. No previous German government used the concept of racial nationalism as a basis for legislation. Previous regimes had sought to Germanise non-Germans, but no legal penalties had been imposed on German Jews. Not only did Hitler believe it was impossible to Germanise peoples of another race, but he also preached their enslavement and annihilation.

Given Germany's preponderance in population and industrial strength her recovery as a great power was only a matter of time. That her restoration was accomplished by 1939 was a measure of Hitler's political genius. The key factor, however, was western sympathy for German grievances. This was an inheritance from the Weimar Republic. Hitler did not need to lay siege to Versailles. Its defenders opened their gates and parleyed before nazi trumpets sounded. The doubts of 1919 were now certainties. It was widely accepted that Versailles was a vindictive settlement (Doc. 1).

Allied to revisionism was internationalism. Men had illusions. 'The stage has ceased to be dominated by the Great Powers . . . the dominant note in the corporate consciousness of communities is a sense of being parts of some larger universe,' wrote Professor Arnold Toynbee.[19] The general detestation of war excluded preventive war. When, in March 1935, Hitler denounced the Versailles disarmament clauses, the foreign editor of *Figaro*, Wladimir d'Ormesson, spoke of his 'anguish'. Hitler and his henchmen were 'gangsters' who were 'capable of anything'. But a war to stop Hitler was too dreadful for words. It would be the 'end of civilisation, the end of the Christian era'.[20]

Sympathy for German claims survived the terrors of Hitler's *Machtergreifung*. The murder of Dollfuss, the Austrian chancellor, in July 1934, made Neville Chamberlain 'hate Nazi-ism, and all its works, with a greater loathing than ever'.[21] Persuasion prevailed because a second European war seemed a much greater evil than nazism. Also the very excesses of nazism fostered faith in Hitler. Nazism, it was plain, was a witches' cauldron and Hitler's violence was necessary in order to restrain his more fanatical followers. As Austen Chamberlain put it, 'the bigger he (*Hitler*) is and the more dominating the more chance there seems . . . of his gradually becoming more reasonable'.[22] Visitors to Germany brought back reassuring reports suggesting that the chancellor could be separated from the 'wild men' of his party. Opposing him, it was feared, might only bring back the old firm of the Junkers.[23] Nazi persecution of the Jews, though criticised, did not provoke unanimous condemnation because anti-semitic currents ran deep in western society. On arrival in Berlin the British ambassador, Sir Horace Rumbold, was 'appalled by the number of Jews in this place'.[24] The French socialist leader, Léon Blum, was assailed on racial grounds.

British sympathy for the underdog persisted. The belief that France was the chief threat to peace lingered on. Lord Allen of Hurtwood wrote: 'It would be a mistake to be on the side of France about the secret rearming of Germany. . . . To do that means . . . that we appear to re-endorse that wicked Treaty and justify the evil policies of France towards world conciliation during the last ten years.'[25] Stories of nazi violence were received with some scepticism. This was the penalty for successful British propaganda about German atrocities in 1914–18. The Germans were respected as a solid, hardworking, Protestant people: 'You Germans work and we don't,' was a common judgment.[26]

Ideological prejudice worked to Hitler's advantage. The growing conflict between left and right in Europe had two consequences. First, it accelerated the decline of democratic ideals. Second, it divided British and French opinion and distracted attention from international perils. Liberal values had been profoundly shaken in the battles of 1914–18. By 1918 the English political thinker and writer Leonard Woolf admitted to an 'iron fatalistic acquiescence in insecurity and barbarism'.[27] T. S. Eliot's lament in *The Waste Land* (1922) on the decadence of Western civilisation attested to a widely felt disillusionment. Society had become 'a heap of broken images'. Historical writing added to the corrosive effect of self-questioning. R. H. Tawney's *Religion and the Rise of Capitalism* (1926) 'greatly assisted in the decline of Protestant self-confidence, in the reaction against capitalism as an economic system'.[28] The world economic crisis increased forebodings about the future of western society. A profound pessimism pervaded the politics and literature of the period. The resulting loss of confidence left opinion extremely vulnerable to ideological pressures. Many intellectuals espoused Marxism. John Strachey considered that Marxism offered the 'sole way of preserving Western civilisation'.[29]

By 1936 every European country had its own fascist party. The domestic activity of fascist and ultra-right organisations diverted attention from the enemy at the gate. The evils of the home front – unemployment, low wages, bad housing – were identified by the left with the international system which had produced the war and peace settlement. The first priority was to fight fascism at home. Many on the left were convinced that even to envisage the possibility of international war would be playing into the hands of the right. In March 1935 the Flandin Cabinet's proposal that military service should be extended from one to two years was vehemently opposed by socialists and radicals.

Hitler's noisy beating of the anti-communist drum evoked a sympathetic response from western conservatives. In his *History of Europe* (1936) the historian H. A. L. Fisher saw in Hitler 'a sufficient guarantee that Russian Communism will not spread westward. The solid German bourgeois hold the central fortress of Europe.'[30] The fascist states appeared purposeful, dynamic and efficient. 'The Prince of Wales was quite pro-Hitler,' recorded one diarist in 1933, '. . . said it was no business of ours to interfere in Germany's internal affairs . . . dictators were popular these days . . . we might want one in England before long.'[31] Four years later, in September 1937, Winston Churchill declared: 'One may dislike Hitler's system and yet admire his patriotic achievement. If our country were defeated I hope we should find a champion as indomitable to restore our courage and lead us back to our place among the nations.'[32]

Confronted with left-wing alliances (Front Populaire in France, Frente Popular in Spain), frightened conservatives gave Hitler and Mussolini the benefit of the doubt. Stalin's Comintern was believed to be busily subverting the social order. The years 1935 to 1938 witnessed the 'great schism' of the French right.[33] Until the end of 1934 the right was, by and large, agreed on the necessity of resisting Germany. But the prospect of a Popular Front electoral victory in April–May 1936 changed right-wing attitudes. In May 1935 a majority of the right supported the signing of the Franco–Soviet pact; nine months later 164 deputies voted against ratification. The reorientation of right-wing views' was completed in October 1938 when a majority of the right endorsed the Munich Agreement.

The very bitterness of the war of creeds supplied a rationale for appeasement. British and French leaders tried to bridge the divisions between the democracies and fascist dictatorships. The means adopted was a so-called realistic, pragmatic diplomacy: 'It was necessary to get rid of ideological prejudices and, in the world as it exists today, employ the type of diplomacy which seeks to have as useful relations as possible with every country,' declared the French foreign minister, Georges Bonnet, in 1938.[34] Taking sides, it was said, would only divide Europe into armed camps and re-create the international anarchy of 1914. Western statesmen also had their eye on the home front. Avoiding an overt ideological bias was a means of maintaining internal peace.

Two fallacies were fostered: the idea that ideological differences were really secondary, and the view that a personal diplomacy of heads of government could over-ride doctrinal divisions. Face-to-face contact, it was felt, would expose insincerity and double-dealing (Doc. 1). The French prime minister, Pierre Laval, had an almost mystical faith in personal meetings: 'He himself would certainly convince the Führer if only he could speak to him personally. Admittedly he spoke no German but the Führer would see that his intentions were honest.'[35]

Eschewing an ideological stance had fatal results. Not only did it prevent an Anglo–French military alliance, but also essential staff talks were delayed. French requests for wider staff talks in April 1938 were refused because British approaches to the Axis powers made 'it necessary to be very careful not to undo any good which had been achieved . . . by exciting Italian and German suspicions that we were devising fresh . . . combinations to injure those two Powers'.[36]

One major misconception about British and French foreign policies has gained currency. There was, it is suggested, a clear choice between stopping or conciliating Hitler. Forewarned is forearmed. If only the statesmen had read *Mein Kampf* their eyes would have been opened. Enough has been said to show that no one at the time was prepared to coerce Germany. French leaders excluded preventive war. There were good reasons for arguing that Germany had legitimate grievances. But the intensive search for a settlement did not mean that Germany was trusted. Early in 1934 the British Cabinet formally recognised Germany as the ultimate potential enemy. Neville Chamberlain, chancellor of the exchequer, described Germany as 'the *fons et origo* of all our European troubles and anxieties'.[37] An unexpurgated text of *Mein Kampf* was placed in the Foreign Office library in 1933.[38] On 26 April 1933 the ambassador, Sir Horace Rumbold, supplied a succinct summary of the 'cardinal points' of the new chancellor's programme.[39] But *Mein Kampf* told western statesmen nothing that they did not already know. The French had always insisted that Germany was the enemy to watch. *Mein Kampf* was alarming but its animus was directed against the Soviet Union and France, not Britain. The central problem of policy making in the six years after 1933 was not one of identifying Germany as the chief mischief-maker but rather one of 'guessing what lay at the other side of the hill'. As Rumbold wrote: 'How far Hitler is prepared to put his fantastic proposals into operation is of course uncertain.'[40]

The premise of British and French policies was that since German rearmament could not be prevented it would have to be legalised in some form. The Versailles disarmament clauses were dead, but time was of the essence: 'If there is to be a funeral it is clearly better to arrange it while Hitler is still in a mood to pay the undertakers for their services,' concluded a Cabinet paper of March 1934.[41] There seemed no alternative to appeasement. Even Sir Robert Vansittart, permanent under secretary, no friend of Germany, admitted in April 1934 that 'a "long-range" policy must aim at the reconciliation of revisionist ideas with anti-revisionist fears and obstinacy' (Doc. 8). The only radical proposal came from Sir Warren Fisher of the Treasury. He argued that since Britain could not fight both Germany and Japan she should work for an understanding with Japan (Doc. 10). But Roosevelt threatened that if Britain 'is even suspected of preferring to play with Japan to playing with us' he would make approaches to the dominions and make them 'understand clearly that their future security is linked with us'.[42]

Hitler skilfully kept alive British and French hopes of *détente*. Western overtures were answered with 'argumentative and essentially negative replies . . . which however never quite closed the door on future discussions'.[43] Acts of defiance of the peace settlement were followed by asseverations of goodwill. On 16 March 1935 Hitler announced the reintroduction of conscription and an army of thirty-six divisions. When British ministers visited Berlin on 25/26 March they received assurances of Hitler's peaceful purposes, his acceptance of the territorial clauses of Versailles, his desire for an eastern pact and for naval and air agreements (Doc. 15).

Why did such experienced observers as the British ambassador, Sir Eric Phipps, and his French colleague, André François Poncet, retain any confidence in the chancellor? Since historians still differ about Hitler's aims it is not surprising that the diplomats sounded an equivocal, inconclusive note. One factor was that the only alternative to negotiations seemed to be sterility. Another reason was that they did not see enough of the chancellor. Over a period of two years Phipps did not have more than three or four serious talks with the Tiger, as he dubbed Hitler. In 1938 his successor, Sir Nevile Henderson, had the same problem: 'It is impossible to know anything for certain in a regime where all depends on the will of a single individual whom one does not see.'[44] Though the ambassadors were kept at a distance, Hitler received a stream of distinguished visitors – politicians, publicists, academics. All came away convinced that Hitler was a reasonable man with reasonable claims. A plausible case could always be argued for taking advantage of 'a last chance' of agreement.[45]

Turning-point, 1935–7

The prewar period that began in 1935 had two distinctive features: extreme rapidity of change, and an atmosphere of undeclared war. The *accelerando* of events made western policy making difficult. The initiative lay with the dictators. As in the approach to the First World War, the cumulative effect of the crises was to speed up the collapse of the international system. An effect became a cause, reinforcing the original cause. The multiplying of tensions and pressure set up intolerable stresses. Moreover there was no sharp transition from peace to war. The outbreak of the Spanish Civil War in July 1936 was the beginning of three years of 'a reign of terror and international lawlessness'.[1] 'We are already in a state of mobilisation and at war, the only difference is that there is no shooting yet,' Field Marshal Hermann Göring announced in 1936.[2] The Sino–Japanese war began in July 1937 without a Japanese declaration of war. The sense of impending doom created by what an American historian has called 'the force of the togetherness of events'[3] made British and French statesmen lean over backwards to stave off disaster. By March 1939, when they at last accepted that Germany might have to be stopped by war, it was too late to convince Hitler that they meant business.

The European security system, already severely strained by Germany's departure from the League of Nations and denunciation of the Versailles disarmament clauses, underwent a decisive test in the Abyssinian crisis of 1935–6. The crisis was not only the 'first great act of appeasement'; it was *the* major step towards war.[4] The consequences of Mussolini's invasion of Abyssinia were far-reaching: the Stresa front of Britain, France and Italy was shattered, as was the Franco–Italian alliance of 1935; the League received its *coup de grâce*, and Britain and France were estranged. Under cover of the crisis Hitler proceeded with the remilitarisation of Germany's western Rhineland frontier a year earlier than he had thought possible. Italy's isolation led directly to the emergence of the Rome–Berlin Axis in October 1936, which in turn brought the abandonment of Italy's interest in preserving Austrian independence. The way was cleared for Germany's annexation of Austria in March 1938.

Italy's invasion of Abyssinia was not a bolt from the blue. It marked the culmination of colonial ambitions entertained for over half a century. Despite Mussolini's sabre rattling, Italian diplomacy followed a peaceful course in the 1920s. Plans for an attack on Abyssinia were not discussed until 1932 because it was only in that year that Italian forces finally completed the subjugation of the Senussi in Libya. Mussolini believed that a 'warlike operation' in Abyssinia would succeed, provided Italy had 'completely free hands in Europe'.[5] Gradually the diplomatic disappointments of 1933–4, beginning with the miscarriage of the Four Power Pact of July 1933, confirmed his resolve to act in Africa. In September 1933 he authorised detailed studies of an invasion, with a deadline for October 1935. Italy's position in Europe continued to deteriorate. The murder of the Austrian chancellor, Dollfuss, in July 1934 and the assassination of King Alexander of Yugoslavia in October brought serious quarrels with Germany and Yugoslavia. A decision on Abyssinia was postponed (Doc. 12).

However on 30 December 1934 Mussolini sent to Marshal Badoglio, chief of the Italian general staff, a directive saying that he had decided to prepare for 'the complete destruction of the Abyssinian army and the total conquest of Abyssinia' (Doc. 14). What decided the issue was the conclusion of an alliance with France. France and Italy had negotiated over Abyssinia in 1931–2. The French foreign minister, Louis Barthou, had courted Italy since early 1934. The *rapprochement* had the blessing of the French general staff. An Italian alliance would protect France's exposed Mediterranean flank and perhaps enable her to send help to her eastern allies. Besides, Austria's independence clearly depended on Italy. In 1934 Mussolini alone of European leaders had shown his willingness to use force to maintain the status quo in central Europe.

Pierre Laval, Barthou's successor, completed the negotiations with Italy. On 7 January 1935 Laval and Mussolini signed the Rome Agreements, promising to consult together in the event of a threat to Austrian independence. They also agreed to consult if Germany should 'modify by unilateral action her obligations in the matter of armaments'. The most controversial of the agreements was a secret one on Abyssinia.[6] With minor reservations France signed over to Italy her economic interests in Abyssinia. In a private conversation with the Duce, Laval used the phrase a 'free hand'. The Italian leader interpreted this gloss as meaning that France would turn a blind eye to the military conquest of Abyssinia, whereas Laval probably assumed that Italy would stop short of war. No record of this colloquy was kept and the ambiguity was no doubt intentional (Doc. 27).

By the spring of 1935 Italy's intentions were common knowledge. But there was no common front against her. The dominant note of Anglo–French diplomacy was conciliation. Italy was needed as a makeweight against Germany. Yet Britain was not prepared to buy Italian support by undertaking new continental commitments. On 8 April the British

Cabinet agreed 'that if France or Italy asked us to join them in a statement that we would not stand a breach of the peace anywhere . . . we ought not to agree to such a proposition unless we were prepared to take action anywhere, e.g., in the event of trouble in Memel' (Doc. 16).

Meeting at Stresa on 11-14 April, Britain, France and Italy merely reaffirmed their Locarno obligations. Stresa was the source of two myths. The final communique declared that the three powers would oppose 'by all practicable means any unilateral repudiation of treaties which may endanger the peace of Europe'. It was believed that the words 'of Europe' were added by Mussolini in order to protect his designs on Abyssinia.[7] In reality the drafting of the communique was entirely the work of the British delegation. The second myth asserted that Abyssinia was not discussed at Stresa. Abyssinia was not on the formal agenda but the delegations did give time to the question.

All the omens were favourable for Mussolini. Laval journeyed to Moscow for the signing of the Franco-Soviet pact on 2 May 1935, but the new Italian alliance had priority. Stalin's proposal for staff talks was side-stepped and parliamentary ratification of the pact was delayed until February 1936. By contrast the Franco-Italian union was soon consummated. On 27 June 1935 General Gamelin, chief of the French general staff, and Marshal Badoglio, Italian chief of staff, signed a military convention providing for concerted action in the event of a German threat to Austria. The possibilities were also discussed of sending an Italian contingent to the Rhine and of French troops crossing Italy *en route* to central Europe.

Anglo-French differences of opinion gave Mussolini additional assurance. Britain's quest for agreement with Germany bore fruit in the Anglo-German Naval Agreement of 18 June 1935, allowing German naval rearmament to up to 35 per cent of British tonnage.[8] French ministers, who had been kept in the dark about Anglo-German naval talks, took umbrage. Britain's attitude was pragmatic. She felt that Germany was going to increase her naval strength whatever happened and that an accommodation was necessary in order to keep this increase as low as possible. Britain seemed saved from the nightmare of having to confront simultaneously the limitless naval ambitions of Germany and Japan. In 1934 Japan insisted on parity with Britain and the United States. France for her part resented British recognition of Germany's violation of Versailles.

The Italian invasion of Abyssinia on 3 October 1935 was answered by League anathemas, followed by the imposition of economic sanctions on 18 November. British and French ministers were unremitting in their efforts to buy off Mussolini. The fruit of their labours was the Hoare-Laval Plan of 8 December, by which two-thirds of Abyssinia would have been ceded to Italy. Abyssinia would have retained a strip of territory as access

to the sea – a 'Corridor for camels', as *The Times* contemptuously described
it. A press leak of the plan brought swift condemnation from British
opinion. The Foreign Office was warned that 'hard-headed businessmen'
in the City 'who waste no time on idealism' were describing the terms 'as
the most miserable document that has ever disgraced the signature of a
British statesman'.[9] Hoare was compelled to resign. Five months later the
Italian conquest was complete. On 2 May 1936 the Emperor Haile Selassie
fled his country and on 9 May the King of Italy was proclaimed Emperor
of Abyssinia.

Why did Britain and France allow Italy to over-run Abyssinia? The
Italian attack on a League member seemed an open-and-shut case of
aggression. There were three major reasons: the desire to retain Italy as
an ally against Germany, military considerations, and divided opinion in
Britain and France (Docs 17, 20, 21). Neither London nor Paris saw any
intrinsic evil in Italian expansion in Abyssinia. Germany, not Italy, was
the main threat to peace. As a Locarno guarantor and guardian of Austria's
independence, Italy had to be wooed, not warned. Military factors were
also relevant. The burden of operations against Italy would fall on the
Royal Navy and the chiefs of staff wanted to keep the fleet intact for use
against Japan. 'A hostile Italy is a real menace to our Imperial communications and defence system. We have relied on practically abandoning the
Mediterranean if we send the Fleet east,' wrote the first sea lord.[10] For
France military considerations were no less important. Italy was the only
major continental power with which France had a military understanding.
The French general staff calculated that in the event of war with Germany
Italian neutrality would release seventeen French divisions from the Alps
and North Africa for service on the Rhine.

Divided opinion on both sides of the Channel imposed a conciliatory
diplomacy. The predominantly Conservative National Government led by
Stanley Baldwin had to reckon with left-wing attachment to the League
and collective security. The results of the British Peace Ballot, announced
on 28 June 1935, attested the strength of League loyalty (Doc. 19). Of
11 million replies 10 million supported the application of economic and
non-military sanctions to stop one nation from attacking another. However,
on the crucial issue of military sanctions (that is, war to stop an aggressor)
opinion was divided. Of those questioned, only 58 per cent (over 6 million)
were prepared to use military sanctions. By contrast many Conservatives,
including senior naval officers, had no love for the League. Baldwin's
slogan was 'all sanctions short of war'. His policy was an attempt to keep
the initiative in foreign affairs out of the hands of the left and to win
support for rearmament. The results of the general election of 14 November
1935, the last before the war, seemed a vindication of his policy, with 492
supporters of the National Government and only 154 Labourites returned.

In France internal tensions were paramount (Doc. 24). The Italian–

Abyssinian war coincided with mounting domestic turmoil. The rise of the ultra-nationalist leagues was countered by the Popular Front alliance of communists, socialists and radical-socialists. Since the Stavisky scandal and the riots of February 1934 right-wing ministries had held office. In June 1935 the Flandin Cabinet was replaced by the Laval administration. Dependent on radical-socialists and right-wing support in the Chamber, Laval's government clung to a precarious parliamentary existence. Political realities presented Laval with an agonising dilemma. France, like Britain, was in a pre-election period, with elections due in April–May 1936. The right sang the praises of the Italian alliance while most radicals favoured the League and collective security. Consequently staunch support for sanctions would have alienated the right and destroyed the government's parliamentary base. Equally the abandonment of the League would have offended the radicals. The fact that many of the radicals had doubts about the wisdom of the Popular Front alliance with socialists and communists made it all the more desirable to retain their support.

British policy added to Laval's difficulties. London demanded a clear-cut decision from Paris. Unequivocal French backing for the League, it was thought, would suffice to secure an Italian withdrawal. The chiefs of staff told the British government that French military help was indispensable. In November growing fears of 'a mad-dog act' by Mussolini, perhaps a sudden swoop on the Mediterranean fleet at Malta, made French co-operation all the more necessary. Alternatively, it was reasoned, a French negative would provide an excuse for British inaction. Faced with British requests for naval co-operation Laval trod water, striving to keep the friendship of both allies (Doc. 25). His tightrope diplomacy came near to success. But for the reactions of British opinion the Hoare–Laval Plan would have been accepted in France.

Would sanctions have sufficed to stop Mussolini? The League sanctions imposed in November 1935 did not include an oil embargo. We now know that if the oil sanction had been imposed, Mussolini, according to his own statement, would have made peace within twenty-four hours.[11] Even those economic sanctions that were applied caused Italy grave distress. Italy's oil needs were met by hundreds of small American operators who took advantage of higher prices for oil to charter tankers to Italy and Red Sea ports. Yet determined Anglo–French naval intervention could have quickly cut off these supplies. What of France's strategic anxieties? Only a British undertaking to underwrite the settlement in eastern Europe could have eased France's predicament. The French in fact tried to secure a new British commitment. On 10 September 1935 Laval asked if Britain would enforce collective security in Europe. In short, Britain was being asked to extend her Locarno undertakings to central and eastern Europe – to include Austria, for example. On 24 September the British Cabinet neatly side-stepped the question, saying that it reserved its liberty of action as to how Article 16 of the League Covenant should be applied (Docs 22, 23).

The failure to restrain Mussolini did not make a second European war inevitable but it did make war highly probable. 'Us today, you tomorrow,' were the Emperor Haile Selassie's parting words at Geneva. Instead of uniting Britain and France in defence of the League, the Abyssinian crisis estranged the two allies. In British eyes France had shown herself unreliable, and the chiefs of staff judged the naval contacts 'profoundly unsatisfactory'.[12]

The Abyssinian crisis delivered a mortal blow to the League. It was already weakened by the departure of Japan in March 1933 and Germany in the October. Italy left in 1937. The assertion that the 'real death' of the League came with the Hoare–Laval Plan in December 1935 is perhaps an oversimplification.[13] The Abyssinian Christmas offensive encouraged League supporters to think that Italy could yet be defeated without an oil embargo. As late as February 1936 the British Cabinet believed that sanctions might still work. Baldwin was ready by that date to accept an oil sanction. Again domestic considerations were uppermost. Without stronger government backing for the League the trade unions would not support rearmament.

While Britain and France were distracted by the Abyssinian war Hitler made his first major move against the territorial order. On 7 March 1936, alleging a contradiction between the Franco–Soviet pact and the Treaty of Locarno, he sent a force of 22,000 men into the demilitarised Rhineland, violating the Versailles and Locarno treaties. His gamble that Britain and Italy, guarantors of Locarno, would remain passive and that France would not dare to act alone proved correct.

The Rhineland *coup* exemplifies Hitler's foreign policy methods: cautious and careful diplomatic preparation, speed and surprise in exploiting opportunities, last-minute hesitations, final firm resolution. The pretext for action was provided by the Franco–Soviet pact of 2 May 1935. In a memorandum of 25 May 1935 the German foreign ministry argued that the pact was incompatible with Locarno. With the return of the Saar to Germany in January 1935 the Rhineland became Hitler's immediate concern. *De facto* remilitarisation had been taking place for several years through the infiltration of paramilitary forces.

In London and Paris it was expected that Hitler would open negotiations for the remilitarisation of the Rhineland. However, instead of negotiating he used force. Before taking action Germany needed a stronger case. This was provided on 11 February 1936, when, after months of procrastination, the Franco–Soviet pact was submitted to the French parliament for ratification. Hitler also needed the neutrality of at least one of the Locarno powers. Italy was the obvious choice. Despite ideological affinities Hitler and Mussolini had been at loggerheads in 1934 and 1935. Hitler even promised aid to Haile Selassie in December 1934, and some German, or German-purchased, arms reached Abyssinia in 1936.[14] Not until the winter of 1935–6 were the first steps taken towards the creation of the Rome–Berlin Axis. Italy was isolated and feeling the effects of economic sanctions. On 7 January 1936 Mussolini informed Berlin that he would not oppose Austria's becoming 'a German satellite' (Doc. 28). In mid-February Hitler sounded out his military advisers about the Rhineland. They urged caution. Von Neurath, foreign minister, also advised delay. Hitler argued that 'passivity was, in the long run, no policy. . . . Attack in this case, too, was the better strategy.'[15] On 22 February Mussolini confirmed that, in the event of a German move, Italy 'would not co-operate with Britain' in any action under Locarno.[16] Mussolini was not, however, told of the nature of the move Hitler had in mind. The way was now clear. Operational orders were issued on 2 March and on the 6th their execution was fixed for the 7th, though even then Hitler asked if the operation could still be postponed.

The Rhineland crisis was the beginning of France's *via dolorosa*. 'If the French government had mobilised,' wrote Winston Churchill, 'there is no doubt that Hitler would have been compelled by his own General Staff to withdraw, and a check would have been given to his pretensions which might well have proved fatal to his rule.'[17] Why, then, did France not expel the German troops from the demilitarised zone? She was not entirely caught off-guard: a German move against the Rhineland had been predicted since the summer of 1935.

France's acquiescence in the *coup* was the result of three factors: Britain's refusal to countenance military action, the state of British and French opinion, and the attitude of the French general staff. In February 1936 the French government decided that no forcible action could be undertaken without the 'full agreement' of the British government.[18] On 7 March, following the German reoccupation, Eden counselled French ministers not to take any action without prior consultation.[19]

'I suppose Jerry can do what he likes in his own back garden,' opined Eden's taxidriver on the morning of 9 March. British reactions to the *coup* were also shaped by the Abyssinian crisis. The estrangement of the two democracies prevented a united front against Germany. Hitler disarmed opposition. He carried not fire and sword but an olive branch. In the morning of 7 March *before* the entry of German troops he offered non-aggression pacts, demilitarisation on both sides of the Rhine frontier, and a pact limiting air forces.

Though Germany's claim that the Franco–Soviet pact and the Locarno treaty were incompatible did not command wide assent, British and French conservatives strongly deplored the ratification of the pact on 27 February.[20] The French right-wing press argued that ratification had needlessly provoked Germany. An outraged and bellicose French public would doubtless have pushed the government into action against Germany, but in fact there was no enthusiasm for chastising Hitler. On 10 March the French Chamber gave a very chilly reception to a suggestion of unilateral action. The Paris press, with few exceptions, rejected a riposte. Given the apathy of opinion, and with a general election only six weeks off, ministers had no choice but to accept the advice of the general staff.

France's passivity was primarily the result of the general staff's refusal to consider unilateral action against Germany (Doc. 30). The government was told that it was not possible to expel the German forces without general mobilisation, involving the risk of a Franco–German war. War with Germany, the generals pointed out, could not be contemplated without the certainty of allied help. Ministers were told that 'the idea of sending quickly into the Rhineland a French expeditionary force, even if only a token force, was a chimera' because the army was a 'static' force and 'no offensive action could be undertaken until the twelfth day of mobilisation'.[21]

The generals were cautious to a fault because they believed that France no longer had a clear lead over her rival. The Haut Comité Militaire was told on 18 January 1936 that 'as regards equipment, Germany is on the point of overtaking us outright' (Doc. 29). The effects of the Abyssinian crisis weakened France on the Rhine. Fourteen divisions, about a fifth of France's total war strength, had been transferred to the Alps and Tunisia. Yet fear of Germany was not perhaps the decisive consideration. With the help of her Czechoslovak and Polish allies France had numerical superiority over Germany. The number of German troops in the Rhineland was grossly overestimated.[22] The fact of the matter was that well before 7 March the generals had tacitly written off the Rhineland. Demilitarisation, it was felt, could not be indefinitely enforced and was not worth the risk of a Franco–German war. Accordingly the attention of the general staff was focused not on ways and means of preventing a reoccupation but on using the Rhineland as a bargaining counter to strengthen ties with Britain. On 18 February the general staff advised the government to seek a defensive alliance with Britain as 'compensation' for the remilitarisation of the Rhineland.[23]

France won the first stage of a defensive alliance. In London on 19 March the four Locarno powers – Britain, France, Belgium and Italy – renewed their obligations and agreed to open staff talks. Anglo–Franco–Belgian staff talks followed on 15–16 April. It was agreed that in the event of an unprovoked German attack on France, and subject to the decision of the government of the day, two infantry divisions would be sent to France. This offer of two divisions was Britain's first permanent military commitment since the First World War.

The Rhineland reoccupation sounded the death knell for France's eastern pacts. The strategic situation was never again as favourable for France. Hitler raced ahead with the building of fortifications in the Rhineland. By closing the gap in Germany's western frontier he could block a French offensive in aid of Poland or Czechoslovakia. He also launched the last stage of German rearmament in the form of the Four Year Plan of August 1936 (Doc. 37). Even if France had possessed an armoured striking force enabling her to deliver a quick riposte without mobilisation it is far from certain that Germany would have retreated from the Rhineland.[24] Resistance might well have been offered. France's passivity sowed dismay in eastern Europe. The shock was all the greater because immediately after 7 March Czechoslovakia and Poland had reaffirmed their loyalty to France. On Italian advice Austria concluded a new agreement with Germany, the *modus vivendi* of 11 July 1936. In return for a German promise to respect Austrian sovereignty Austria acknowledged herself 'a German state'.

Europe's sorrows did not come singly but in battalions. On 18 July 1936 the Spanish Civil War began.[25] It was to last almost three years. Rapidly the war became an international issue. On 20 July the government of the Spanish Republic asked France for arms, and at the same time General Franco, leader of the military insurrection, requested help from Germany and Italy. Within a few months Germany, Italy and the Soviet Union were supplying men and arms. For the rest of 1936 and well into 1937 it seemed likely that Spain would spark off a general conflagration.

Spain's significance was ideological, economic and strategic. It was the beginning of a war of creeds. The conflict between left and right, hitherto confined to street skirmishes, strikes and slogans, now occupied a real battlefield where the 'blunt Ideals' of the left found not 'their whetstones' but a graveyard.[26] In 1944, after the liberation of France, General de Gaulle inspected the partisan forces of Toulouse. 'Stopping before one raggedly dressed man, he asked: "And when did you join the *Résistance*, my friend?" The partisan replied: "*Bien avant vous, mon général*" – he had fought in the Spanish civil war.'[27] The Spanish economy was a valuable pawn since it supplied a large share of world requirements in quicksilver and iron pyrites. Spain's strategic importance lay in the fact that she controlled the entrance to the western Mediterranean and Atlantic approaches.

Contrary to what has often been supposed, Germany's primary motive for intervention in Spain was ideological – the desire to prevent the emergence of a Bolshevik regime. Italy's motives were ideological and military. Popular Front regimes in France and Spain threatened her Mediterranean interests. Intervention in Spain, it was thought, might bring military bases in the Balearics. Soviet intentions are far from clear. Ostensibly Stalin wanted to support the Frente Popular. Following her admission to the League in 1934 the Soviet Union had supported collective security and Popular Front alliances. Soviet policy was extremely cautious. Stalin delayed sending substantial help until the scale of Axis intervention became known in the autumn of 1936.

Of the myths created by the Spanish Civil War two that have been effectively exploded are, first, the idea that Hitler's main motives for intervention were economic and military and, second, the belief that British pressure forced an unwilling Front Populaire to adopt a policy of non-intervention. Without prompt help from Germany Franco's rising would have been a fiasco. A week after the rebellion he was marooned in Morocco with the Spanish African Army. The success of his *pronunciamiento* depended on transporting the elite units of the Spanish Foreign Legion across the Straits of Gibraltar to the mainland. But the Spanish fleet, loyal to the Republic, barred the way. Lacking aircraft, Franco was powerless to join the Spanish Southern Army in the drive to Madrid. He sent envoys to Berlin and to Rome to ask for aircraft. Hitler's decision to intervene brought immediate relief: twenty Junker JU-52 transport planes ferried Franco's forces across the Straits of Gibraltar. Italian help soon followed. By October 1937 there were 60,000 Italian 'volunteers' in Spain, together with 5–6,000 men of the German Condor Legion. Axis assistance, especially in the air, greatly outweighed Soviet help and made a crucial contribution to Franco's victory in March 1939.

Most writers have seen in German intervention the outcome of a plot between Franco and agents of the nazi Auslandsorganisation in Spain. Hitler's objects, it is said, were to secure Spanish iron ore for Germany's war economy and to use Spain as 'a testing ground' for German armaments.[28] In reality Hitler's decision was quite unconnected with economic or military considerations, though these became important in the course of the war.[29]

Franco's rising took Hitler and Mussolini by surprise.[30] The request for help reached Hitler at Bayreuth in the night of 25 July 1936. Hitler, who had just attended a performance of *Siegfried*, summoned Göring and Blomberg, war minister. It was decided to send transport and fighter aircraft. Three features of Hitler's decision deserve attention. First, its personal nature. Göring and Blomberg were consulted on the practicalities of intervention but, before seeing them, Hitler had made up his mind. The foreign minister, Neurath, was not at Bayreuth. Second, the ideological motive of anti-Bolshevism. Third, Hitler's awareness that the war might be a long one. It has been suggested that Hitler intervened only because he thought the war would be short. This is very questionable. The German embassy in Madrid had already warned Berlin of the possibility of a long war.[31] By 25 July Hitler also knew that France had promised help to the Republic. His decision therefore flowed from long-range policy goals. In a memorandum of August 1936 on the Four Year Plan he reasserted his belief in the need to secure living space in the east (Doc. 37). This expansion was imperilled by events in 1936. At the beginning of the year the Soviet Union had more than doubled its defence spending; in February the Frente Popular came to power in Spain and France ratified the Franco–Soviet pact; in June the Front Populaire took office in France. With the left seemingly going from strength to strength Hitler judged that German intervention was necessary to maintain freedom of action in eastern Europe. If Germany did not act, France and Spain would form a Bolshevik bloc encircling Germany.

Only speedy and substantial French aid could have saved the Spanish Republic. 'Arms for Spain' was the cry in London and Paris. On 20 July the Spanish government asked for help and received a promise of assistance. However, on 2 August France, seconded by Britain, proposed a Non-Intervention Agreement. Though Germany, Italy and the Soviet Union signed the agreement it proved a complete farce. Britain alone respected it. The left in Britain and France claimed that the Front Populaire had been bullied by Britain into accepting non-intervention.[32]

Some British pressure was applied on French ministers, but the decisive factors which led the French prime minister, Léon Blum, to adopt non-intervention were domestic. The only record of a British *démarche* in Paris is an interview of 7 August between the ambassador, Sir George Clerk, and the French foreign minister, Yvon Delbos (Doc. 36). The interview, however, came *after* the French initiative of a Non-Intervention Agreement. Also Clerk acted without instructions and stressed the personal nature of his representations.[33] There are other indications of British pressure before 7 August but the evidence is scrappy and inconclusive.[34]

The major considerations which weighed on Blum were the danger of a general war and the risk of civil war in France. With Germany and Italy committed in Spain it seemed likely that French aid would lead to a European war. In France the Spanish war fanned the flames of class conflict and threatened to sweep away what remained of national unity. The president of the Republic, the presidents of the Chambers and the foreign minister all impressed on Blum the danger of a general conflict. The paroxysms of left and right convinced the prime minister that sending arms to Spain might topple his own government and destroy its social reforms. Charity began at home.

It would be hard to exaggerate the impact of the Spanish Civil War on French policy. The subsequent political and strategic anxieties virtually determined the capitulations in central and eastern Europe in 1938. The military situation was a terrifying one. Ministers and their advisers assumed that in the event of a Franco victory France would be encircled by a triple alliance of Germany, Italy and Nationalist Spain. As well as the threat to the Pyrenees land frontier, sea and air links with French North Africa were endangered. A third of the French army was stationed in

North Africa and survival in war depended on the speed and safety with which troops could be transported across the western Mediterranean. The nightmare of encirclement made France cleave closer to Britain. Presented with almost simultaneous threats to her Mediterranean flank and to geographically remote allies in eastern Europe, France gave priority to her own frontiers.

To everyone Spain was an example. Stalin's intervention increased British and French suspicions of his intentions. The democracies decided that it was best to keep the Soviet Union at a safe distance. As for the Soviet Union, her 'experience in the Non-Intervention Committee and in the diplomatic proceedings arising from the Spanish Civil War was . . . a major factor in convincing her of the bankruptcy of her collective security policy . . . and opened the way to the Russo–German pact of August, 1939'.[35] Spain confirmed Hitler's and Mussolini's intuitive readings of British and French foreign policies. France would not stir without British backing and both powers preferred accommodation to resistance. Two general conclusions were drawn from the conflict: one was the immense destructive potential of air power, demonstrated in the bombing of Guernica[36] and other Spanish towns; the other the likelihood that a European war would be a long one. Japan's new attack on China in July 1937 confirmed these conclusions.

The obsession with Spain diverted attention from Hitler. The hatreds unleashed killed any hopes of restoring national unity. The polarisation of politics proceeded apace. More people than ever before were politically active, signing manifestos, subscribing aid for Republican Spain, serving in the International Brigades. The left believed that it was in Spain, not central Europe, that fascism had to be fought. Spain offered salvation from a class-ridden, capitalist society. 'If Spain goes communist, France is bound to follow. And then Britain,' reasoned Louis MacNeice.[37] The left's advocacy of violence as necessary to achieve social justice illustrated the increasing contamination of liberal values. In the event Spain was an ulcer that drained the left's• crusading zeal. The intellectuals returned disillusioned, and the struggle with Hitler came as an anticlimax.[38]

Lastly Spain created a climate of war. In 1934 and 1935 articles were being written about the 'next war'. By the autumn of 1936 international war was no longer a possibility but an overwhelming probability. The French in particular felt the change of climate. Negotiations with Germany for a settlement were punctuated by cries of alarm: 'Europe is on the verge of general war,' said Delbos in November 1936.[39] From Berlin François-Poncet signalled in September 1937: 'The present state of affairs in reality was no longer peace but undeclared war.'[40]

In Britain and France the proposition was still peace. The Rhineland *coup* did not stop the quest for agreement. Indeed Britain had hoped to use remilitarisation as a bargaining counter. Eden told the Cabinet on 9 March 1936: 'Hitler had deprived us of the possibility of making to him a concession which might otherwise have been a useful bargaining counter . . . in the general negotiations with Germany.'[41] Hitler's carrot of twenty-five years non-aggression pact and a return to the League was sufficient to keep negotiations ticking over until the late summer of 1936. But endeavours to fasten Hitler down to practical proposals were met by evasions and excuses. Plans for a secret meeting between Hitler and Baldwin on a ship near Dover came to nought. The distinctive feature of the post-Rhineland approaches was the stress on economic and colonial concessions. In August 1936 Dr Schacht, German minister for economic affairs, met Blum and aroused French interest in a colonial bargain. Eden, however, vetoed separate colonial talks, insisting that discussions must take place within the mainstream negotiations for a new western security pact in place of Locarno.

Why did Britain and France continue to seek *détente*? Chiefly because France's fear of Germany and the general horror of war were the ruling emotions. Also there remained a lingering hope in Hitler's ultimate reasonableness. As Winston Churchill said in 1937, 'the Angel of Peace is unsnubbable'. For France the Rhineland added urgency to the search for *détente*. 'The best that we can expect', wrote the editor of *Figaro* on 3 April 1936, 'is an almost immediate germanisation of central and eastern Europe.'[42] During the summer of 1936 a new note was sounded in British policy – the need to gain time for rearmament.

British approaches to Italy resulted in the Gentlemen's Agreement of January 1937 according Italy equality of rights in the Mediterranean. Blum's Popular Front ministry refused to make any overtures. Blum believed that the Abyssinian crisis had wedded the two dictators for better or for worse. The German–Austrian agreement of 11 July 1936 seemed to confirm that Italy did not intend to oppose Germany in central Europe. But Blum may well have missed an opportunity of reconciliation with Mussolini. As late as June 1936 the Italians still regarded the 1935 military convention as valid (Doc. 33).

By the summer of 1937 French leaders were nearly at the end of their tether. Not only were they no nearer to agreement with Germany, but also their efforts to resurrect the eastern pacts had failed. An added misfortune was Belgium's new stance in international affairs. In the autumn of 1936 Belgium abandoned a 1920 military agreement with France and returned to her pre-1914 policy of full neutrality.[43] The Maginot line did not extend to the Franco–Belgian frontier and the French general staff had assumed that in the event of war French troops would at once advance into Belgium to meet a German attack. To have extended the Maginot line in 1937 would have been ruinously expensive. Belgium might still ask for French help but there could be no certainty. Arguably only a

Franco–Soviet military alliance could have repaired the breaches in France's security system. Secret negotiations in 1936–7 for a military convention were probably France's last chance of a real alliance. But the French general staff had no stomach for the talks and repeatedly advised against them. And Britain firmly warned France against staff talks with Moscow (Doc. 39).

Appeasement, 1937–8

From late 1937 the immediate origins of the Second World War can be discerned. Hitler set Germany on a course of territorial expansion in central Europe. The response of the democracies was a renewed effort at *détente*. Only after Hitler's annexation of rump Czechoslovakia in March 1939 did Britain and France begin to consider stopping him by force. By encouraging Hitler to think that his territorial ambitions would not be opposed, Anglo–French appeasement contributed to the making of the Second World War.

It used to be believed that appeasement was the personal policy of Neville Chamberlain, who became prime minister in May 1937. It was, in fact, the policy followed since 1919: namely, the reconciliation of the four major European powers – Britain, France, Germany and Italy – leading ultimately to general disarmament. The essential error of the policy lay in a readiness to make concessions without asking for reciprocal advantages. The offer of a colonial settlement to Germany in March 1938 and the dismemberment of Czechoslovakia in September were the main instances of this misjudgment.

Underlying this misjudgment were two ideas: an assumption that in politics there can be no final incompatible aspirations, where the wishes of one man are wholly irreconcilable with those of another, and a conviction that the 1919 treaty structure was bound to collapse. The difference of values between the dictatorships and the democracies was a much more fundamental cleavage than western leaders supposed. Liberal democracy and nazism were really incompatible worlds. The belief that the peace treaties were doomed stemmed partly from the feeling that they were unfair and unenforceable, partly from the belief that, as new nations, Germany and Italy had the initiative. The tide of expansion, it was thought, could only be ridden, not reversed. Unreciprocated concessions were unavoidable. According to R. A. Butler, parliamentary under secretary at the Foreign Office, 'the man in possession when challenged must eventually inevitably part with something'.[1]

The ethos of British policy was reinforced by the temperaments of the prime minister and foreign secretary. Critics delighted in denigrating

Chamberlain as a Birmingham businessman, inexperienced in foreign affairs, manipulated by the *éminence grise*, Sir Horace Wilson, chief industrial adviser to the government. However, as chancellor of the exchequer since 1931 and heir-apparent to Baldwin since 1935, Chamberlain was closely concerned in the formulation of foreign and defence policies. He was suspicious of the Foreign Office and occasionally bypassed it, but in this respect he was no more guilty than his predecessors. Asquith had his 'Shadow Cabinet', Lloyd George his 'Garden Suburb'. Wilson admittedly knew little of foreign policy but his role was much more that of *fidus Achates* than *éminence grise*. Chamberlain's real weakness, it would seem, 'lay in his willingness to be guided by mediocre advice, not in his alleged aloofness from official advice'. More importantly, the essential flaw in policy making was structural, not personal. 'Meaningful debate . . . was not generated because the policy-making machinery was too centralised in its formal workings and too clubby in its informal workings.'[2]

What distinguished Chamberlain's premiership from that of Baldwin was a belief in a personal mission and a sense of urgency. The sense of mission was partly family tradition – a desire to achieve the Anglo–German alliance which had eluded his father, Joe Chamberlain – partly an instinct to save the soul of conservatism through Tory democracy. Armaments, he told Hitler in September 1938, were 'eating up the capital which ought to be employed on building houses, on better food and on improving the health of the people'.[3] His awareness of time running out reflected his own age – 68 in 1937. It was also a natural reaction to the drift of Baldwin's last year when the abdication crisis paralysed foreign policy. The speeding-up of appeasement was a response to the darkening international scene in 1936–7. But perhaps the most important consideration was party politics. With a general election looming ahead not later than 1940, *détente* was urgent if the Labour Party was to be kept out of office and Tory democracy fulfilled.

As 'a practical man' Chamberlain saw negotiations as part of the natural order, almost therapeutic in themselves: 'If only we could sit down at a table with the Germans and run through all their complaints and claims with a pencil, this would greatly relieve all tension.'[4] But he was not to be bullied. His reaction to the *Anschluss* was that 'for the moment we must abandon conversations with Germany, we must show our determination . . . by announcing some increase or acceleration in rearmament'.[5] Chamberlain's approach rested on the premise that Hitler and Mussolini were reasonable, rational men at heart, who would keep their word, provided their reasonable claims were met. 'I got the impression that here was a man who could be relied upon when he had given his word,' he wrote after the Berchtesgaden meeting with Hitler.[6] 'Herr Hitler's objectives', he told Cabinet colleagues, 'are strictly limited.'[7] Excessive reliance on his own judgment and abilities led him to make an act of faith

in a political fanatic. After talking to Hitler at Godesberg he was convinced
that Hitler 'would not deliberately deceive a man whom he respected . . .
he thought that he had now established an influence over Herr Hitler and
that the latter trusted him'.[8]

Halifax, who succeeded Eden as foreign secretary in February 1938,
was pre-eminently a conciliator. A former viceroy of India and a leading
high churchman, his first impulse was towards reconciliation. His father,
the first Lord Halifax, had played a major role in the Malines Conversations
of 1922-3 – the bid to reconcile Canterbury with Rome. Such was
Halifax's personal integrity that, like the Miss Lydgate created by
Dorothy L. Sayers, he 'embraced the irregularities of other people in a
wide unquestioning charity'.[9] Sincerity was all. In Germany in November
1937, despite the evidence he saw of a 'different set of values', he found
Hitler 'very sincere' and 'liked all the Nazi leaders'. After the discussions
he felt 'more than ever the tragedy of Versailles' and concluded that it
was 'essential for us to get on with them'.[10] He utterly failed to fathom the
wickedness of Hitler's myrmidons. Göring was compared to 'a modern
Robin Hood . . . film star, gangster, great landowner . . . head gamekeeper
at Chatsworth'.[11] However, Halifax grew with office and showed a will of
his own. In September 1938, at the height of the Czechoslovak crisis, he
was persuaded to oppose Hitler's Godesberg terms and parted company
with Chamberlain on this issue (Doc. 57). After Munich there was more
evidence that he had a mind of his own.[12]

The idealistic considerations which had always guaranteed Germany
some sympathy still applied – horror of war, the need for treaty revision.
'In war there are no winners, but all are losers,'[13] declared Chamberlain.
The peace treaty prohibition on an *Anschluss* between Germany and
Austria was considered unjust. Sir Nevile Henderson, who took over from
Phipps as ambassador in Berlin in late 1937, 'always, from 1920 onwards,
held the view that Austria could not but be swallowed up in the end'.[14]
Czechoslovakia was condemned as an artificial, unstable structure, 'part
of a French plan to keep Germany under control'.[15] 'Czechoslovakian rule
in the Sudeten areas for the last 20 years has been marked by tactlessness,
intolerance and discrimination,' wrote the Liberal leader Lord Runciman
in September 1938.[16]

With Japan's attack on China in July 1937 the latent problem of British
power became explicit. By her departure from the Second London Naval
Conference in 1936 Japan had already challenged the leading naval powers,
Britain and the United States. 'We cannot', Chamberlain wrote in 1934,
'provide simultaneously for hostilities with Japan and Germany.'[17] After
Abyssinia, Italy was now numbered among the potentially hostile powers.
In the summer of 1937 Italian submarines were attacking British and
French ships trading with Spanish Republican ports. 'There were limits
to our resources both physical and financial,' Chamberlain told the

Committee of Imperial Defence on 5 July 1937, 'and it was vain to contemplate fighting singlehanded the three strongest powers in combination.'[18] Though there was no military alliance between Germany, Italy and Japan, there were grounds for supposing that the three would act together. In November 1937 Italy joined the Anti-Comintern Pact which Germany and Japan had signed the previous year. Mussolini's visit to Berlin in September 1937 seemed to set the seal on the Axis.

Yet it would be quite wrong to assume that the Chamberlain government kowtowed to Japan. It can be argued that, notwithstanding appeals from the British embassy in Tokyo for a conciliatory line, 'the Chamberlain government gave surprisingly little sustained consideration during the 1937–9 period to a policy of appeasement'.[19] In fact, consideration was given to the idea of a demonstration of naval strength to deter the Japanese.

Imperial defence was an added anxiety for the Chamberlain government. At the 1937 Imperial Conference an undertaking was given to New Zealand and Australia that in the event of a crisis a British fleet would be sent to the Far East. Since Britain did not have the naval strength to send fleets to both the Far East and the Mediterranean, it was reasoned that some effort must be made to reach agreement with Germany and Italy. Hopes that American help might be enlisted in blocking Japan were dashed by the failure of the Nine Power Brussels Conference on the Far East in November 1937.

In Chamberlain's view Britain's allies were no armour against the dictators. France was deemed politically and militarily unreliable (Doc. 44). Though the French army was acknowledged the finest in Europe, Chamberlain and his advisers had serious doubts about the French air force. The United States offered no salvation. The extension of the Neutrality Act in February 1936 confirmed American isolationism and made it impossible for the United States to supply arms even to League members combating an aggressor. The dominions were more a hindrance than a help. Attempts to persuade them to share the burden of imperial defence failed. The 1937 Imperial Conference revealed Canadian and South African suspicions of European affairs. The one common factor in imperial foreign policy – recognition of the League – was destroyed. The Soviet Union was a potential ally, but Chamberlain was deeply suspicious of Stalin's motives. The aim of Soviet intervention in Spain, it was thought, was to stir up a general war in western Europe. It was known that purges had taken a heavy toll of the Russian military leaders. Three out of five marshals had vanished, and hosts of lesser commanders.

Massive armaments were rejected on financial and political grounds. An arms race, it was held, would be self-defeating, acting not as a deterrent but as cause of war. The assumption that a war with Germany would be a long one made it seem axiomatic that financial reserves should be husbanded, not squandered on great armaments. In the First World War the United States had served as an arsenal for the two democracies, but the neutrality legislation of 1935–6 meant that Britain and France would have to pay for a war entirely out of their own pockets. For Chamberlain, therefore, financial and economic strength was the 'fourth arm of defence'. 'Nothing', Sir Thomas Inskip, minister for the co-ordination of defence, wrote in February 1938, 'operates more strongly to deter a political aggressor from attacking this country than our (*economic*) stability.'[20] The Chamberlain government was haunted by the spectre of the financial and economic collapse of 1931. Rising prices in 1937 led Chamberlain to voice his fears 'that we might easily run . . . into a series of crippling strikes . . . a feverish boom followed by a disastrous slump, and finally the defeat of the Government . . . the advent of an ignorant, unprepared and heavily pledged Opposition, to handle a crisis as severe as that of 1931'.[21]

Financial and economic constraints weighed heavily on French ministers. The French economy showed no signs of recovery until 1938–9. In 1936–7 and for much of 1938 ministers battled to save the franc. Apprehensive of the Front Populaire, French investors had sold francs for United States dollars or pounds sterling. In May 1938 the franc was devalued for the third time in less than two years. In August a financial crisis erupted and resulted in the resignation of two ministers. Foreign observers did not pull their punches. Lending money to France, declared Henry Morgenthau, secretary to the United States treasury, was 'just like flowing money into the Atlantic . . . someone has to tell the French that they are a bankrupt, fourth class power'.[22] In August 1938 the French foreign minister warned that 'if France should continue to arm at the present rate it would be necessary to regiment the entire country, placing the civilian population on soldiers' wages and soldiers' rations'.[23]

Appeasement was also a response to social and political pressures. The Front Populaire deeply divided French society. The Spanish Civil War injected fresh venom into the body politic. For French conservatives Blum's government was an unmitigated disaster – sit-in strikes, nationalisation measures, wage increases, a 25 per cent devaluation of the franc, a forty-hour week and paid holidays. Hence the slogan 'Better Hitler than Blum'.[24] Blum's conciliatory approaches to Berlin in 1936–7 were motivated by the desire to save his social programme. International *détente* was needed for domestic *détente*. After Blum's fall in June 1937 a right-wing reaction gathered pace. His successors, Camille Chautemps and Edouard Daladier, were intent on exorcising the demons of the Popular Front. That Blum's second administration in March–April 1938 lasted barely four weeks testified to the strength of right-wing attitudes. Like Blum, Chautemps and Daladier worked for *détente* but for different reasons. A settlement with the fascist dictators, it was hoped, would divide the left and assuage the anxieties of the propertied classes. Given peace abroad, Popular Front social legislation could be quietly dismantled. War with

Germany, it was feared, would only strengthen the left and bring social revolution. In September 1938, when war seemed imminent, Joseph Caillaux, president of the Senate finance committee, warned that 'heavy air bombardments of factories around Paris may well cause another Commune'.[25]

In Britain party politics and foreign policy were closely intertwined. Indeed Maurice Cowling argues that 'in the late thirties foreign policy was the form that party conflict took. Politicians conducted it in the light of party considerations; it can only be understood if these considerations are reconstructed.'[26] Briefly put, his thesis is that the central concern of politics in the 1930s was keeping Labour out. In 1931 the Labour Party was broken and the predominantly Conservative National Government in office. By 1934 Labour was recovering its strength and a new policy was needed to keep it at bay. The answer was an initiative in foreign policy. In the Abyssinian crisis Baldwin championed the League and thereby captured the floating vote. The policy carried no serious risks. If it failed, the failure could be blamed on the League and on France. The government's support for sanctions in November 1935 undoubtedly helped to give it a massive majority in the election of that month. Within a month, however, the Hoare–Laval Plan discredited the government and badly damaged the League. After two wasted years under Baldwin the government was no nearer a settlement with Germany. Neville Chamberlain tried a new initiative. The recipe was reconciliation and rearmament. Britain would work for the reconciliation of the three major continental powers – Germany, France and Italy. Treaty revision would satisfy Germany's genuine needs and rearmament would convince her of the uselessness of general war.

Hitler's occupation of Prague in March 1939, argues Mr Cowling, killed *détente*. Chamberlain was reluctant to change course but was saved by Halifax, 'the embodiment of Conservative wisdom who decided that Hitler must be obstructed because Labour could not otherwise be resisted'.[27] However, the new firmness had flaws. The articles of faith of Chamberlain's pre-Munich policy had been preservation of the empire, detachment from Russia, defence of the Low Countries and a stable economy. After March 1939 both the empire and the economy were at risk. None the less Chamberlain survived. It was Hitler's invasion of the Low Countries and of France in May 1940 that finally toppled him and traditional conservatism. The need to fight the war produced a new consensus: Churchill's centre coalition of May 1940. Its triumph had two major consequences: the establishment of the Labour Party as the dominant political force after 1945 and the disestablishment of the British empire.

The main fault with appeasement, Mr Cowling implies, was that it was not properly followed through. A Britain which had rearmed could have pursued an isolationist foreign policy which, it is suggested, would have saved her empire. Chamberlain's mistake was not the abandonment of Czechoslovakia but the giving of a guarantee in September 1938. Though the guarantee was merely a tactical move to induce the French and Czechs to accept dismemberment it marked the beginning of a fatal course of continental involvement culminating in the post-Prague guarantees to Poland, Greece, Romania and Turkey. By avoiding commitments until September 1938, Chamberlain's diplomacy had been consistent and coherent. Isolation, it is asserted, would have been practicable because Hitler did not really threaten British interests at all:

> Hitler may have wanted to destroy the British Empire. But this was not obvious then and is far from obvious now. It is at least as likely that he aimed primarily to fulfil promises about Germany's economic and world role and was compelled to attack Britain only by British action in May and September 1938. Even if it is assumed that his aims were from the start to 'purify' Germany, destroy Russia and colonise the Ukraine, that suggests nothing about his attitude to Britain.
>
> It may be that Hitler was the 'beast from the abyss' whom Britain had a duty to destroy. It may be that victory over Russia would have been followed by an attack on the West. It is possible to deny the duty, to question the sequence or to believe that success, or failure to succeed against Russia, would have affected the character of the regime in Germany. . . .[28]

These are assertions, not arguments. While it is conceivable that Hitler might have been content with mastery of Europe and his regime might have changed as a result of his conquests, the sequence is in fact far from likely. Late in 1937 Hitler made clear his intention of turning on the west after the destruction of Czechoslovakia. The long-term naval preparations for a conflict with Britain date from November 1937. The priority given to the navy in the allocation of armour plate at the Hossbach conference on 5 November 1937 showed a significant change of attitude towards Britain.[29] Thus *before* the Czechoslovak crisis of 1938 Hitler was thinking of an attack on the west.

It is true that Hitler's regime *might* have changed after conquests in the east but there is no reason to think that it would have been in the direction of consolidation and stability. To have allowed Germany to over-run much of eastern Europe and then trusted in Hitler's moderation would have been a suicidal course. Once Germany dominated the east, Britain and France were effectively trapped because the resources harnessed by Germany gave her an overwhelming superiority in the west. Complete isolation for Britain was a chimera. A refusal to guarantee Czechoslovakia in September 1938 or Poland in March 1939 would not have saved Britain from war. France would have been so demoralised that she would have come to terms with Germany and thereby endangered the Low Countries – always recognised as a major British interest. Alternatively, France would have gone to war in September 1939 in defence of Poland and Britain would have had to support her in order to protect the Low Countries. Britain lacked the strength to pursue an isolationist foreign policy. Isolation meant powerlessness, as 1940 showed. Only the wartime Anglo–American alliance enabled Britain to re-establish some world influence.

Conceivably the doctrine of appeasement might have been challenged by the chiefs of staff. Before 1914 the generals had fuelled the 'will to war' mood. By contrast, in the late 1930s none of the general staffs regarded the prospect of war with enthusiasm. The timidity of the politicians was sustained by the reluctance of their military advisers to prepare for war.[30]

The French army had no plans to help the eastern allies. The defensive principle was unchallenged. Following a declaration of war the French army planned to mobilise within the shelter of the Maginot line. Faced by the prospect of war for Czechoslovakia in 1938 Gamelin, chief of the French general staff, pursued a double line.[31] With his civilian masters he was pessimistic about the possibilities of helping Czechoslovakia, stressing the difficulties of a war – the strength of the Siegfried line, uncertainty of allied help, especially of Poland and the Little Entente, Belgian neutrality. With the British he was optimistic, contrasting German weaknesses: unfinished fortifications, shortage of trained reserves and of raw materials, especially oil – with allied strength: 5-million-strong French forces, a powerful defensive position, Czechoslovak military power. His object was to keep the army out of trouble. Abroad it was necessary to speak up for Czechoslovakia for the sake of French honour; at home it was essential to discourage the politicians, because another Franco–German war might well mean defeat and internal collapse for which the army would be blamed.

The British chiefs of staff were also pessimistic to the point of defeatism (Doc. 44). The defence review of late 1937 gave priority to home defence. The idea of a continental field force on the model of 1914 was abandoned. So too was bomber parity with Germany. The emphasis was on providing a fighter force and navy to make Britain impregnable. Germany, it was reasoned, would not be able to deliver a 'knockout blow' and then British naval and economic strength would prove decisive in a long war. The chiefs of staff warmly seconded the doctrine of limited liability. They opposed staff talks with France, though 'the refusal to accept a Continental commitment was a nonsense in military terms'.[32]

The Chamberlain government's assessment of the international situation in 1937–8 may be criticised on several counts. Optimism about the prospects of *détente* with Germany and Italy contrasted with the gloomy opinions about Britain's principal allies: France and the United States.

France certainly had her troubles but the Chamberlain Cabinet's thinly veiled contempt and refusal to hold staff talks strengthened the hand of those Frenchmen who wanted to withdraw from eastern Europe.[33] Both countries had common interests and ideals and a full partnership might have solved their dilemmas. Anglo–French military co-operation, though exiguous before March 1939, could produce decisive results. The Nyon Conference in September 1937 instituted joint Anglo–French destroyer patrols in the Mediterranean which stopped Italian submarine attacks on ships trading with Republican Spain. Indeed, Italy's strength was over-estimated. 'The British', it is argued, 'were bluffed again and again by Italy because they over-estimated Mussolini's ability to act in defiance of the sheer realities of power. By acting on the unproved but generally accepted assumption that he would commit a "mad dog" act rather than lose face they were bound to lose the war of nerves in every Mediterranean crisis.'[34]

Much was made then and later of American isolationism and in particular of the weakness of President Roosevelt's initiative of January 1938. In a message of 11 January Roosevelt informed Chamberlain that he proposed to make a major speech on international dangers with a suggestion for a conference. Without British backing he would not go ahead. Chamberlain's chilly reply of 13 January concealed elements of fear and jealousy of American economic and naval power.[35] The feeling of British and French statesmen was that European affairs were best settled by Europeans. American co-operation was needed but only on Europe's terms. Despite the fragility of Anglo–American relations the progress that was made in 1938–9 suggests that given determination and goodwill much more might have been achieved. In May 1938 the Admiralty authorised the regular exchange of secret technical information with Washington; in September American cruisers were kept in British waters in order to impress Germany; in October Roosevelt sent a message to Chamberlain, promising that in the event of war with the dictators he would do his utmost to ensure that Britain had the help of American industry; in April 1939 the American fleet was transferred from the Atlantic to the Pacific in response to Anglo–French requests.[36]

Chamberlain's intense distrust of the Soviet Union (Doc. 47) meant the cold-shouldering of what may have been genuine initiatives; for example, the Soviet appeal in March 1938 for a four-power conference to consider measures against aggression. Contrary, however, to what Soviet and Marxist historiography alleges, western statesmen did not scheme to turn Hitler against the Soviet Union. There is no evidence for the belief that Chamberlain and Halifax were plotting to give Germany a free hand in the east.[37] Baldwin's remark that if there was 'any fighting in Europe to be done' he would like to see the 'Bolshies' and the 'Nasties' doing it was an expression of opinion, not a statement of policy.

Dominion attitudes also influenced the Chamberlain government's foreign policy.[38] In conversations with French ministers in 1937-8, British leaders stressed that the dominions would not support a strong line against Germany. In particular, there would be no sympathy for a British guarantee to Czechoslovakia. Now although it is true that the dominion high commissioners were almost wholly against a commitment for Czechoslovakia in 1938, it is significant that when the dominions followed the same line in 1939 – only Australia gave support for the Polish guarantee – British policy was not deflected. This suggests that the influence of the dominions was not a major constraint on British policy. Indeed, 'dominion opinion only confirmed Chamberlain on a course of action on which he had already decided . . . Their opinions [Dominions] were considered . . . But care was taken to sift information on the European situation going to the Dominions' (Doc. 53).[39] Arguably a government determined to resist Germany might have brought about a change of attitude in the dominions.

One major assumption behind Chamberlain's thinking was that it was necessary to play for time because Britain was best fitted to wage a long war. The longer Britain had to finish her rearmament the better her prospects of survival and ultimate victory. It is argued that Chamberlain underestimated the rapidity and extent of Britain's post-1931 recovery. According to one historian, 'had we rearmed more intensively between 1934 and 1938 . . . it seems likely that not only would there have been no Munich but Britain would have been able to keep out of war'.[40] Yet economic historians question whether there was in fact an 'economic recovery' after 1931.[41] Also, it seems inconceivable in the context of world depression and continuing hopes for disarmament that a British government could have begun rearmament in 1934. More plausibly, it can be said that Chamberlain was wrong in thinking that Britain had the stamina to fight a long war. In July 1939 Sir John Simon, chancellor of the exchequer, told the Cabinet that the effect of rearmament on the balance of payments and the level of taxation would be such that the war for which they were preparing would be lost before it began.[42] The Treasury's view was that neither Britain nor Germany could sustain a major war. If the Treasury's analysis was sound – and by the autumn of 1940 Britain had exhausted almost all her American assets – it might have been better to fight Germany in 1938.

From the autumn of 1937 a new aggressive note was sounded in German policy. On 5 November Hitler summoned his leading advisers to a secret conference at the Reich chancellery. The only extant record of the conference is the much-disputed Hossbach Memorandum drawn up by Hitler's adjutant, Colonel Hossbach (Doc. 40).[43] In the Nuremberg Trials the prosecution cited the Memorandum as evidence of premeditated aggression against Austria and Czechoslovakia in 1938. However, the document is not a full and accurate record of the 5 November meeting. It is not the original record or even a first copy, but a copy of a copy. Nor is it an official record. It was composed several days after the conference and covers only part of the proceedings. Moreover, the conference was not called to discuss foreign policy but to decide on priorities in the allocation of armaments between the three armed services. This said, there is no reason why the Memorandum should not be accepted as a guide to Hitler's ideas on foreign policy.

The Hossbach Memorandum confirms the continuity of Hitler's thinking: the primacy of force in world politics, conquest of living space in the east, anti-Bolshevism, hostility to France. It also offers evidence of long-range goals. Germany's problems, Hitler said, would have to be solved by force by 1943–5 at the latest. If Germany did not act by that date her armaments would be obsolescent, nazism would lose its momentum, economic and financial pressures would become intolerable. More important though was the confession of immediate aims – the seizure of Austria and Czechoslovakia. Hitler envisaged two opportunities for German expansion in central Europe: 'the crippling of France by civil war', or an 'Anglo–French–Italian war' arising out of Mediterranean tensions. A Mediterranean conflict, Hitler thought, might come as early as 1938. Whatever Hitler's ultimate destination, his warlike intentions were now explicit.

The sequel to the Hossbach conference affords conclusive evidence of its significance in foreign policy. Until the winter of 1937–8 German military planning had been defensive in character. Strategic planning was based on a general directive of 24 June 1937, providing for two deployments: Plan Red to defeat a major French attack in the west while holding the defensive against France's eastern allies; Plan Green according priority to a pre-emptive attack on Czechoslovakia while remaining on the defensive in the west. The June 1937 directive gave priority to Plan Red. However, an amendment of 7 December 1937 reveals a crucial change of emphasis (Doc. 43). Green was now given precedence over Red. The purpose of planning was no longer the defence of the Reich but the conquest of Czechoslovakia.[44]

A prerequisite of expansion was the complete concentration of power in Hitler's hands. The diplomats and officer corps had retained considerable independence. In February 1938 Hitler reorganised the military leadership. Field Marshal von Blomberg, war minister, and General von Fritsch, commander-in-chief of the army, were dismissed.[45] The war ministry was abolished and replaced by a new armed-forces organisation, the OKW (*Oberkommando der Wehrmacht*). Hitler assumed personal command of the armed forces on 4 February. Ribbentrop's appointment as foreign minister in place of von Neurath marked the final subordination of the foreign ministry. With the resignation of General Beck, army chief of staff, in August 1938, the elimination of moderate and independent counsels was complete.

Within the *Wehrmacht* a small group of officers formed an anti-Hitler opposition. But the intermediaries sent to London in the summer of 1938 were met with incredulity. Chamberlain likened them to the 'Jacobites at the Court of France in King William's time'.[46] Such scepticism was understandable since the emissaries could offer no evidence of an efficient military conspiracy or of an attractive political programme for a future Germany.

'With dictators nothing succeeds like success,' Hitler boasted.[47] The new tempo of policy was a natural extension of previous successes. 'The sight of means to do ill-deeds' had its usual effect. The Mediterranean tensions generated by the Spanish Civil War offered Hitler an unprecedented opportunity for expansion. The new dynamism was based in part on a conviction that Germany did not now need a British alliance. Until 1936–7 Hitler assumed that Britain could be wooed or forced into an alliance. But 'by the summer of 1937 it was clear that Ribbentrop's mission as ambassador in London had failed. Therefore, though still willing to enter into an alliance, as Ribbentrop's appointment had been intended to emphasise, he made up his mind to start German expansion on the Continent "without England", confident that the British government would have no option but to accept this development.'[48] In *Mein Kampf* and the *Secret Book* Hitler had stressed the need for a British alliance, but at the 5 November conference Britain and France were referred to as 'our enemies who both hate us'. Hitler gave practical effect to this change of heart. The decision was taken on 5 November to give priority in the allocation of armour plate to the navy.

To what extent were economic pressures pushing Hitler towards war? The search for an economic motive has produced three main interpretations: first, the prewar interpretations of nazism and fascism as the final aggressive stage of capitalism leading inevitably to war; second, the argument that German rearmament imposed such enormous strains on the economy that a war for plunder was the only escape; third, the contention that the social and economic tensions that gave rise to national socialism implied in the long run the economic reconstruction of European society.

The first interpretation is one which post-1945 communist historians have adopted.[49] The difficulty is that although industrialists supported the Third Reich it was not a 'big-business' government. Often the regime seemed to act against the interests of big business. National socialism had distinct anti-capitalist undertones. Its most loyal adherents – middle-class white-collar workers and poorly paid agricultural workers – were the two groups who felt most threatened by industrialisation. Also, the Marxist interpretation does not explain why the two leading capitalist states, Britain and the United States, were the most anxious to avoid war.

More plausible is the second view. Its chief proponent, Dr Tim Mason, writes: 'The Third Reich was the first modern state to face the many new problems raised by permanent full employment . . . the economic, social and political tensions within the Reich became steadily more acute after the summer of 1937 . . . a war for the plunder of manpower and materials lay square in the dreadful logic of German economic development under Nazi rule.'[50] There is certainly evidence of economic difficulties in 1937–8, and many contemporaries believed that Germany was in a serious plight. But there is no evidence that these tensions played a part in Hitler's decision making. As Dr Mason concedes: 'The existence in the winter of 1937–8 of a conscious connection in Hitler's mind between this general crisis and the need for a more dynamic foreign policy cannot yet be established.'[51] It is also puzzling that Hitler should have ignored western offers of colonial, financial and economic concessions in 1938–9.

The strength of the third interpretation is that the economic and political factors are seen as a whole. 'Hitler's determination to conquer Russia', writes Mrs Carroll, 'stemmed not merely from political fanaticism but also from his "substitute for an economic theory" and his analysis, in its terms, of Germany's economic situation.'[52] More fundamentally, as Professor Milward believes, the very problems of industrialisation which created national socialism implied ultimately the conquest and reorganisation of Europe.[53]

German rearmament in 1938–9 sheds some light on Hitler's intentions. The level of armaments has been cited as 'the decisive proof that Hitler was not contemplating general war, and probably not intending war at all'.[54] Before 1939 foreign observers pictured Germany as a vast armed camp, geared for total war. After 1945 studies of the effect of strategic bombing on Germany showed that she did not have a total war economy until 1942. But the prewar image of German armaments was not without some foundation. Germany's pre-1939 war effort was much greater than that of Britain, France or the United States. Britain's military expenditure rose from 3 per cent of her national income in 1933 to 8 per cent in 1938; in the same period Germany's military spending rose from 3 per cent of her gross national product to 17 per cent. The conclusion of one analysis is that 'in 1933 the economy of the Third Reich was still "peace orientated". From 1934 it was moving in the direction of a "war economy". . . . Beginning in 1936 Germany's economy was "dominated" in certain key respects . . . by armaments, but should still not be called a "war economy". From 1938 on however that designation can legitimately be used.'

Yet Hitler was not preparing for general war. In 1939 Germany had an army of fifty-one divisions but only six weeks' supply of munitions. The key question therefore is: what kind of a war did Hitler envisage? The answer is a series of short wars – against Czechoslovakia in 1938, Poland in 1939, Russia in 1941. The war that Britain and France expected and planned for – a war of attrition on the lines of the First World War – was the war Hitler wanted to avoid. Not until the first defeats in Russia in 1941–2 did Hitler reluctantly abandon the *Blitzkrieg* strategy for one of total war.

As Hitler speeded up his programme of territorial expansion, Chamberlain launched new initiatives to secure *détente*. Halifax's visit to Germany in November 1937 was 'a great success', holding out hopes of a bargain: 'I don't see why we shouldn't say to Germany "give us satisfactory assurances that you won't use force to deal with the Austrians and Czechoslovakians and we will give you similar assurances that we won't use force to prevent the changes you want, if you can get them by peaceful means" ' (Doc. 41). Letters were exchanged with Mussolini and agreement was reached on the holding of Anglo–Italian talks.

The Anglo–French conversations of 29–30 November 1937 offered France a last chance of saving her Czechoslovak ally (Doc. 42). British ministers refused to guarantee Czechoslovakia. Chamberlain told the Cabinet afterwards: 'At one time it looked as though the French were going to press for some more forthcoming attitude on central Europe' but 'no encouragement had been given them . . . finally they had agreed that appropriate concessions might be made and that an attempt should be made to reach a general settlement with Germany'.[55] It was agreed that the initiative in approaches to Berlin and Rome should rest with London.

The demotion of Vansittart in January 1938 and the resignation of Eden as foreign secretary in February gave Chamberlain full control of policy making. The changes did not reflect any fundamental difference of principle between the prime minister and the Foreign Office. Quite the contrary: disagreements were concerned with procedure and timing rather than principle.[56] Both Eden and Vansittart conceded the need for a settlement with Germany. But their inclination was to delay concessions and settlement until rearmament was completed. Chamberlain and the chiefs of staff argued that the only way to gain time was by concessions and a settlement. Hankey explained: 'Van has got on a good many people's nerves and there is an idea about that FO suspiciousness has prevented us from taking advantage of opportunities to get on better terms with Italy and perhaps Germany.'[57]

On the eve of the *Anschluss* Britain was preoccupied with approaches to Germany and Italy. No thought was spared for the Austrians. 'Personally I almost wish Germany would swallow Austria and get it over,' wrote Sir Alexander Cadogan, Vansittart's successor as permanent under secretary.[58] French pressure for a diplomatic stand on Austria aroused Cadogan's wrath: 'I want to stop the French butting in.'[59] Anglo–Italian talks started in the second half of February, and on 3 March Henderson submitted to Hitler proposals for a general settlement, including colonial concessions. Hitler showed no interest, dismissing the colonial offer with the comment that opinion was not 'ripe' to give it consideration.[60] Despite efforts to persuade Britain to join her in sending a warning to Germany, France had no military plans to help Austria and was without a government on 12 March.

The improvisation and opportunism that characterised Hitler's annexation of Austria on 12 March 1938 need no emphasis. As an Austrian, Hitler stated his goal of *Anschluss* on the first page of *Mein Kampf*. After the abortive *putsch* of July 1934 the strategy followed was an evolutionary one – German economic and political pressures would pull Austria inexorably into Germany's orbit. The Berchtesgaden Agreements of 12 February 1938, by which the Austrian chancellor, Schuschnigg, agreed to include Austrian nazis in his government, represented an acceleration of tactics, not a change of strategy. As late as 26 February the leader of the Austrian nazis was told that Hitler 'did not now desire a solution by violent means'.[61] The use of force on 12 March was precipitated by Schuschnigg's decision to hold a plebiscite. An Austrian majority for independence would have sabotaged Hitler's goal. Invasion plans were improvised in the night of 9–10 March.

However, there are two aspects of the *Anschluss* that have not been sufficiently stressed: one was the interplay of Hitler's foreign and domestic policies in February–March 1938; the other was the key role played by Göring. As early as 31 January 1938 Colonel Jodl of the general staff noted in his diary: 'Führer wishes to divert the spotlight from the *Wehrmacht*, keep Europe in a ferment. . . . Schuschnigg should not gain courage but tremble.'[62] Four weeks later Hitler told another officer: 'I shall launch an undertaking against Austria in the very near future. It will go smoothly.'[63] Hitler welcomed the Austrian crisis as a means of diverting attention from the domestic repercussions of the Fritsch–Blomberg affair and the reorganisation of the armed forces. The march on Vienna on 12 March was due 'in large measure to Göring, who grasped with both hands the lead vacated by the vacillating Hitler'.[64]

The Approach of War, 1938–9

After Austria, Czechoslovakia was next on the menu. With an army of thirty-five divisions and alliances with France and the Soviet Union, Czechoslovakia was a formidable barrier to German expansion. Of the successor states Czechoslovakia alone possessed a real parliamentary democracy. Hitler found a convenient stalking horse in the grievances of the 3·5 million Sudeten Germans led by Konrad Henlein.

British policy towards Czechoslovakia was singularly ill-informed and unsympathetic. Czechoslovakia constituted not a bastion to be defended but 'a last chance' for Anglo–German understanding.[1] British ministers assumed that virtually nothing had been done to satisfy Sudeten German claims. They ignored the fact that in 1937 the Prague government included three Sudeten German ministers and that in elections 33 per cent of the German electorate supported the government.[2] The tales of misery and oppression purveyed by Henlein were accorded almost complete credence in London while the declarations of Edward Beneš, president of Czechoslovakia, were received with polite disbelief.

Anglo–French policies towards Czechoslovakia were finalised in the week following the *Anschluss*. Without consulting Paris and without full benefit of military advice, the British Cabinet decided that Czechoslovakia was indefensible and that no guarantee should be given to France in respect of her ally (Doc. 47).[3] Blum's second Popular Front administration searched for some way of saving Czechoslovakia. On 15 March the Comité Permanent de la Défense Nationale (Permanent Committee of National Defence) concluded that France could not help Prague directly (Doc. 46). Buffeted by storms on all sides – the loss of his wife, political intrigues to unseat him, industrial unrest, Senate opposition to his financial reforms, ill-concealed British antipathy – Blum, and his foreign minister, Joseph Paul-Boncour, offered only a token resistance to British pressures.

The story of the Czechoslovak crisis of 1938 has been told and retold. Rather than retrace old ground I have singled out three themes for scrutiny: French intentions, the origins of the weekend crisis of 20–1 May, and Munich. On 28–9 April 1938 the first of three Anglo–French conversations on Czechoslovakia took place in London. Outwardly the object was the working out of an agreed policy. In reality both governments were concerned to shuffle off the responsibility for unpleasant decisions. British ministers saw the April conference not as a genuine discussion leading to joint decisions but as a means of inducing French colleagues to accept a predetermined policy.

Edouard Daladier, Blum's successor as prime minister, posed as an opponent of German expansion. Resistance was in part for the record. Uppermost was the desire to preserve French honour. France wanted Britain to take the initiative in putting pressure on Prague to reach a settlement with the Sudeten Germans so as to save her 'from the cruel dilemma of dishonouring her agreements or becoming involved in war'.[4] Moreover, French ministers had to keep watch on their parliamentary majority – largely a Popular Front majority sympathetic to Czechoslovakia. A public admission in London or Paris that the government was preparing to abandon Czechoslovakia would have been political suicide. France also needed insurance. Daladier feared that in the event of a German attack on Czechoslovakia France would be without British backing. War for Czechoslovakia without Britain would be a catastrophe. Britain's Locarno obligations covered only unprovoked German aggression against France. Speaking in the House of Commons on 24 March, Chamberlain had refused to widen this commitment to include a Franco–German war arising out of the operation of the Franco–Czechoslovak treaty. Nevertheless his statement closed on an equivocal note: 'Where peace and war are concerned, legal obligations are not alone involved. . . .'[5] What Daladier wanted, therefore, in the Anglo–French conversations was an unequivocal pledge of British support. By insisting that France would fulfil her treaty obligations Daladier won substantial concessions – Chamberlain's promise on 18 September of a British guarantee for Czechoslovakia and on the 26th a pledge of British support in the event of France's going to war. Despite recriminations and reproaches in both capitals (Doc. 58) the Czechoslovak crisis led to a strengthening and consolidation of the *Entente*. Within its terms French policy was highly successful. The responsibility for the abandonment of Czechoslovakia was shared, and France was within sight of a full defensive alliance.

On 30 May 1938 Hitler issued a new directive on Plan Green, code name for an attack on Czechoslovakia. It was his 'unalterable decision to smash Czechoslovakia in the near future'. Military preparations were to be completed by 1 October 1938 'at the latest' (Doc. 50). In March–April Hitler had seemed in no hurry to solve the Czechoslovak problem. On 28 March Henlein was instructed 'not to drive things to the limit' but always to demand 'so much that we can never be satisfied' (Doc. 48). Why did Hitler change his mind? The answer to this question depends on the interpretation of the crisis of 20–1 May. On 19 May persistent reports of German troop movements against Czechoslovakia caused an international panic. A partial Czechoslovak mobilisation was followed by a British *démarche* in Berlin. The commonly accepted interpretation of the crisis is that it was the result, not of German troop movements, but of international nervousness.[6] Hitler, it is said, was so infuriated by the belief that Germany had retreated under a show of force that he issued the new directive for an attack on Czechoslovakia.

Alternatively it can be argued that the crisis was of Hitler's making. The *Anschluss* had been improvised in two days. Similarly, Hitler, it is suggested, believed that in mid-May conditions were ripe for a lightning descent on Czechoslovakia. Those who argue that the crisis was none of Hitler's doing cite a draft of 20 May for Plan Green: 'It is not my intention to smash Czechoslovakia by military action in the immediate future without provocation.'[7] An undated entry in the diary of Colonel Jodl of the general staff reads: 'The intention of the Führer not to touch the Czech problem is changed because of the Czech strategic troop concentration of 21 May which occurs without any German threat. . . . Because of Germany's self-restraint its consequences lead to a loss of prestige which the Führer is not willing to take once more. Therefore the new order is issued for Green on 30 May.'[8] This evidence is not in fact as conclusive as it might seem. The draft orders of 20 May for Green were sent to Hitler by General Keitel, head of the OKW; they summarised discussions held on 21 April and do not necessarily represent Hitler's intentions in mid-May. Furthermore, the precise wording of the draft orders is important: 'It is not my intention to smash Czechoslovakia by military action in the immediate future without provocation unless an unavoidable development of the political conditions within Czechoslovakia forces the issue, or political events in Europe create a particularly favourable opportunity which may perhaps never reoccur.' In short, far from excluding an attack on Czechoslovakia Hitler was concerned to define the conditions for such an attack. As for the entry in Jodl's diary, it is undated and sandwiched between entries for 11 March and 22 May, and must therefore be treated with caution.

By mid-May Hitler seemed to have the conditions he needed: municipal elections in Czechoslovakia were to be held on 22 May; the international situation was favourable. Acting on instructions, Henlein visited London on 12–14 May and reported back to Hitler on the 15th. His impressions of a sympathetic British government may have encouraged Hitler to think that Britain would accept a *fait accompli*. The other element in the situation was Italy. Hitler's policy was linked to Mussolini's Mediterranean interests. His bid for a military alliance with Italy in the first week of May was unsuccessful but reports from Rome in the second week were encouraging. Hitler may have felt that it was safe to proceed without Italy. Professor Wallace writes: 'On 16 May a series of telegrams flashed between Hitler and his supreme command. "Which divisions on the Green frontiers ready to march within 12 hours, in the case of mobilisation? . . . Please send the numbers of the divisions." . . . Three days later, on 19 May, came the reports of German troop movements.[9] Hitler may not have intended a full-scale invasion, but simply a show of strength on the frontier while paramilitary SA and SS units crossed into Czechoslovakia to join up with Sudeten German groups.[10]

Whatever the origins of the May crisis, its results were indisputable. Contrary to what Hitler had assumed in November 1937, Britain had not completely 'written off the Czechs'. Almost any settlement of the Czecho-slovak issue would be acceptable to London provided it was a peaceful one. Hitler drew two conclusions. One was that in attacking Czechoslovakia time was of the essence. British and French opinion must not be given time to react. While the 20 May draft for Green stated that the hopelessness of Czechoslovakia's military position must be demonstrated 'in the first four days', the 30 May directive insisted that this must be made clear 'within the first two or three days'.[11] The other conclusion was that Germany must prepare for a possible conflict with Britain. On 24 May Admiral Raeder, chief of naval staff, received a telephone call from Hitler's naval adjutant. The note of that telephone call reads: 'On Friday 27 May the Führer intended to put questions . . . on the development of the Navy. The reason for this is the diplomatic situation from which the Führer must reckon that Britain and France will be among his enemies.'[12] This was the genesis of the Z-Plan, the naval building programme, designed to give Germany by 1944-6 'favourable prospects of a conclusive solution of "the British question"'.

The conference in Munich on 29 September 1938 was almost a non-event because agreement virtually preceded it. The Italian plan, which Britain and France accepted as a working draft, had been drafted by the Germans and was itself largely based on a British timetable proposed by Chamberlain on the 27th and seconded by Daladier.[13] The fact that both Chamberlain and Daladier left their foreign ministers at home signalled the supersession of the foreign ministries. The Agreement signed in the early hours of 30 September provided for: German occupation of the Sudetenland in ten days from 1 October; an international commission of representatives of Britain, France, Germany, Italy and Czechoslovakia to supervise the operation; and a Four Power guarantee of the dismembered state to replace the Franco–Czechoslovak treaty once Polish and Hungarian claims on Czechoslovakia had been settled. In the event German pressure on the international commission ensured that the final settlement was even more generous to Germany than the Munich Agreement had allowed.

For Chamberlain the chief justification of Munich lay not in the peaceful and orderly settlement of the Sudeten dispute but in the Anglo–German Declaration of 30 September. Before leaving Munich and without saying anything to Daladier, Chamberlain and Hitler met privately and signed a statement that Anglo–German relations were 'of the first importance for the two countries and for Europe'. The two countries would 'never . . . go to war with one another again' and were resolved 'that the method of consultation shall be the method adopted to deal with any other questions that may concern the two countries'.[14] This was the real fruit of Chamberlain's labours, the foretaste of *détente* which led Chamberlain on his return to London to speak of 'peace for our time'.

Hitler accepted Munich because his brinkmanship gave him a bloodless victory. All his public demands had been met in full. Others had done his work for him. Historians have disputed whether Hitler was bluffing during the crisis. There is no doubt that despite the reservations of his military advisers Hitler made all the preparations for an invasion of Czechoslovakia.[15] If Britain and France had not given way Czechoslovakia would probably have been attacked. But Hitler was not committed to the use of force for its own sake. The combination of political, military and psychological pressure was designed 'to wreck the nerves of those gentlemen in Prague' (Doc. 62). The Munich Agreement dismembered Czechoslovakia, depriving her of defences and much industrial potential besides. The absorption of rump Czechoslovakia could await Hitler's pleasure. Hitler's acceptance of a peaceful settlement was influenced by the fact that the assumptions of Plan Green were no longer valid. With the Czech mobilisation on 23 September and partial French mobilisation on the 24th the vital element of surprise had gone. In the morning of the 28th the British fleet was mobilised. Contrary to Hitler's expectations Britain was pledged on the 26th to support France in the event of a German attack on Czechoslovakia.

The clue to Beneš's acceptance of Munich is to be found in his fear of civil war. The enemies within were almost as dangerous as those without. Since the *Anschluss* Czechoslovakia had been increasingly torn by factional strife. Beneš was afraid of his country's becoming a Spanish-type question. Accepting Munich and salvaging some independence seemed the lesser of two evils. Fear of civil war was probably the determining element in Beneš's attitude towards the Soviet Union. The operation of the Czechoslovak–Soviet alliance was dependent on the previous implementation of the Franco–Czechoslovak pact. To have invited Soviet aid after France had in effect renounced her alliance would have precipitated civil war.

Although the hysterical relief which greeted Munich testified to the strength of support for appeasement, this does not mean that no other policy was possible at the time. Enough attention has not been paid to the question whether, given other men in power in Britain and France, with other conceptions guiding them, the climate of opinion might not have been different. Winston Churchill's 'grand alliance' against Germany offered an alternative to appeasement.[16] The Cabinet Foreign Policy

Committee discussed the idea in the week after the *Anschluss*. No one spoke up for it and it was never thoroughly explored because it ran completely counter to the goal of *détente*. Any glimmers of light on the international scene were immediately blacked out. In the first week of September the French foreign minister, Georges Bonnet, did his best to suppress a Soviet offer of staff talks (Doc. 52).[17]

Militarily there was a case for resisting Germany in September 1938. France had a last chance of fighting Germany on better or at least even terms.[18] With Germany nearing the peak of her rearmament and amassing more trained reserves, France's position could only deteriorate. At sea the two democracies were more than a match for Germany. Their weakness lay in air power and air defences. Only the Thames estuary was protected by radar. France had 1,454 aircraft of all types, Britain 1,550 and Germany 3,356. But there was no danger of the much feared knock-out blow from the air. The Luftwaffe was a tactical air force, designed for close support of ground forces. Without bases in the Low Countries it could not mount an effective bombing offensive against Britain. Germany's shortcomings were serious – shortage of trained reserves and of essential resources such as oil, for which she was heavily dependent on purchases from the west. Though known at the time, Germany's lack of oil reserves was never brought to the notice of the British Cabinet.[19] Moreover, the bulk of the German army had to be deployed against Czechoslovakia. By 30 September there were only ten German divisions in the west facing the French army. Since the concrete in the Siegfried line was not dry there was little to stop a determined French offensive.

Why, then, in the approach to Munich did Anglo–French diplomacy encounter so little domestic criticism? While the deep-seated hatred of war and condemnation of Versailles were powerful influences, they were not the only forces at work. Analyses of Munich have neglected the inter-relation between public opinion and government. Writing after the Rhineland *coup* an American diplomat signalled: 'The facts with respect to Germany are known, but they have not been consistently faced. In some countries there has been an effort through press control . . . to keep the facts from people' (Doc. 31). Two years later a State Department official observed: 'Through all this crisis [*Munich*] what has surprised me is that the governments of the democracies have not taken their people or their parliaments into their confidence.'[20] Beyond an inner circle of ministers and officials little was known of the pressure put on Prague. Faced with signs of stiffening resistance to concessions to Germany French ministers sought to limit and guide public discussion of the issues (Doc. 59). From the middle of September the French Cabinet banned all public meetings on international affairs.

Although the British government's approach to the press was based on persuasion rather than on direct intervention, considerable influence was exercised. On 17 September 1938 the American ambassador cabled home: 'When I saw Sir Samuel Hoare [*Home Secretary*] he had just finished seeing the editor of the *Daily Herald* and Sir Walter Layton, the editor of the *News Chronicle*, and he was trying to persuade them to have the papers strong on the side of peace.' Following Eden's resignation in February 1938 the American newsreel firm Paramount allowed a leading critic of the government to air his views. Within hours the newsreel firm was ordered to delete the item from reels. Paramount again fell foul of the government over Munich. They filmed interviews with critics of the Agreement. The Foreign Office approached the American government and the offending reel was withdrawn.[21]

The secrecy of Anglo–French policy went unchallenged because society in Britain and France was profoundly hierarchical and class-ridden. A passion for secrecy was built-in to British government. Deference to authority remained strong. A full knowledge of foreign affairs was thought to be the prerogative of the ruling class. Politicians and diplomats inhabited a world which had very little contact with ordinary life. Confronted with challenges at home and abroad the political elite clung to the traditions of the past. For the state visit of President Lebrun of France in March 1939 no effort was spared to stress the style and continuity of British life. It was both a bid to boost morale and a gesture of defiance against the alien ways of the dictators. This closing of the ranks brought self-censorship. In this respect the BBC sinned more than most. Conformity was the order of the day and contentious issues were shunned or soft-pedalled. When 'the unusually independent-minded programme head of North Region . . . allowed the corrosive opinions of some hunger-marchers to go out in interview form on the air, the Director General warned him that there must be no repetition of so grave an "error of judgement" '.[22] Finally, it must be remembered that many people were not greatly troubled about national, let alone international, affairs. Local, regional concerns came first.

The post-Munich period has been depicted as the 'golden age' of appeasement, followed by the 'awakening' of Hitler's entry into Prague in March 1939.[23] The truth was at once less dramatic and more complex. In reality the post-Munich winter was one of disquiet, of 'confused alarms' about German intentions, giving rise to a British request to France for staff talks. Hitler's Prague *coup* shattered some illusions but not all. The guarantees which Britain and France gave to Poland, Greece and Romania in March–April were not a decision for war but a final effort to avoid it: demonstrations of strength designed to bring about a resumption of negotiations.

On both sides of the Channel even the most fervent advocates of appeasement were united on the need to remedy military weaknesses.[24] But rearmament, it was also agreed, had to be subordinated to *détente* (Doc. 61). There was no suggestion that Britain and France should try to check

German expansion in the east. Halifax defined the object of Anglo–French policy as being 'to uphold their preponderant position in Western Europe . . . they should also firmly maintain their hold on the Mediterranean and the Near East . . . also keep a tight hold on their Colonial Empires and maintain the closest possible ties with the United States'.[25]

No Anglo–German political talks took place. There was nothing comparable to the negotiations of November 1937–March 1938. The Anglo–German economic negotiations in the winter of 1938–9, though designed to lead to political conclusions, did not affect the political climate.[26] There were two reasons for the absence of political initiatives: Hitler offered no openings, and intelligence reports indicated that he regarded Munich as a defeat and blamed Britain. These reports were considered by the Cabinet Foreign Policy Committee on 14 November 1938. Germany, it was suggested, was planning the destruction of the British empire. Chamberlain, though impressed by the evidence, was not dismayed: 'There was no suggestion that Herr Hitler contemplated any immediate aggressive action.'[27] His conclusion was that efforts at *détente* should be directed at Rome rather than Berlin. Mussolini, he believed, 'might be extraordinarily valuable in making plans for talks with Germany'.[28]

Plans were made for a Rome visit in January 1939. The approach to Italy was complicated by the Franco–Italian quarrel. Despite efforts at *rapprochement* made by Daladier and Bonnet in May 1938 relations had rapidly deteriorated after Munich. An anti-French demonstration in the Italian Chamber on 30 November culminated in shouts of 'Nice, Corsica and Tunis'. *En route* for Rome, Chamberlain and Halifax stopped off in Paris to reassure Daladier and Bonnet that Britain would not play the honest broker. France refused to concede any territory and feared British mediation. The Rome visit was a disappointment to both sides. 'Effective contact', wrote Count Ciano, Italian foreign minister, 'has not been made. How far apart we are from these people. It is another world.'[29]

A new departure in British policy came in January 1939. Secret reports suggested that Hitler was planning to invade the Low Countries and attack Britain (Doc. 65). On 1 February 1939 the British Cabinet reversed its policy of the past twelve months. It decided that a German attack on the Netherlands or Switzerland would constitute a *casus belli* because it would offer clear evidence of a bid to dominate Europe by force.[30] Two conclusions followed: a return to a continental field force and Anglo–French staff talks – in sum an Anglo–French military alliance. No secret reports seem to have reached Paris. The French were preoccupied with Italy. Both countries were concentrating troops in North Africa. On 6 February Chamberlain promised France 'immediate co-operation in the event of a threat to her vital interests from whatever quarter'.[31] This was a major extension of Britain's Locarno obligations. Britain was now pledged to defend France against Italy as well as Germany.

Pessimism soon gave way to optimism. 'All the information I get seems to point in the direction of peace,' Chamberlain wrote on 19 February.[32] There were general reasons for the change of mood: the ending of the Spanish Civil War brought hopes of an easing of Franco–Italian tension; the strengthening of Anglo–French defences, especially in the air, was encouraging; and Chamberlain continued to believe that Mussolini would exercise a moderating influence on Hitler. More particularly, Chamberlain believed he had evidence that Hitler still wanted a settlement. Conciliatory references which Henderson was told Hitler had inserted into a speech at an Anglo–German fellowship dinner in Berlin renewed Chamberlain's hopes.[33]

Munich opened a new chapter in Franco–British relations. During the Czechoslovak crisis France allowed Britain to act as pacemaker because it was essential to share responsibility for the solution to the Sudeten dispute. In the winter of 1938–9 France played a much more independent role than hitherto. The change in French policy was a direct consequence of Munich. Throughout the crisis France had been fully aware of the military value of Czechoslovakia. On 27 September Gamelin warned Daladier that if France did not save Czechoslovakia then within a decade she would be 'a second class power'.[34] On 12 October Gamelin reminded the government that 'German occupation of the Sudetenland' had brought about 'a reversal of the general situation in central Europe'.[35] A major redistribution of power had taken place, and France realised that only a full Anglo–French alliance could compensate for the loss of thirty-five Czechoslovak divisions. In the autumn of 1938 France pressed for a continental field force instead of the promised two divisions, and from January 1939 on French ministers demanded the introduction of conscription. The other area of Anglo–French disagreement was Italy. Such was the shock and humiliation of Munich that no French government could have considered making territorial concessions to Italy (Doc. 64). The mere mention by British ministers of negotiations with Italy aroused Daladier's anger.

France took a major political initiative towards Germany. In Paris on 6 December Ribbentrop and Bonnet signed a Franco–German declaration. It comprised three clauses: a declaration of friendship and goodwill, a confirmation of the existing Franco–German frontier as fixed and final, an undertaking to consult together on matters of common interest. The Bonnet–Ribbentrop discussions that accompanied the declaration, like the Laval–Mussolini conversations of January 1935, generated more heat than light (Doc. 63). At the time and after the French foreign minister was accused of giving Germany a 'free hand' in eastern Europe. But, with the exception of a single ambiguous phrase in the German record of the Paris conversations of 6–7 December, the French and German archives contain no evidence of such an assurance.[36]

No assurance was given because none was needed. The mere fact of the signing of the declaration in the wake of Munich was tantamount to a tacit acquiescence in Germany's claim to dominance in the east. Though the drift of French policy was clear there was no hasty retreat from the east. Despite Bonnet's wish *in petto* to abandon France's pacts with Poland and the Soviet Union, the alliances were maintained and even reaffirmed on 26 January 1939. A belated effort was made to assert an economic presence. French leaders had no intention of allowing Germany complete freedom of action. Preservation of some French interests, especially the Polish pact, was judged essential to France's survival as a great power. German expansion was accepted as inevitable but French ministers considered that it must be gradual and peaceful. Rapid and violent expansion would endanger Anglo–French security in western Europe.

Yet there was some ambiguity about the 6 December declaration because Germany wrongly concluded that France was ready to liquidate all her interests in the east. A degree of confusion was unavoidable since France needed time to take stock of her post-Munich position. Ambiguity was a response to the uncertainty surrounding German intentions. Germany, it was believed, would expand in the east, perhaps in the Ukraine, but there was no certainty. Until Hitler showed his hand it was prudent to postpone major policy decisions. But the ambiguity of French diplomacy was also dictated by the need to retain a bargaining position *vis-à-vis* Germany and Italy. The Franco–German accord was viewed as a possible lever against Italy. In return for French acceptance of German policy in eastern Europe Hitler might be persuaded to muzzle Mussolini. It was imperative, therefore, not to surrender too much too soon. Ambiguity was a necessary stratagem.

Secret information about Hitler's intentions had a major effect on British policy. How accurate was this information? Hitler's animus towards Britain in general, and Churchill, Eden and Duff Cooper in particular, was common knowledge, but there is no evidence that Hitler was actually planning a war against Britain. The secret reports of an imminent German invasion of the Netherlands, coupled with an air attack on London, were the work of the German opposition, notably the conservative industrialist, Carl Goerdeler.[37] The alarmist reports were taken seriously because of Hitler's declared hostility. However, Hitler did take one concrete step against Britain. In January 1939 the Z-Plan was approved, giving priority to the construction of a large fleet.

Hitler's immediate concerns in the winter of 1938–9 were the negotiation with Poland of an agreement on Danzig and the Polish Corridor, an attempt to secure military alliances with Italy and Japan, and the settlement of the Czechoslovak issue. In negotiations with Japan Germany tried hard to commit her to action against Britain and the United States in the Far East.[38] Military directives for the annexation of rump Czechoslovakia were

issued in October and December 1938.[39] In the event it was the Czechoslovak issue which was settled first. Hitler found a 'fifth column' in the
Slovaks. Their separatist claims were encouraged. Like Austria, Czechoslovakia provided the pretext for German intervention. On 9 March 1939
in a last bid to prevent his country's disintegration President Hácha
dismissed the autonomous governments of the Carpatho–Ukraine and
Slovakia and proclaimed martial law. On the 15th Germany occupied
Prague and announced the annexation of Bohemia and Moravia. The
same day Hungary occupied the Carpatho–Ukraine. Slovakia survived as
a vassal state. Militarily and politically Germany now controlled central
Europe.

Prague precipitated a diplomatic revolution. Anglo–French guarantees
were showered on eastern Europe and the Balkans: on Poland on 31 March,
on Greece and Romania on 13 April, on Turkey on 12 May. In mid-April
Britain and France opened negotiations with the Soviet Union for a
treaty of mutual assistance. The guarantees had no foundation in recent
Foreign Office thinking. Improvisation was the key note of the month
that followed Prague. Though the British Cabinet's decision in February
to regard a German attack on the Netherlands or Switzerland as a *casus
belli* had been a new departure it had operated within the defensive peri-
meter of western Europe and the Mediterranean laid down after Munich.

By annexing non-Germans Hitler at a stroke destroyed the moral
justification which his policy had hitherto enjoyed. Prague was proof that
he was bent on European domination. Parliamentary and public opinion
in Britain and France clamoured for immediate measures to deter Germany
from further adventures. But the guarantees were not designed as the
mainspring of a grand alliance against Germany. The aim remained
détente, but henceforth with more of the stick than the carrot. Chamberlain
sought 'to gain time' because he refused 'to accept the view that war is
inevitable'.[40] Given time Hitler might die or be replaced, and Anglo–
French defences would become so strong that Hitler would think twice
about going to war.

Militarily there was almost nothing to be said for the guarantees. The
chiefs of staff warned that Poland and Romania would be easily conquered,
perhaps in a matter of weeks. However, in the light of secret intelligence
reports the government believed that Germany was unable to fight a
major war. The practical value of the guarantees was that they imposed a
two-front war on Germany and the strain of such a war, it was argued,
would be too great. But in the last analysis military considerations were
secondary in the guarantees. Arguably they were flawed from the outset
because they were given without a real attempt to establish Soviet support.
Resistance to Germany could be effective only if the Soviet Union were
drawn in.

Sullenly and slowly the two democracies changed gear. Policy making went in fits and starts. First reactions to the Prague *coup* were muted. London and Paris cancelled official visits to Berlin. Halifax even saw a 'compensating advantage' in that Hitler's action 'had brought to an end the somewhat embarrassing commitment of a guarantee'.[41] The four-power guarantee promised to Czechoslovakia under the Munich Agreement was never honoured. Public pressures then changed British and French policies. Chamberlain's mild rebuke to Germany in his Commons statement on 15 March was followed by the firmness of his Birmingham speech on the 17th. On the same day London and Paris recalled their ambassadors. The stiffer note of the Birmingham speech was very much Halifax's doing.[42] Alert to the political mood, especially Labour criticism, Halifax counselled sternness. But sternness had its limits. In Birmingham Chamberlain spurned fresh commitments and his tone was interrogatory, not minatory: 'Is this the end of an old adventure or the beginning of a new ?'[43]

The most important factor shaping the new course was the atmosphere of imminent European war. On 23 March Hitler occupied Memel and on 7 April Mussolini invaded Albania. As in January false alarms provoked policy changes. Informed on 17 March that Germany had given Romania an ultimatum, London took the first stumbling and hesitant steps towards guarantees. Romania's oil and agricultural wealth made her a tempting prey. Though no evidence of an ultimatum came to light, that did not matter. The Romanian scare was a chance 'to take a stand' (Doc. 70). The Soviet Union, Poland, Yugoslavia, Greece and Turkey were asked to define their attitude in the event of German aggression against Romania. In reply to the question 'What will you do ?' their reply was 'What will you ?' On the 20th Chamberlain unveiled a new plan. France, the Soviet Union and Poland were invited to join Britain in a four-power declaration pledging themselves to consult together in the event of a threat to their security. The French pooh-poohed the idea, and Cadogan admitted that 'there is some force in . . . objection. We propose to publish a declaration that in the event of a further outrage we will consult. *Point c'est tout.*'[44] Faced with Poland's refusal to be associated with the Soviet Union, Halifax conceded that Britain would have to give Poland 'a private undertaking that, if Poland came in, they (*Britain*) would . . . come in also'.[45] Then came another false alarm. Reports of German troop movements against Poland in the last week of March prompted the announcement of a British guarantee on 31 March.

The impact of Prague revitalised French policy.[46] On three important issues – the Romanian guarantee, conscription and negotiations with Italy – France had her own way. Though Britain considered that the announcement of a guarantee to Romania was best left until the conclusions of negotiations with Poland and Turkey, Daladier demanded and obtained an announcement on 13 April. French appeals for the introduction of conscription reached a crescendo after the Albanian *coup*. The help of Roosevelt was enlisted. Alexis Léger, secretary general of the French foreign ministry, insisted on the urgency of an announcement before Hitler's Reichstag speech on 28 April. Britain was in no position to withstand both France and the United States. Renewed Japanese expansion early in 1939 – occupation of Hainan and the Spratly Islands – together with the Mediterranean alarms, meant that Britain could not fulfil her promise of naval assistance to Australia. On 9 April France had concentrated her fleet in the Mediterranean and asked Britain to do the same. Roosevelt agreed to a British request for the transfer of the United States fleet from the Atlantic to the Pacific but asked for an announcement of conscription before 28 April. On the 26th Chamberlain made the announcement. As for Italy, Chamberlain still believed that Mussolini might be persuaded to use his influence with Hitler. But the continuing Franco–Italian fracas prevented a firm understanding. Yet in spite of repeated requests, culminating in a personal appeal from Chamberlain in July, Daladier refused to make an approach to Rome (Doc. 75).

Rivers of ink have been spilt over the failure of the Anglo–Franco–Soviet negotiations and over the origins of the Nazi–Soviet non-aggression pact of 24 August 1939.[47] The Nazi–Soviet pact rendered the Second World War inevitable. Thanks to the Soviet Union's benevolent neutrality Hitler was freed from the danger of a war on two fronts. He could attack Poland in safety and then deal with the western powers. The much vaunted diplomatic deterrent of the guarantees had failed.

The story of the Anglo–Franco–Soviet negotiations can be quickly told. On 14 April Britain asked the Soviet Union to make a public declaration stating that in the event of any aggression against a European neighbour Soviet assistance would be given if desired. On 18 April the Soviet Union proposed a three-power pact of mutual assistance with immediate staff talks. Throughout the summer the Soviet government maintained its proposal and the course of negotiations was marked by a series of reluctant concessions to the Soviet view. By mid-July agreement on a political pact had been virtually achieved. Military conversations opened in Moscow on 12 August only to break down two days later on the key issue of the passage of Soviet forces across Poland and Romania.

Two questions which emerge from a study of the lengthy negotiations are: first, to what extent were Britain and France responsible for the breakdown of the talks in August; second, when did the Soviet leaders decide to embark on political talks with Germany? Obviously the western powers had some responsibility for the failure of the alliance talks. Their protracted nature was due in part to the ambivalence of British policy. The peace front in eastern Europe was a diplomatic, not a military, deterrent. 'We should not act in such a way as to forgo the chance of Russian help in war: we should not jeopardise the common front with Poland, and we should not jeopardise the cause of peace,' [48] Halifax advised colleagues on 24 April. He opposed the Soviet proposal for a full alliance because it 'would make war inevitable'.[49] 'P.M. says he will resign rather than sign alliance with Soviet,' recorded Cadogan on 20 May.[50] Not until the end of May did Britain accept in principle the Soviet proposal for a three-power pact.

Soviet suspicions might have been allayed if Britain had been prepared to send a senior minister to lead the talks. Halifax declined an invitation to go to Moscow, and Eden's offer to go in his place was opposed by Chamberlain.[51] Another opportunity was lost when the military missions went to Moscow. Britain dredged up Admiral Sir Reginald Aylmer Ranfurly Plunkett-Ernle-Erle-Drax as leader of the British mission. Though 'he had more to recommend him than . . . his name' he was hardly a leading military figure.[52] During the months of haggling in Moscow the one question that really mattered, namely, whether Poland and Romania would allow Soviet forces to cross their frontiers, was never raised. It was left to Marshal Voroshilov, commissar for defence, to ask this key question at the third session of the military talks on 14 August (Doc. 76). The failure of the western negotiators to give a satisfactory answer led directly to the suspension of the military conversations. Why did London and Paris evade the issue for so long? Almost certainly because they knew in advance that the Polish reply would be negative. The Moscow negotiations were partly a means of gaining time, and it seemed therefore only sensible to postpone for as long as possible an obvious sticking point. Also, it was argued that if and when an emergency arose the Poles would have no choice but to accept Soviet aid.

Analysis of Soviet intentions is gravely handicapped by the fragmentary evidence. A German–Soviet *rapprochement* lay in the logic of Versailles. Both states had reason to be dissatisfied with the peace treaties. The Treaty of Rapallo in 1922 initiated German–Soviet political and military co-operation. But the likelihood of a return to Rapallo does not explain why the *rapprochement* came in 1939. One suggestion is that the first move towards an understanding came with Molotov's speech to the Central Executive Committee of the Soviet Communist Party on 10 January 1936.[53] Conversations took place between the Soviet trade commissioner in Berlin and German leaders in December 1936–January 1937.[54] What this indicates, however, is that Stalin was keeping his options open, not that he had decided on a pact with Germany.

Much more convincing is the view that Munich marked the start of a real *rapprochement*. Isolated and excluded from a major European settlement, the Soviet Union conducted a post-mortem on the policy of Popular Fronts and collective security followed since 1934. Potemkin, deputy commissar for foreign affairs, told the French ambassador, Robert Coulondre: 'My poor friend, what have you done? For us I see no other solution but a fourth partition of Poland.'[55] Coulondre cabled on 18 October: 'We must expect early action by the Kremlin, doubtless semi-official and indirect, to approach Berlin and sound its intentions.'[56] In November came the final Soviet withdrawal from the Spanish Civil War. The Soviet leaders wanted to repair relations with Germany but Germany was not ready. The Soviet Union and Germany signed a trade agreement on 19 December 1938 but there was no political outcome. In Berlin German–Polish negotiations had priority. Ribbentrop cancelled the visit of a German financial mission to Moscow because of its effect on talks with Warsaw.

Stalin's speech on 10 March 1939 to the Eighteenth Congress of the Soviet Communist Party has often been seen as another milestone on the road to German–Soviet *rapprochement* (Doc. 69). The speech was note-worthy for three reasons: condemnation of western appeasement, stress on 'the strengthening of business relations with all countries', the conclusion that the Soviet Union would not allow herself to be 'drawn into conflict by warmongers who are accustomed to have others pull their chestnuts out of the fire'. It seems likely, however, that Stalin was speaking not to Germany but to Britain and France. His remarks about warmongers were an answer to British and French attempts in February and early March to mend their fences with Moscow. Chamberlain, for example, had actually dined for the first time at the Soviet embassy. It was also proposed to send a trade mission to Moscow.[57]

What proved decisive for German–Soviet relations were the diplomatic effects of Prague. Hitler's seizure of Memel on 23 March convinced Poland that a German *coup* was imminent. Beck ordered partial mobilisa-tion. The resulting breakdown in German–Polish negotiations brought a fundamental change in Hitler's policy. While on 25 March Hitler had still hoped to win Danzig by peaceful means, on 3 April he ordered plans to be prepared for an invasion of Poland by 1 September 1939. By the end of April the change of course was completed. In his speech of 28 April denouncing the German–Polish non-aggression pact of 1934 and the Anglo–German naval agreement of 1935, Hitler omitted any attack on the Soviet Union. In the second half of April both countries signalled their readiness for an agreement. Of these signals the most significant was the dismissal on 3 May of Maxim Litvinov, commissar for foreign affairs. Litvinov had always been a champion of collective security. The first warnings to the west of a German–Soviet *rapprochement* date from the second half of April. It is clear that Göring was closely involved in pro-moting the German–Soviet understanding.[58] Another month, however, elapsed before economic and commercial talks were resumed, and discus-sion of political issues did not take place until mid-July.

Stalin's primary consideration in embarking on talks with Germany was security. Faced with severe internal stresses and the danger of a war on two fronts – Soviet and Japanese forces clashed on the Mongolian-Manchurian frontier in 1938 and a minor war developed in the summer of 1939 – Stalin insured himself by talking to both sides. But it would be rash to conclude that the negotiations with Britain and France were merely a manoeuvre to make the Germans bid higher. Stalin's first reaction to Prague was to resurrect the policy of collective security. The rejection of the Soviet proposal for a six-power conference in March and the response to the offer of a tripartite pact in April probably convinced him that the British were still hedging, harbouring hopes of conciliating Hitler. The intense Soviet suspicions of western policy were confirmed (Docs 68, 71). At some stage Stalin made up his mind to sign an agreement with Germany. All we know is that from June onwards the tone of the Soviet press suggested that Stalin was preparing opinion for the breakdown of negotiations with the West.

Would a greater effort have regained a Soviet commitment to an anti-Nazi front? This is an open question. It is true that Germany was able to outbid the western powers by offering German–Soviet control of the Baltic states and Poland, but in April Stalin was not to know that Hitler would pay such a high price. An immediate and unconditional acceptance of the Soviet proposal of 18 April for a tripartite alliance might have saved the day.

'A guarantee a day keeps Hitler away,' it was said. But Count von Schwerin of German military intelligence warned his English hosts in early July: 'Hitler took no account of words, only of deeds.'[59] The guarantees did not deter Hitler because they were unenforceable without a Soviet alliance, and British leaders fought a long delaying action against such an alliance. Practical measures of preparation for war were tardy and ineffective. Anglo–French staff talks did not begin until early April. The Ministry of Supply, announced in April, did not begin to function until July and had no responsibility for the Admiralty and Royal Air Force. Its impact was deadened by the appointment of a political lightweight, Leslie Burgin, minister of transport, as its head. Conscription, announced in April, was limited to men of 20 and 21. Only four divisions of the continental field force were ready by September 1939. Chamberlain kept the door open for negotiations with Germany. In May Anglo–German economic talks were restarted secretly in Berlin and transferred to London in June. On 8 June Halifax announced that if confidence could be re-established 'any of Germany's claims are open to consideration round a table'.[60] Britain's readiness to discuss a settlement was confirmed in the secret talks which Helmuth Wohlthat, Göring's representative, had with Sir Horace Wilson and others in London on 6–7 June and again on 19–20 July.[61]

Hitler's strategy was the same as in 1938 – a war of nerves. Military directives of 3 and 11 April 1939 initiated preparations for an attack on

Poland. In his Reichstag speech of 28 April Hitler demanded the return of Danzig to the Reich and a route and railway line through the Polish Corridor. The failure of the lengthy negotiations for a military alliance with Japan was compensated by the conclusion of the Pact of Steel on 22 May which pledged Italy to support Germany with all her military forces. But the Axis was not as solid as it seemed. In a secret memorandum of 30 May Mussolini confirmed in writing what he had already told Hitler in conversation, namely, that Italy would not be ready for war for four years (Doc. 74).[62] Hitler too was cautious. Poland, he told his generals on 23 May, would be attacked 'at the first suitable opportunity' but 'it must not come to a simultaneous showdown with the West' (Doc. 73). The 'showdown with England' was a 'matter of life and death' but it would have to await the completion of German armaments in 1943–4.

Until 25 August Hitler was under the illusion that Britain and France would not fight for Poland. His assurance stemmed from the German–Soviet negotiations for a non-aggression pact. The Nazi–Soviet pact of 24 August had a secret protocol delimiting German and Soviet spheres of influence in Poland and the Baltic states. In contrast to the caution of his 23 May address to the generals, his words on 22 August were clear and confident (Doc. 77). Orders were issued on 23 August for an invasion of Poland on the 26th. In the evening of the 25th the orders were cancelled. Had Hitler 'lost his nerve'?[63] On the contrary, he was simply pursuing the war of nerves. The effect of the Nazi–Soviet pact on British and French opinion was not as shattering as expected. Since they had never had much faith in Stalin, western statesmen were not demoralised by the pact. On the 25th Hitler made 'a last attempt' to achieve an Anglo–German alliance. At 1.30 p.m. he outlined to Henderson 'a large comprehensive offer': settlement of the Polish question, German hegemony in eastern Europe, guarantees for the British empire.[64] Despite the offer to Henderson the orders for the attack were confirmed shortly after 3 p.m. Two events then caused Hitler to postpone the invasion. In the afternoon of the 25th Hitler was informed that Mussolini would not go to war immediately without very large supplies from Germany. At the same time news arrived that the Anglo–Polish treaty of 6 April 1939 was about to be ratified. Instead of softening, British policy appeared to be hardening. That evening Hitler cancelled the orders for the 26th and strengthened his diplomatic initiative. On the 26th the Swedish industrialist, Birger Dahlerus, was given proposals for London.[65]

Hitler's instinct was sound. Western leaders were anxious to avoid war over Poland. They demonstrated this in three ways: pressure on Poland, efforts to enlist Mussolini's mediation, secret discussions with Hitler and Göring through the Swedish intermediary, Dahlerus. One suggestion was that 'it would be a good idea to relay to Germany "the famous song of the nightingale" in Bagley Woods as a token of Britain's peace-loving intentions'.[66] The French foreign minister was more practical. On the eve of the Nazi–Soviet pact he made a desperate effort to wriggle out of the Polish alliance. At Bonnet's behest Daladier summoned on 23 August a special meeting of service ministers and chiefs of staff (Doc. 78). Bonnet planned 'to corner' Gamelin by extracting from him an admission that the armed forces were not ready for war.[67] Gamelin gave no ground. If France did not fulfil her obligations her security in western Europe would be impaired. More circumspectly, Daladier was also looking for a peaceful solution to the Polish crisis. The Poles, he told the French Cabinet on 24 August, 'must sacrifice Danzig. They ought to have done so earlier.'[68] His letter of 26 August to Hitler was conciliatory and offered his services as mediator.[69] French representations on 29 August induced the Poles to postpone their mobilisation for several hours. These few hours were crucial, since they meant that a quarter of the army never reached the units at the front.[70]

Where Hitler miscalculated was in thinking that September 1938 would be repeated, with Chamberlain and Daladier on their knees for compromise. This was in fact the very situation that Chamberlain and Daladier were determined to avoid. What they wanted to do was to replay September 1938 in the light of the lessons learnt and the military strength gained during the year. The aim was *détente* but negotiated from strength. News that Hitler had postponed the attack on Poland led to the conclusion that he was 'wobbling'.[71] Reading Hitler's letter of 29 August Halifax saw 'a man . . . trying to extricate himself from a difficult situation'.[72] When the British Cabinet met on 30 August Hitler was said to be in an 'awful fix'.[73] British and French intelligence reports indicated discontent in Germany and the probability of a palace revolution, with Göring replacing Hitler. Late on the 31st, within hours of the German invasion, it seemed to Cadogan that Hitler was 'hesitant and trying all sorts of dodges, including last minute bluff. We have got to stand firm.'[74]

By the evening of the 30th Hitler had practically abandoned the bid to seduce Britain. He was prepared to wait until the early hours of 2 September for negotiations with the Poles but not later. At 4 p.m. on the 31st the order for the attack was given and at dawn on 1 September German troops crossed the Polish frontier. Was Hitler sincere in his offer of an Anglo–German alliance? Or was it merely a manoeuvre to confuse the enemy and gain time for military preparations? The answer is both. Hitler very much preferred to avoid a European war and thought it worthwhile to make a last effort to bribe Britain. But he wanted a settlement on his terms only. He did not want another Munich. Thus there was misjudgement on both sides. Hitler believed that the western powers would waver and surrender and then he would dictate a settlement. Western statesmen wanted to avoid war but were resolved not to repeat the surrender of 1938. Any suggestion of a second Munich would have swept them from power. They believed that Hitler was wavering and that all they had to do was stand firm and indicate willingness to talk. But Hitler did not stumble into war. He wanted a war with Poland and was prepared 'if the worst comes to the worst' to fight 'a war on two fronts'.[75]

Mussolini remained neutral. In the morning of 31 August Britain was told: 'Italy will not fight against either England or France.'[76] At midday Mussolini proposed a conference for 5 September to discuss the revision of Versailles (Doc. 79). Though the conference proposal failed Italy stayed neutral until after the German attack on France in May 1940. It would be mistaken, though, to conclude that Chamberlain's courtship of Italy had 'paid off'.[77] Chamberlain had worked for Italian neutrality as a means of dissuading Hitler from war and also in the hope of reducing Britain's potential enemies. The probability, however, is that Mussolini would have opted for neutrality whatever Chamberlain's policy. On the evidence Mussolini's decision was taken on military grounds – shortage of raw materials and munitions.[78] Moreover, Italian neutrality did not alter Hitler's decision for war.

While Poland fought for her life, the British and French Cabinets pondered Mussolini's conference idea. Warnings demanding the withdrawal of German troops were delivered in Berlin in the evening of 1 September but they were open-ended without time limits. The British ultimatum was not delivered until 9 a.m. on 3 September, with a time limit of 11 a.m. that day. The French ultimatum was delivered at noon on the 3rd, with a time limit of 5 p.m. the same day. The delays surrounding the declaration of war and the failure to synchronise the ultimatums have been blamed almost entirely on the French, especially Bonnet. More recently it has been argued that 'on 2 September . . . the house of commons revolted and forced war on a reluctant government'.[79]

The truth was that neither government was in a hurry to go to war. But there was no plot to betray Poland and surrender to Germany. The assumption in London and Paris was that the war would be a long one but that nothing could be done to save Poland. There was no need, therefore, to rush into a war which would last several years. More particularly, much confusion prevailed on 1 September because Hitler did not declare war on Poland and information was hard to come by. From the French record it is clear that for military and political reasons Daladier and Gamelin were as keen as Bonnet to delay the delivery of an ultimatum. And Bonnet was not the only French minister who favoured Mussolini's conference proposal. Though suspicious of Mussolini, Daladier considered that the door should be kept open (Doc. 80). In the morning of 1 September the French Cabinet cautiously accepted the Italian proposal, whereas the British Cabinet virtually rejected it. Telephoning Chamberlain in the evening of the 2nd Daladier pointed out that his Cabinet wished to wait until noon next day in order to give Germany time to accept or reject the

Italian proposal (Doc. 81). As for Chamberlain and Halifax, there is no evidence that they were reverting to appeasement. They showed only lukewarm interest in the conference idea and insisted on the need for a German withdrawal before a conference could meet. By midday on the 1st negotiations with Dahlerus had virtually ended. Chamberlain has not been given enough credit for his desire to synchronise matters with the French.

To recapitulate briefly the argument of this essay. Though the settlement that ended the First World War was a patched-up peace it was not fore-doomed to failure. A solid Anglo–French alliance might have contained Germany. The reasons for the rapid breakdown of the European security system erected in 1919 are to be found in the explosive mixture of power politics and ideology that propelled Germany, in the general detestation of war and in the appreciation of economic, political and military weaknesses that weighed down western statesmen. Essentially it was a failure to envisage alternative political and military strategies. But the failure was not inevitable. It has become almost axiomatic in assessments of British and French leaders to see them as realistic statesmen, oppressed by the know-ledge of their countries' weaknesses and the strength of potential enemies. The uncritical premise of these assessments is that the policy pursued was the only practicable one at the time. In fact there were many variables, and ministerial appraisals were the product of prejudice and opinion. 'The outstanding feature' of the international situation, Eden minuted in late 1937, was 'its extreme fluidity'.[80] Different initiatives in 1937 might have completely altered the international scenario of 1938-9. Even 'after the crisis of May 1938 the Government could have emphasised, rather than undermined, its firmness and warned the British public as well as Germany'.[81] Statesmanship was the nub of the problem. 'Never did our people require more guidance and advice than at present,' Lord Tyrell, ambassador in Paris, had written in 1934.[82] The historian, Marc Bloch, analysing the causes of the fall of France, stressed the failure of successive governments to inform opinion.[83] The feebleness and timidity of British and French foreign policies in the late 1930s were symptomatic of the shortsighted selfishness of a ruling class set on self-preservation: 'Everyone is smiling, the weather is glorious, but I feel that our world or all that remains of it, is committing suicide, whilst Stalin laughs and the Kremlin triumphs.'[84]

Notes and References

The following abbreviations are used for some sources frequently cited in the notes.

DBFP – *Documents on British Foreign Policy, 1919–1939*, ed. E. L. Woodward and Rohan Butler, 2nd series, vol. V (London, 1956), vol. VI (1957); ed. W. N. Medlicott and Douglas Dakin, 2nd series, vol. XII (1972); ed. E. L. Woodward and Rohan Butler, 3rd series, vol. I (1949), vol. II (1949), vol. III (1950), vol. IV (1951), vol. VI (1953), vol. VII (1954).

DDF – *Documents diplomatiques français, 1932–1939*, 2nd series, 1936–9, vol. I (Paris, 1963), vol. II (1964), vol. III (1966).

DGFP – *Documents on German Foreign Policy, 1918–1945*, series C, vol. IV (London, 1962), vol. V (1966); series D, vol. I (1949), vol. II (1949), vol. III (1951), vol. IV (1951), vol. VI (1956), vol. VII (1956).

FRUS – *Foreign Relations of the United States: Diplomatic Papers 1936*, vol. I (Washington, 1953), vol. II (1954); *1937*, vol. I (1954); *1938*, vol. I (1955).

AC – Austen Chamberlain Papers (University of Birmingham Library).

CAB – Cabinet Papers (Public Record Office, London).

FO – Foreign Office Papers (Public Record Office, London).

Cadogan Diaries – David Dilks (ed.), *The Diaries of Sir Alexander Cadogan, 1938–1945* (London, 1971).

Harvey Diaries – John Harvey (ed.), *The Diplomatic Diaries of Oliver Harvey, 1937–1940* (London, 1970).

The following sources, also frequently cited, are given in a short form in the notes.

Avon, the Earl of, *The Eden Memoirs*, vol. I: *Full Circle* (London, 1962); vol. II: *Facing the Dictators* (London, 1960).

Carr, William, *Arms, Autarky and Aggression: A Study in German Foreign Policy, 1933–1939* (London, 1972).

Cowling, Maurice, *The Impact of Hitler: British Politics and British Policy, 1933–1940* (Cambridge, 1975).

Feiling, Keith, *The Life of Neville Chamberlain* (London, 1946).

Medlicott, W. N., *Britain and Germany: The Search for Agreement, 1930–1937*, The Creighton Lecture in History, 1968 (University of London, 1969).

Robertson, Esmonde M. (ed.), *The Origins of the Second World War: Historical Interpretations* (London, 1971).

Roskill, Stephen, *Hankey: Man of Secrets*, vol. II (London, 1972), vol. III (London, 1974).

Taylor, A. J. P., *The Origins of the Second World War* (London, 1963).

Watt, D. C., *Too Serious a Business: European Armed Forces and the Approach to the Second World War* (London, 1975).

Other sources repeated in the notes are given in full within the preceding notes for the same chapter.

CHAPTER 1

1 Gordon Wright, *The Ordeal of Total War, 1939–1945* (London, 1968), p. 263. Far Eastern casualties are difficult to assess; see Peter Calvocoressi and Guy Wint, *Total War* (London, 1972), pp. 553, 889.

2 Paul Addison, *The Road to 1945: British Politics and the Second World War* (London, 1975).

3 Ralf Dahrendorf, *Society and Democracy in Germany* (London, 1967).

4 For the British sources see C. L. Mowat, *Great Britain since 1914* (London, 1971).

5 See Nicholas Pronay, 'British newsreels in the 1930s', part 1: 'Audiences and producers', *History*, 56 (1971), pp. 411–18, and part 2: 'Their policies and impact', *History*, 57 (1972), pp. 63–72; Paul Smith (ed.), *The Historian and Film* (Cambridge, 1976).

6 Some British material judged sensitive is still sealed for another sixty years. For example, correspondence relating to the Duke of Windsor's stay in Portugal in 1940 is closed, though in this and other instances the researcher can gain a good idea of the contents because the censors omitted to purge the relevant index summarising each document. In Italy a fifty years rule remains in force. In 1970 France adopted the principle of a thirty years rule but in practice many files for the late 1930s are still closed.

7 Pieter Geyl, *Debates with Historians* (London, 1975), p. 278.

8 See the correspondence between Christopher Hill and J. H. Hexter in the *Times Literary Supplement*, 24 October, 7 November, 28 November 1975.

9 No trace has been found of a meeting of armed forces leaders called by Hitler on 10 February 1939 Robertson, *Origins of the Second World War*, p. 23.

10 Ritchie Ovendale, *'Appeasement' and the English Speaking World: Britain, the United States, the Dominions and the policy of 'Appeasement', 1937–1939* (Cardiff, 1975), p. 21.

11 Sir Alexander Cadogan's phrase, permanent under secretary of state for foreign affairs, 1938–45, quoted in David Dilks, 'Appeasement revisited' (Inaugural Lecture, University of Leeds, December 1971), *University of Leeds Review*, 15 (1972), p. 34.

12 F. W. Winterbotham, *The Ultra Secret* (London, 1974). However, Winterbotham is in many respects unreliable and should be read in conjunction with the *Times Literary Supplement*, 28 May, 25 June, 9 July 1976, and *Naval Review* (April 1975), pp. 185–8.

13 Anthony Adamthwaite, *France and the Coming of the Second World War, 1936–1939* (London, 1977).

14 Sir Maurice Hankey to Sir Eric Phipps, 11 January 1938, Sir Eric Phipps Papers (Churchill College, Cambridge) 3/3.

15 *Toynbee on Toynbee: A Conversation between Arnold J. Toynbee and G. R. Urban* (New York, 1974), p. 24.

16 *DBFP*, 2nd series, vol. VI, no. 452; vol. XII, no. 637.

17 Medlicott, *Britain and Germany*, p. 4; Alan J. Sharp, 'The Foreign Office in eclipse, 1919–22', *History*, 61 (1976), pp. 198–218.

18 For an example of how memoirs can mislead see Sir Robert Vansittart's account of the Stresa conference of 1935: *The Mist Procession* (1958), p. 520; *DBFP*, 2nd series, vol. XII, no. 722, n. 43.

19 Quoted in *The Collected Writings of John Maynard Keynes*, vol. X: *Essays in Biography* (London, 1972), p. 53.

20 Avon, *Eden Memoirs*, vol. II. For assessments of Eden see Sidney Aster, *Anthony Eden* (London, 1976); Lawrence R. Pratt, *East of Malta, West of Suez: Britain's Mediterranean Crisis, 1936–1939* (London, 1975); R. A. C. Parker,

'Great Britain, France and the Ethiopian crisis 1935–6', *English Historical Review*, 89 (1974).

21 Ross Terrill, *R. H. Tawney and his Times* (London, 1974), p. 229.

22 F. H. Hinsley, *Nationalism and the International System* (London, 1973), p. 167. Robert Skidelsky argues that the politicians in 1939 'sensed that parliamentary democracy could only survive through war, however terrible the cost, because only war could give it the sinews and will to rejuvenate itself' ('Going to war with Germany', *Encounter*, 39 (1972), p. 65).

23 Samuel Hynes, *The Auden Generation: Literature and Politics in England in the 1930s* (London, 1976), p. 41; Robin Skelton (ed.), *Poetry of the Thirties* (London, 1964), p. 18.

24 Margaret Storm Jameson, *A Kind of Survivor: The Autobiography of Guy Chapman* (London, 1975), p. 183.

25 Cato (pseudonym, M. Foot and M. Howard), *Guilty Men* (London, 1940).

26 L. B. Namier, *Diplomatic Prelude, 1938–39* (London, 1948); *Europe in Decay* (London, 1950); *In the Nazi Era* (London, 1952).

27 The painful exhumation of France's past has continued; see Michel Mitranis's film *Les Guichets du Louvre* (1974) on the events of July 1942 when French police rounded up 130,000 Paris Jews.

28 'Falsificators of history (an historical note)', Moscow, 1948, quoted in John L. Snell (ed.), *The Outbreak of the Second World War: Design or Blunder?* (Boston, 1962), p. 29. See also Georges Deborin, *Secrets of the Second World War* (Moscow, 1971).

29 Ernest R. May, *Lessons of the Past: The Use and Misuse of History in American Foreign Policy* (London, 1974); Avon, *Eden Memoirs*, vol. II, foreword.

30 Taylor, *Origins of the Second World War*, p. 9; Robertson, *Origins of the Second World War*; D. C. Watt, 'Sir Lewis Namier and contemporary European history', *The Cambridge Journal* (July 1954), pp. 579–600; D. C. Watt, 'Appeasement: the rise of a revisionist school?', *Political Quarterly* (April–June 1965), pp. 191–213.

31 Franklin Reid Gannon, *The British Press and Germany, 1936–39* (Oxford, 1971); Neville Thompson, *The Anti-appeasers: Conservative Opposition to Appeasement in the 1930s* (Oxford, 1971).

32 Meir Michaelis, 'World power status or world domination?', *Historical Journal*, 15 (1972), pp. 331–60.

33 H. R. Trevor-Roper, *Hitler's Table Talk, 1941–1944* (London, 1953), pp. vii–xxxv.

34 Taylor, *Origins of the Second World War*, p. 172.

35 Helen M. Cam, *Selected Historical Essays of F. W. Maitland* (London, 1957), p. xix.

36 It is in this sense, not the pejorative sense of surrender, that the word is employed throughout this eassy.

CHAPTER 2

1 The Germans played on the fear of Bolshevism: 'They [German delegation] dwelt on the fact that Germany is on the verge of Bolshevism unless we assist them to resist and that we ourselves will subsequently be invaded by the same scourge' (Clemenceau to Lloyd George, 9 November 1918, Lloyd George Papers (House of Lords), LG/F/50/3/46).

2 Treaty of St Germain (Austria), 10 September 1919; Treaty of Neuilly (Bulgaria), 27 November 1919; Sèvres (Turkey), 20 April 1920; Trianon

(Hungary), 4 June 1920. See J. A. S. Grenville, *The Major International Treaties, 1914–1973: A History and Guide with Texts* (London, 1974).
3 Martin Gilbert, *The Roots of Appeasement* (London, 1966), pp. 30–1.
4 Lord Balogh, Keynes Seminar, November 1974, University of Kent at Canterbury, quoted in the *Times Literary Supplement*, 10 October 1975, p. 1211. For a refutation of Keynes see Etienne Mantoux, *The Carthaginian Peace* (London, 1946).
5 Taylor, *Origins of the Second World War*, p. 56.
6 The most recent study of the peace conference is Howard Elcock, *Portrait of a Decision* (London, 1972). For French policy see David Robin Watson, *Georges Clemenceau: A Political Biography* (London, 1974); for French opinion see P. Miquel, *La Paix de Versailles et l'opinion publique française* (Paris, 1972). See also Roskill, *Hankey*, vol. II; Arno J. Mayer, *Politics and Diplomacy of Peacemaking: Containment and Counter-revolution at Versailles, 1918–1919* (London, 1968).
7 Quoted in Gordon Wright, *Rural Revolution in France* (Stanford, 1968), p. 28.
8 For this paragraph see Sally Marks, 'Reparations reconsidered: a reminder', *Central European History* (December 1969); David Felix, 'Reparations reconsidered with a vengeance', ibid. (June 1971), pp. 171–9; Sally Marks, 'Reparations reconsidered: a rejoinder', ibid. (December 1972), pp. 358–61; Eckhard Wandel, *Die Bedeutung der Vereinigten Staaten von Amerika für das Deutsche Reparationsproblem 1924–1929* (Tübingen, 1971).
9 J. Néré, *The Foreign Policy of France, 1914–1945* (London, 1975), pp. 52–62.
10 Thomas Mann, 'Inflation: the witches' sabbath, Germany 1923', *Encounter* (February 1975), pp. 60–3.
11 C. J. Lowe and M. L. Dockrill, *The Mirage of Power: British Foreign Policy, 1902–1922*, 3 vols (London, 1972).
12 Ian H. Nish, *Alliance in Decline: A Study in Anglo–Japanese Relations, 1908–1923* (London, 1972).
13 Roskill, *Hankey*, vol. II, pp. 536–8.
14 Correlli Barnett, *The Collapse of British Power* (London, 1972).
15 Judith M. Hughes, *To the Maginot Line: The Politics of French Military Preparation in the 1920s* (Cambridge, Mass., 1971).
16 *Harvey Diaries*, p. 222.
17 Barnett, op. cit., p. 195.
18 ibid., p. 273.
19 Austen Chamberlain to Lord Crewe (ambassador in Paris), 20 January 1925, AC 50/28.
20 Taylor, *Origins of the Second World War*, p. 64.
21 Jon Jacobsen and John T. Walker, 'The impulse for a Franco–German entente: the origins of the Thoiry Conference, 1926', *Journal of Contemporary History*, 10 (1975), pp. 157–81.
22 René Massigli's comment, quoted in Sir Hughe Knatchbull-Hugessen, *Diplomat in Peace and War* (London, 1949), p. 53. For Locarno see Jon Jacobsen, *Locarno Diplomacy: Germany and the West, 1925–1929* (Princeton, 1972).
23 Austen Chamberlain to Eyre Crowe, 8 March 1925, AC 52/50.
24 For evaluations of Stresemann see Robert Grathwol, 'Gustav Stresemann: reflections on his foreign policy', *Journal of Modern History*, 45 (1973), pp. 52–70; Michael Olaf Maxelon, *Stresemann und Frankreich 1914–1929* (Düsseldorf, 1973); Werner Weidenfeld, *Die Englandpolitik Gustav Stresemanns* (Mainz, 1973). For the documents see *Akten zur deutschen auswärtigen Politik 1918–1945*, series B, 1925–33 (Göttingen, 1966–), Band II, i (1967) and Band II, ii (1967). For German–Soviet military co-operation see F. L. Carsten, *The Reichswehr and Politics, 1918- 1933* (Oxford, 1966).

CHAPTER 3

1 Charles P. Kindleberger, *The World in Depression, 1929–1939* (London, 1973), pp. 174–7.
2 Claude Fohlen, 'France 1920–1970', *The Fontana Economic History of Europe*, 6, 2 (London, 1973); T. Kemp, *The French Economy, 1913–1939* (London, 1972); Alfred Sauvy, *Histoire économique de la France entre les deux guerres*, 3 vols (Paris, 1966–72).
3 Kindleberger, op. cit., p. 210.
4 The opinion of Vincent Auriol, minister of finance in Blum's Popular Front government of 1936: *FRUS 1936*, vol. I, p. 564.
5 Oliver Stanley, president of the board of trade, 11 September 1938, quoted in Harold Nicolson, *Diaries and Letters, 1930–1939*, ed. Nigel Nicolson (London, 1966), p. 359.
6 The opinion of William Strang, head of the central department of the Foreign Office, and of Oliver Harvey, Halifax's private secretary, 18 November 1938: *Harvey Diaries*, p. 222.
7 Quoted in Christopher Thorne, *The Limits of Foreign Policy: The West, the League and the Far Eastern Crisis of 1931–1933* (London, 1973), p. 4.
8 Quoted in Roskill, *Hankey*, vol. III, p. 27.
9 See Z. J. Gasiriowski, 'Did Pilsudski attempt to initiate a preventive war in 1933?', *Journal of Modern History* (June 1955), pp. 135–51.
10 Paul Reynaud, *Mémoires*, vol. II: *Envers et contre tous* (Paris, 1963), p. 219.
11 For recent biographies see Colin Cross, *Adolf Hitler* (London, 1973); Joachim C. Fest, *Hitler* (London, 1974); Werner Maser, *Hitler* (London, 1973); Robert Payne, *The Life and Death of Adolf Hitler* (London, 1973); J. P. Stern, *Hitler: The Führer and the People* (London, 1975).
12 See Jacques Barzun's comments on Walter C. Langer's *The Mind of Adolf Hitler* (London, 1972), in *Clio and the Doctors* (Chicago and London, 1974), pp. 45, 70–1.
13 Stern, op. cit., p. 216.
14 ibid.
15 For Hitler's foreign policy see Carr, *Arms, Autarky and Aggression*; Klaus Hildebrand, *The Foreign Policy of the Third Reich* (London, 1973); Hans-Adolf Jacobsen, *Nationalsozialistische Aussenpolitik* (Frankfurt, 1969); Gerhard L. Weinberg, *The Foreign Policy of Hitler's Germany: Diplomatic Revolution in Europe, 1933–1936* (Chicago, 1971). A. J. P. Taylor's review of Weinberg is in *Journal of Modern History*, vol. 44, no. 1 (March 1972), pp. 140–3.
16 'Hitler and the origins of the Second World War', in Robertson, *Origins of the Second World War*, p. 193.
17 For *Mein Kampf* see Adolf Hitler, *Mein Kampf*, trans. by Ralph Manheim, intro. by D. C. Watt (London, 1969); *Hitler's Secret Book* (London, 1963).
18 After the *Anschluss* Weizsäcker wrote: 'Yesterday in Vienna is indeed the most significant date since January 18, 1871. To see the Austrian cavalrymen defile together with our troops to the tune of the Prince Eugene March and then the proclamation from the balcony of the Hofburg are impressions which I would have wished upon you all' (Leonidas E. Hill (ed.), *Die Weizsäcker-Papiere, 1933–1950* (Berlin, 1975), p. 123). See also Leonidas E. Hill, 'Three crises 1938–1939', *Journal of Contemporary History*, 3 (1968), pp. 113–44.
19 A. Toynbee, *A Study of History*, vol. I (London, 1934), pp. 14–15.
20 Letter of 30 March 1935, AC 41/1/12.
21 Feiling, *Neville Chamberlain*, p. 253.
22 Quoted in Neville Waites, 'The Depression years', in Neville Waites (ed.),

Troubled Neighbours: Franco–British Relations in the Twentieth Century (London, 1971), p. 145.

23 Cowling, *Impact of Hitler*, pp. 67–8. Thomas Jones, a former deputy secretary to the Cabinet, described Hitler as 'a factor for peace' (letter of 1 March 1934, *A Diary with Letters 1931–1950* (London, 1954), p. 125). The bloodbath of 30 June 1934 was considered to have had a salutary effect on the regime. Sir Eric Phipps, ambassador in Berlin, wrote: 'The old regime has been modified . . . the wild men have been shot . . . One might also say that the country is being ruled by the permanent officials while Hitler looks on benevolently' (quoted in Medlicott, *Britain and Germany*, p. 89).

24 Martin Gilbert, *Sir Horace Rumbold: Portrait of a Diplomat, 1869–1941* (London, 1973), p. 319. In December 1938 Lord Beaverbrook wrote: 'The Jews have got a big position in the press here [*London*] . . . The Jews may drive us into war' (A. J. P. Taylor, *Beaverbrook* (Harmondsworth, 1974), p. 503). In 1940 Churchill's proposal that Hore-Belisha should be minister of information was over-ruled by Halifax because he 'was a Jew' (A. J. P. Taylor, *English History, 1914–1945* (Oxford, 1965), p. 460, no. 1).

25 Quoted in Correlli Barnett, *The Collapse of British Power* (London, 1972), p. 393.

26 The words of Sir Robert Bruce Lockhart in an interview with the ex-Kaiser at Doorn in 1929: Kenneth Young (ed.), *The Diaries of Sir Robert Bruce Lockhart, 1915–1938* (London, 1973), p. 112.

27 Leonard Woolf, *Downhill All the Way* (London, 1967), p. 9. The most recent study of the impact of the First World War is Paul Fussell, *The Great War and Modern Memory* (London, 1976).

28 Professor G. R. Elton, quoted in Ross Terrill, *R. H. Tawney and his Times* (London, 1974), pp. 59–60.

29 Terrill, op. cit., p. 139.

30 H. A. L. Fisher, *History of Europe* (London, 1936), p. 1209.

31 Young, op. cit., p. 263.

32 Quoted in Neville Thompson, *The Anti-appeasers: Conservative Opposition to Appeasement in the 1930s* (Oxford, 1971), p. 59. Lord Reith, director-general of the BBC 1922–38, was a consistent admirer of Hitler and Mussolini: Charles Stuart (ed.), *The Reith Diaries* (London, 1975). Conservative ideological sympathy for Italian fascism was considerable. Winston Churchill, chancellor of the exchequer, told Italian journalists in 1927: 'If I had been an Italian, I am sure that I should have been whole-heartedly with you . . . in your triumphal struggle against the bestial appetites . . . of Leninism' (P. G. Edwards, 'The Foreign Office and fascism, 1924–1929', *Journal of Contemporary History*, vol. 5, no. 2 (1970), p. 157). Austen Chamberlain, foreign secretary 1924–9, was a great admirer of the Duce. He wrote in 1925: 'I am confident that he is a patriot and a sincere man; I trust his word when given' (Sir Charles Petrie, *The Life and Letters of the Right Hon. Sir Austen Chamberlain*, vol. II (London, 1940), p. 296).

33 René Rémond, *La Droite en France: de la première restauration à la Vᵉ République*, 2 vols (Paris, 1968).

34 *FRUS 1938*, vol. I, p. 102. 'Our policy is not one of dividing Europe into two opposing *blocs* of countries' (Neville Chamberlain, 8 April 1938, in *In Search of Peace: Speeches, 1937–1938* (London, 1939), p. 171).

35 *DGFP*, series C, vol. IV, no. 430.

36 *DBFP*, 3rd series, vol. I.

37 Feiling, *Neville Chamberlain*, p. 254.

38 Medlicott, *Britain and Germany*, p. 6.

39 *DBFP*, 2nd series, vol. V, no. 36.

40 ibid.
41 *DBFP*, 2nd series, vol. VI, no. 363.
42 Quoted by Stephen Roskill in a letter to the *Times Literary Supplement*, 26 July 1974.
43 *DBFP*, 2nd series, vol. XII, p. vii.
44 *DBFP*, 3rd series, vol. II, no. 643, n. 3. In January 1937 the French prime minister, Léon Blum, complained that 'it was impossible for Poncet to see Hitler frequently' (*FRUS 1937*, vol. I, p. 27).
45 In June 1935 Hankey was worried lest through loyalty to France Britain should let slip 'this possibly last chance for years of obtaining a settlement' (Medlicott, *Britain and Germany*, p. 17).

CHAPTER 4

1 President Roosevelt, 'Quarantine Speech', 5 October 1937, *Survey of International Affairs 1937*, vol. I (London, 1938), pp. 273–6.
2 Quoted in Carr, *Arms, Autarky and Aggression*, p. 61.
3 J. H. Hexter, *The History Primer* (London, 1972), p. 156.
4 Frank Hardie, *The Abyssinian Crisis* (London, 1974), p. 3.
5 Esmonde M. Robertson, *Mussolini as Empire Builder* (London, 1977). This is the most recent account of the Abyssinian crisis. Extremely valuable also is Daniel Waley, *British Public Opinion and the Abyssinian War 1935–6* (London, 1975).
6 See William C. Askew, 'The secret agreement between France and Italy on Ethiopia, January 1935', *Journal of Modern History*, 25 (1953), pp. 47–8; D. C. Watt, 'The secret Laval–Mussolini agreement of 1935 on Ethiopia', *The Middle East Journal*, 15 (1961), reprinted in Robertson, *Origins of the Second World War*, pp. 225–42.
7 *DBFP*, 2nd series, vol. XII, no. 722, n. 43.
8 D. C. Watt, 'The Anglo–German naval agreement of 1935: an interim judgement', *Journal of Modern History*, 28 (1956), pp. 155–75.
9 Quoted by R. A. C. Parker, 'Great Britain, France and the Ethiopian crisis 1935–1936', *English Historical Review*, 89 (1974), pp. 322–3. For Laval see Geoffrey Warner, *Pierre Laval and the Eclipse of France* (London, 1968).
10 Quoted in Michael Howard, *The Continental Commitment: The Dilemma of British Defence Policy in the Era of Two World Wars* (London, 1972), p. 104.
11 Avon, *Eden Memoirs*, vol. II, p. 297.
12 A. J. Marder, 'The Royal Navy and the Ethiopian crisis of 1935–36', *American Historical Review*, 75 (1970), p. 1350.
13 Taylor, *Origins of the Second World War*, p. 128. For the League see Ruth B. Henig (ed.), *The League of Nations* (Edinburgh, 1973); F. Walters, *A History of the League of Nations* (London, 1952); J. Barros, *Betrayal from Within* (New Haven and London, 1969); P. Raffo, *The League of Nations* (Historical Association, London, 1974).
14 Robertson, op. cit.
15 *DGFP*, series C, vol. IV, no. 575.
16 ibid., no. 579.
17 Winston Churchill, *The Second World War*, vol. I: *The Gathering Storm* (London, 1964), p. 170. See John C. Cairns, 'March 7 1936, again: the view from Paris', in H. W. Gatzke (ed.), *European Diplomacy between two Wars, 1919–1939* (Chicago, 1972), pp. 172–92; Maurice Baumont, 'The Rhineland crisis: 7 March 1936', in Neville Waites (ed.), *Troubled Neighbours: Franco–British Relations in the Twentieth Century* (London, 1971), pp. 158–69.

18 *DDF*, 2nd series, vol. I, no. 196.

19 ibid., no. 301.

20 On 28 March 1936 Sir Austen Chamberlain wrote to Wladimir d'Ormesson (editor of *Figaro*): 'There is a great fear of France's entanglements in the East and a general feeling that the occupation of the demilitarised zone by Germany was a certainty sooner or later . . . Some of our Right wing politicians feel very much as yours do about the Franco–Soviet Pact. They regard it as almost a betrayal of our Western Civilisation' (AC 4/3/27).

21 *DDF*, 2nd series, vol. I, no. 525; vol. II, no. 113.

22 Total German strength, including police, was 36,000 (*DGFP*, series C, vol. V, no. 189). French estimates put German strength at six to seven divisions – about 90,000 men (*DDF*, 2nd series, vol. I, no. 392).

23 *DDF*, 2nd series, vol. I, nos 187, 202.

24 See D. C. Watt, 'German plans for the reoccupation of the Rhineland: a note', *Journal of Contemporary History* (October 1966), pp. 193–9.

25 For a general survey see Gabriel Jackson, *A Concise History of the Spanish Civil War* (London, 1974). Dante A. Puzzo, *Spain and the Great Powers, 1936–1941* (New York and London, 1962) is now outdated by three recent specialist studies: Hans-Henning Abendroth, *Hitler in der Spanischen Arena* (Paderborn, 1973); John F. Coverdale, *Italian Intervention in the Spanish Civil War* (Princeton, 1976); Angel Vinas, *La Alemania nazi y el 18 de julio* (Madrid, 1974). Major essays in English and German on the international significance of the war are reprinted in Wolfgang Schieder and Christof Dipper (eds), *Der Spanische Burgerkrieg in der Internationalen Politik 1936–1939* (Munich, 1976).

26 Louis MacNeice, 'Autumn journal', in Robin Skelton (ed.), *Poetry of the Thirties* (Harmondsworth, 1964), p. 163.

27 A. J. P. Taylor, 'The Second World War', Creighton Lecture in History, 1973 (University of London, 1974), p. 10.

28 For example, Jeremy Noakes and Geoffrey Pridham (eds), *Documents on Nazism, 1919–1945* (London, 1974), pp. 518–19.

29 See Glen T. Harper, *German Economic Policy in Spain* (The Hague, 1967).

30 This paragraph is based on Abendroth, op. cit., and Vinas, op. cit.

31 *DGFP*, series D, vol. III, no. 4.

32 For the origins of non-intervention see Geoffrey Warner, 'France and non-intervention in Spain, July–August 1936', *International Affairs*, vol. 1, no. 38 (April 1962), pp. 203–20; David Carlton, 'Eden, Blum and the origins of non-intervention', *Journal of Contemporary History*, 6 (1971), pp. 40–55; M. D. Gallagher, 'Leon Blum and the Spanish Civil War', *Journal of Contemporary History*, 6 (1971), pp. 56–64. There is no authoritative study of the impact of the Spanish Civil War on British and French opinion. K. W. Watkins, *Britain Divided: The Effect of the Spanish Civil War on British Political Opinion* (Edinburgh, 1963) predates the massive release of governmental and private papers at the end of the 1960s. David Wingeate Pike, *Conjecture, Propaganda, and Deceit and the Spanish Civil War: The International Crisis over Spain, 1936–1939, as Seen in the French Press* (Stanford, Calif., 1968) is based entirely on a rather uncritical reading of the French press. The same author's *Les Français et la guerre d'Espagne, 1936–1939* (Paris, 1975) is a translation of the earlier English work.

33 But the Foreign Office approved Clerk's action: FO 371/20528. W7964/62/41. For the French record of Clerk's *démarche* see *DDF*, 2nd series, vol. III, no. 108.

34 See Anthony Adamthwaite, *France and the Coming of the Second World War, 1936–1939* (London, 1977).

35 David T. Cattell, *Soviet Diplomacy and the Spanish Civil War* (University of California, Berkeley and Los Angeles, 1957; reprinted 1971), p. 131.
36 For the controversy about the bombing of Guernica see Herbert Southworth, *La Destruction de Guernica* (Paris, 1975); Max Morgan-Witts and Gordon Thomas, *The Day Guernica Died* (London, 1975); Klaus A. Maier, *Guernica 26.4.1937: Die Deutsche Intervention in Spanien und der 'Fall Guernica'* (Freiburg, 1975); the *Times Literary Supplement*, 13 June, 20 June, 11 July, 18 July, 25 July 1975.
37 Louis MacNeice, *The Strings Are False* (London, 1965), p. 161.
38 See George Watson, 'Were the intellectuals duped?', *Encounter* (December 1973), pp. 20–30. In his poem 'Where are the war poets?' (1940) C. Day Lewis summed up the mood:

> They who in folly or mere greed
> Enslaved religion, markets, laws,
> Borrow our language now and bid
> Us to speak up in freedom's cause
> (*Word Over All* (London, 1943))

39 *FRUS 1936*, vol. II, p. 578.
40 *FRUS 1937*, vol. I, p. 124.
41 Medlicott, *Britain and Germany*, pp. 24–5.
42 AC 41/3/28.
43 David Owen Kieft, *Belgium's Return to Neutrality* (Oxford, 1972).

CHAPTER 5

1 Robert Rhodes James (ed.), *Chips: The Diaries of Sir Henry Channon* (Harmondsworth, 1967), p. 207.
2 Cowling, *Impact of Hitler*, p. 203; Lawrence R. Pratt, *East of Malta, West of Suez: Britain's Mediterranean Crisis, 1936–1939* (London, 1975), p. 105.
3 *DBFP*, 3rd series, vol. II, no. 1228.
4 Keith Middlemas, *Diplomacy of Illusion: The British Government and Germany, 1937–1939* (London, 1972), p. 53.
5 Feiling, *Neville Chamberlain*, p. 342.
6 ibid., p. 367.
7 CAB 23/95, 17 September 1938.
8 CAB 23/95, 24 September 1938.
9 'Gaudy night', in *Sayers Holiday Book* (London, 1963), p. 17.
10 Cowling, *Impact of Hitler*, pp. 273–4.
11 The Earl of Birkenhead, *Halifax: The Life of Lord Halifax* (London, 1965), p. 372.
12 Cowling, *Impact of Hitler*, pp. 289–91.
13 Middlemas, *Diplomacy of Illusion: The British Government and Germany, 1937–1939* (London, 1972), p. 47.
14 Letter of 22 April 1938 to Lord Lothian, 1st Marquess of Lothian Papers (Scottish Record Office, Edinburgh), 205.
15 Letter of 10 October 1938 from Sir John Simon to J. A. Spender, 1st Viscount Simon Papers (Institute of Historical Research, London).
16 Prime Minister's Office (Public Record Office, London), PREM 1/266A.
17 Feiling, *Neville Chamberlain*, p. 253.
18 Quoted in David Dilks, 'Appeasement revisited', *University of Leeds Review*, 15 (1972), p. 40.
19 Bradford A. Lee, *Britain and the Sino-Japanese War, 1937–1939: A Study in the Dilemma of British Decline* (London, 1973), p. 207. For British and American

policy in the Far East see Wm Roger Louis, *British Strategy in the Far East, 1919–1939* (Oxford, 1971); Stephen E. Pelz, *Race to Pearl Harbour: The Failure of the Second London Naval Conference and the Onset of World War II* (Cambridge, Mass., 1974); Ann Trotter, *Britain and East Asia, 1933–1937* (London, 1975); Stephen Lyon Endicott, *Diplomacy and Enterprise: British China Policy, 1933–1937* (Manchester, 1975).

20 Quoted in Watt, *Too Serious a Business*, p. 113.

21 Feiling, *Neville Chamberlain*, p. 292.

22 John Morton Blum (ed.), *From the Morgenthau Diaries*, vol. 1: *Years of Crisis, 1928–38* (Boston, 1959), p. 460.

23 *FRUS 1938*, vol. I, p. 65.

24 General M. G. Gamelin, chief of the French general staff, wrote: 'The crisis of May–June 1936 terrorised a great section of the French bourgeoisie. It made many of us lose sight of the dangers of Hitlerism and Fascism . . . because behind the Popular Front one saw the spectre of Bolshevism' (*Servir*, vol. II: *Le Prologue du drame (1930–1939)* (Paris, 1946), p. 219).

25 *DBFP*, 3rd series, vol. II, no. 1083.

26 Cowling, *Impact of Hitler*, p. 5.

27 ibid., p. 9.

28 ibid., pp. 8–9.

29 Watt, *Too Serious a Business*, p. 115.

30 In this and the following two paragraphs I have drawn on Watt, *Too Serious a Business*, and Michael Howard, *The Continental Commitment: The Dilemma of British Defence Policy in the Era of Two World Wars* (London, 1972).

31 Gamelin, op. cit., vol. II, pp. 344–7, 351–2.

32 Watt, *Too Serious a Business*, p. 130.

33 Feiling, *Neville Chamberlain*, p. 323; Middlemas, op. cit., p. 55.

34 Pratt, op. cit., p. 117.

35 Berndt-Jürgen Wendt, *Handel und Finanz in der Britischen Deutschland-Politik, 1933–1939* (Düsseldorf, 1971); C. A. MacDonald, 'Economic appeasement and the German "moderates", 1937–1939: an introductory essay', *Past and Present* (April–August 1972), pp. 105–35.

36 Lawrence R. Pratt, 'The Anglo–American naval conversations on the Far East of January 1938', *International Affairs* (October 1971), pp. 745–63.

37 Donald N. Lammers, *Explaining Munich: The Search for Motive in British Policy* (Stanford University, 1966); Keith Middlemas and John Barnes, *Baldwin: A Biography* (London, 1969), p. 955.

38 The most recent study is Ritchie Ovendale, *'Appeasement' and the English Speaking World: Britain, the United States, the Dominions and the policy of 'Appeasement', 1937–1939* (Cardiff, 1975). See also R. G. Neale (ed.), *Documents on Australian Foreign Policy, 1937–49*, vol. I: *1937–38* (Australian Government Publishing Service, 1976); D. C. Watt, *Personalities and Policies: Studies in the Formulation of British Foreign Policy in the Twentieth Century* (London, 1965); Keith Middlemas, 'The effect of dominion opinion on British foreign policy, 1937–38', in *The Dominions Between the Wars*, collected seminar papers, Institute of Commonwealth Studies (University of London, 1970–1), no. 13.

39 Ovendale, op. cit., p. 319.

40 Roskill, *Hankey*, vol. III, p. 389.

41 B. W. E. Alford, *Depression and Recovery? British Economic Growth, 1918–1939* (London, 1972), p. 81.

42 CAB 23/100, 5 July 1939. For the economic factor see MacDonald, op. cit.; F. Coghlan, 'Armaments, economic policy and appeasement: background to British foreign policy, 1931–1937', *History*, 57 (1972), pp. 205–16.

43 For interpretations of Hossbach see Robertson, *Origins of the Second World War*, pp. 112–14, 168–71.
44 For German military planning see R. O'Neill, *The German Army and the Nazi Party* (London, 1966); Esmonde M. Robertson, *Hitler's Pre-war Policy and Military Plans, 1933–1939* (London, 1963); Carr, *Arms, Autarky and Aggression*.
45 The 'initiatory role' in the Blomberg–Fritsch affair was played by Göring, not Hitler. Göring wanted to be war minister. See Harold C. Deutsch, *Hitler and his Generals: The Hidden Crisis January–June 1938* (Minneapolis, 1974), p. 77.
46 *DBFP*, 3rd series, vol. II, app. IV, p. 686; A. P. Young, *The 'X' Documents*, ed. Sidney Aster (London, 1974); Watt, *Too Serious a Business*, pp. 126–7.
47 Interview with Sir Eric Phipps on 26 May 1936, quoted in Medlicott, *Britain and Germany*, p. 27.
48 Andreas Hillgruber, 'England's place in Hitler's plans for world domination', *Journal of Contemporary History* (January 1974), p. 13; J. Henke, *England in Hitlers Politischen Kalkül, 1935–1939* (Boppard am Rhein, 1973).
49 See Dietrich Eichholtz, *Geschichte der Deutschen Kriegswirtschaft, 1939–1945*, vol. I (Berlin, 1969).
50 T. W. Mason, 'Some origins of the Second World War', in Robertson, *Origins of the Second World War*, p. 123; Taylor's reply, ibid., pp. 136–41.
51 ibid., p. 124.
52 Berenice A. Carroll, *Design for Total War: Arms and Economics in the Third Reich* (The Hague, 1968), p. 104. See also John D. Heyl, 'Hitler's economic thought: a reappraisal', *Central European History*, vol. VI, no. I (March 1973), pp. 83–96.
53 A. S. Milward, *The New Order and the French Economy* (Oxford, 1971).
54 For this paragraph see Taylor, *Origins of the Second World War*, p. 267; B. H. Klein, *Germany's Economic Preparations for War* (Cambridge, Mass., 1959); Carroll, op. cit., pp. 185, 189–90; A. S. Milward, *The German Economy at War* (London, 1965).
55 CAB 23/90, 1 December 1937.
56 Cowling, *Impact of Hitler*, pp. 156–9, 170–6.
57 Letter of 11 January 1938 to Sir Eric Phipps, Sir Eric Phipps Papers (Churchill College, Cambridge), 3/3. There was no love lost between Eden and Vansittart. 'He (Van) was quite catty about Eden, who, he said had been trying to edge him out for a long time' (1st Lord Dalton Papers (London School of Economics), diary, 12.4.1938).
58 *Cadogan Diaries*, p. 47.
59 FO 371/22311.
60 Robertson, *Hitler's Pre-war Policy*, op. cit., p. 113.
61 *DGFP*, series D, vol. I, no. 328.
62 Deutsch, op. cit., p. 338.
63 ibid., p. 339.
64 ibid., p. 343.

CHAPTER 6

1 Henderson to Lord Lothian, 22 April 1938, 1st Marquess of Lothian Papers (Scottish Record Office, Edinburgh), 205.
2 J. W. Bruegel, *Czechoslovakia Before Munich: The German Minority Problem and British Appeasement Policy* (Cambridge, 1973), p. 166. However, Henlein, it must be noted, was never completely in Hitler's pocket: Ronald M. Smelser, *The Sudeten Problem 1933–1938: 'Volkstumspolitik' and the Formulation of Nazi Foreign Policy* (Folkestone, 1975).

3 Keith Middlemas, *Diplomacy of Illusion: The British Government and Germany, 1937-1939* (London, 1972), p. 192.
4 *DBFP*, 3rd series, vol. I, no. 219, n. 2.
5 ibid., vol. I, no. 114.
6 Cowling, *Impact of Hitler*, p. 181. A. J. P. Taylor states that the Czechoslovaks deliberately started the rumours: *Origins of the Second World War*, p. 206. For conflicting interpretations see W. V. Wallace, 'The making of the May crisis of 1938', *Slavonic and East European Review* (June 1963), pp. 368-90; D. C. Watt, 'The May crisis of 1938: a rejoinder to Mr Wallace', ibid. (July 1966), pp. 475-80; W. V. Wallace, 'A reply to Mr Watt', ibid. (July 1966), pp. 481-6; D. C. Watt, 'Hitler's visit to Rome and the May weekend crisis: a study in Hitler's responses to external stimuli', *Journal of Contemporary History*, 9 (1974), pp. 23-32.
7 *DGFP*, series D, vol. II, no. 175.
8 Quoted in Watt, in *Journal of Contemporary History*, op. cit., p. 25.
9 Wallace, in *Slavonic and East European Review*, op. cit., p. 389.
10 General Moravec, head of Czechoslovak military intelligence in 1938, claims that their star informant, agent A54, a high Abwehr officer, informed them on 12 May that the Germans were planning an anti-Czechoslovak coup in the Sudetenland on the eve of municipal elections on the 22nd (*Master of Spies: The Memoirs of General František Moravec* (London, 1975), p. 126).
11 *DGFP*, series D, vol. II, no. 221.
12 Watt, in *Journal of Contemporary History*, op. cit., p. 31.
13 *DBFP*, 3rd series, vol. II, nos 1140, 1151, 1157, 1177, 1224, 1227; *DGFP*, series D, vol. II, nos 655, 669-70, 674-5; *Memoirs of Ernst von Weizsäcker* (London, 1951), p. 154.
14 *DBFP*, 3rd series, vol. II, no. 1228 and app. to no. 1228.
15 *DGFP*, series D, vol. II, nos 338, 424, 448, 654.
16 In the debate on the *Anschluss* in the House of Commons on 14 March 1938 Winston Churchill called for a 'grand alliance' around Britain and France: 'If that were sustained . . . and if it were done in the year 1938 – and . . . it may be the last chance there will be for doing it – I say you might even now arrest this approaching war' (*333 HC Deb. 5s.*, cols 93-100; Middlemas, op. cit., p. 186).
17 *DBFP*, 3rd series, vol. II, no. 791.
18 For the military situation see R. G. D. Laffan (ed.), *Survey of International Affairs, 1938*, vol. III (London, 1953), pp. 460-603; for Anglo–German air strengths see Roskill, *Hankey*, vol. III, app. 3, pp. 664-5. The estimate for France given here is from British air ministry figures in FO 371/21710. The picture of French air strength is confused because conflicting figures were put out by the opposing groups of *bellicistes* and *pacifistes* in September 1938 (Doc. 59). According to one recent account: 'Daladier left for Munich with General Vuillemin's parting words, that the French air force had only 700 front line planes' (Watt, *Too Serious a Business*, p. 120). In fact what the chief of air staff told the government was that the air force strength 'at present available' in *Metropolitan* France was 700 aircraft and that up to 40 per cent of air strength might be lost at the end of the first fortnight of hostilities. But Vuillemin's assumption in making this evaluation was that Hitler would at once launch an air offensive against France: Vuillemin to Guy la Chambre (air minister), 26 September 1938, *Les Evénements survenus en France de 1933 à 1945: Témoignages et documents récueillis par la commission d'enquête parlementaire*, vol. II (Paris, n.d.), p. 313.
19 Roskill, *Hankey*, vol. III, p. 387.
20 Nancy Harvison Hooker (ed.), *The Moffat Papers: Selections from the Diplo-*

matic Journals of Jay Pierrepont Moffat, 1919–1943 (Cambridge, Mass., 1956), p. 214. Arguably, the government's failure to educate opinion in the Abyssinian crisis of 1935–6 made the task of alerting it to German intentions in the later 1930s all the more difficult: Daniel Waley, *British Public Opinion and the Abyssinian War, 1935–6* (London, 1975), pp. 139–40.

21 *FRUS 1938*, vol. I, p. 611; Nicholas Pronay, 'British newsreels in the 1930s', *History*, 57 (1972), pp. 66, 68.

22 Asa Briggs, *The History of Broadcasting in the United Kingdom*, vol. III: *The War of Words* (London, 1970), p. 83; Andrew Boyle, *Only the Wind will Listen: Reith of the BBC* (London, 1972), p. 253. Lord Home's memoirs provide many examples of the gulf between the leisured social and political elite and the rest of the nation: *The Way the Wind Blows* (London, 1976).

23 Sir John Wheeler-Bennett, *Munich: Prologue to Tragedy* (London, 1963).

24 Henderson called for a major effort to finish Britain's air defences: *DBFP*, 3rd series, vol. III, app. I (ii). On 6 October 1938 Jacques Chastenet, editor of *Le Temps*, wrote to Duff Cooper who had just resigned as first lord of the admiralty in protest against Munich: 'I confess I am not in agreement with you on the essentials of the matter and I think that, having regard to the circumstances, and particularly to the present state of British and French armaments, M. Chamberlain was right to act as he did . . . I believe that we are in any case agreed on one point; that it is necessary to strengthen Britain and France to such a point that we will no longer be forced to accept further retreats.' (I am indebted for this reference to Mr Martin Gilbert who holds a small collection of papers of the 1st Viscount Norwich.)

25 *DBFP*, 3rd series, vol. III, no. 285. For British policy see Donald Lammers, 'From Whitehall after Munich: the Foreign Office and the future course of British policy', *Historical Journal*, 16 (1973), pp. 831–56.

26 Cowling, *Impact of Hitler*, p. 205.

27 *Cadogan Diaries*, 14 November 1938, p. 125.

28 Cowling, *Impact of Hitler*, p. 478, n. 143.

29 Malcolm Muggeridge (ed.), *Ciano's Diary, 1939–1943* (London, 1947), p. 9.

30 CAB 23/97, 1 February 1939.

31 *Cadogan Diaries*, 6 February 1939, p. 147.

32 Feiling, *Neville Chamberlain*, p. 396.

33 *DBFP*, 3rd series, vol. IV, pp. 591, 594.

34 General M. G. Gamelin, *Servir*, vol. II (Paris, 1946), p. 353.

35 ibid., vol. I, pp. 124–5. See Robert J. Young, 'The aftermath of Munich: the course of French diplomacy, October 1938–March 1939', *French Historical Studies*, 8 (1973), pp. 305–22.

36 *DGFP*, series D, vol. IV, nos 370, 372.

37 A. P. Young, *The 'X' Documents*, ed. Sidney Aster (London, 1974), p. 239.

38 See J. M. Meskill, *The Hollow Alliance: Germany and Japan* (New York, 1966); Ernest L. Presseisen, *Germany and Japan: A Study in Totalitarian Diplomacy, 1933–1941* (New York, 1969).

39 *DGFP*, series D, vol. IV, nos 81, 152.

40 Feiling, *Neville Chamberlain*, p. 401. The best study of British policy after Prague is Sidney Aster, *1939: The Making of the Second World War* (London, 1973).

41 *DBFP*, 3rd series, vol. IV, no. 280.

42 Cowling, *Impact of Hitler*, pp. 289–91, 294.

43 Feiling, *Neville Chamberlain*, p. 400.

44 *Cadogan Diaries*, p. 161.

45 *DBFP*, 3rd series, vol. IV, no. 484. For Poland see Anne M. Cienciala, *Poland and the Western Powers, 1938–39* (London, 1968).
46 See C. A. MacDonald, 'Britain, France and the April Crisis of 1939', *European Studies Review*, 2 (1972), pp. 151–69.
47 See Gerhard L. Weinberg, *Germany and the Soviet Union 1939–41* (Leiden, 1954); Gustav Hilger and Alfred G. Meyer, *The Incompatible Allies: A Memoir History of German–Soviet Relations, 1918–1941* (New York, 1953); Ivan Maisky, *Who Helped Hitler?* (London, 1964); Walter Laqueur, *Russia and Germany: A Century of Conflict* (London, 1965); D. C. Watt, 'The initiation of the negotiations leading to the Nazi–Soviet Pact: a historical problem', in C. Abramsky (ed.), *Essays in Honour of E. H. Carr* (London, 1974), pp. 152–70.
48 CAB 23/98.
49 CAB 23/98, 3 May 1939.
50 *Cadogan Diaries*, 20 May 1939, p. 182.
51 Aster, op. cit., p. 265.
52 ibid., p. 291.
53 Jane Degras (ed.), *Soviet Documents on Foreign Policy*, vol. III (Oxford, 1953), pp. 151–8.
54 L. Kochan, 'Russia and Germany, 1935–1937: a note', *Slavonic and East European Review*, 95 (1962), pp. 518–20.
55 Robert Coulondre, *De Staline à Hitler* (Paris, 1950), p. 165.
56 ibid., p. 171.
57 Aster, op. cit., pp. 154–5.
58 Watt, in Abramsky, op. cit., p. 164.
59 *DBFP*, 3rd series, vol. VI, no. 269.
60 Aster, op. cit., p. 233.
61 Aster describes the conversations between Sir Horace Wilson and Wohlthat solely from Wilson's point of view (op. cit., pp. 244–8). For the German record see *DGFP*, series D, vol. VI, no. 716; for the British, *DBFP*, 3rd series, vol. VI, no. 354. For talks between Wilson and the German ambassador, Dirksen, see *DBFP*, 3rd series, vol. VI, no. 533; Ministry for Foreign Affairs of the USSR, *Soviet Peace Efforts on the Eve of World War II (September 1938–August 1939): Documents and Records*, ed. V. M. Falin et al. part 2 (Moscow, 1973), no. 396. The Foreign Office files relating to Wohlthat's selection to attend the London whaling conference in July 1939 – his excuse for visiting London – are closed until the year 2015.
62 Mario Toscano, *The Origins of the Pact of Steel* (Baltimore, 1967), pp. 384–7.
63 Aster, op. cit., p. 336.
64 *DBFP*, 3rd series, vol. VII, no. 283.
65 For Dahlerus see his memoirs, *The Last Attempt* (London, 1947); *DBFP*, 3rd series, vol. VI, app. IV; vol. VII, *passim*.
66 The suggestion came from the director-general of the BBC: Briggs, op. cit., vol. III, p. 81.
67 Georges Bonnet, *Dans la Tourmente* (Paris, 1971), p. 167.
68 Edouard Herriot Papers (by courtesy of M. Michel Soulié).
69 *Le Livre jaune français: documents diplomatiques, 1938–1939* (Paris, 1939), no. 253.
70 Nicholas Bethell, *The War Hitler Won* (London, 1972), p. 28.
71 *Harvey Diaries*, 27 August 1939, p. 306.
72 Cowling, *Impact of Hitler*, p. 309.
73 *Cadogan Diaries*, p. 205.
74 ibid., p. 206.

75 Esmonde M. Robertson, *Hitler's Pre-war Policy and Military Plans 1933–39* (London, 1963), p. 188.
76 *DBFP*, 3rd series, vol. VII, no. 621.
77 Aster, op. cit., p. 366.
78 See Mussolini's letter listing Italian requirements for a war lasting twelve months: *DGFP*, series D, vol. VII, no. 301.
79 A. J. P. Taylor, *Beaverbrook* (Harmondsworth, 1974), p. 513. See R. A. C. Parker, 'The British government and the coming of war with Germany, 1939', in M. R. D. Foot (ed.), *War and Society: Historical Essays in Honour of J. R. Western, 1928–1971* (London, 1973), pp. 1–15.
80 Avon, *Eden Memoirs*, vol. II, p. 520.
81 Middlemas, op. cit., p. 455.
82 Letter of 2 March 1934, AC 40/6/14.
83 Marc Bloch, *L'Etrange Défaite* (Paris, 1946).
84 Robert Rhodes James (ed.), *Chips: The Diaries of Sir Henry Channon* (Harmondsworth, 1967), 3 September 1939, p. 265.

DOCUMENTS

1932–6

1. Ramsay MacDonald's attitude towards Germany, 10 October 1932

From Documents diplomatiques français, 1932–1939, *1st series, 1932–5, vol. I (Paris, 1964), no. 235. Letter from Ramsay MacDonald, English prime minister, to Edouard Herriot, French prime minister.*

London, 10 October 1932

I. Private. Personal.

My dear Herriot,

I was very glad to get your letter of October 6th when I reached London on the evening of the 8th, and should like to thank you for the efforts which you are making to reach agreement with us as to the meeting which we suggested to overcome the difficulty arising from Germany's withdrawal from the disarmament discussions. I need hardly say that I warmly welcome your suggestion for a preliminary exchange of views with Sir John Simon and myself on this situation. I am told that you have no objection to coming to London, and as I have begun a series of cabinet meetings in preparation for the meeting of the House of Commons, which will tie me to London until they are finished, I am most grateful to you for helping me in this way. You know how welcome you will be.

I am not at all happy as regards the immediate future, and feel that letters and dispatches will never brighten it. We must all meet and face up to the problems which fate has given us to deal with.

As I expect to see you soon I shall not go into any details, but I feel in my blood and bones that the first thing we have to do is to be perfectly clear in our own minds about the general outlook before we begin to make any specific proposals. Europe has been undoubtedly drifting recently into militarist hands, and a great part of the impetus has certainly come from the psychological reaction upon the german mind of germany's economic and political position. I think this ought to have been foreseen some years ago so that resentment would have been prevented from accumulating. Metaphorically, we have now to face a bow drawn to the utmost stretch, instead of one only slightly drawn. One day when both of us have more leisure and less responsibility, so that we can open our hearts more fully to each other, I should like to discuss with you upon whose shoulders the blame lies and what events produced the unfortunate results; but it is sufficient to say at the moment, I do not believe that any of us can rigidly resist the german claim that the treaty of Versailles must in some respects be reconsidered. Supposing you were to continue to repeat 'No' to those claims, and Germany said 'Then as we are not to be released by agreement we shall appeal to the sense of fair play of the whole world and release ourselves reasonably', what would you do? That would put you in a very serious dilemma, and would be a heavy blow to treaty observance and to european stability.

There is another point: my own feeling is that Germany wants to rearm, but it has put its request in such a way as to delude many people on both sides of the Atlantic, and the attitude of 'we will not listen' has swung a great many more people into sympathy with Germany. I am sure that very great harm will be done if we continue to address notes to Berlin and to receive replies from Berlin. That method will harden a situation which must be kept fluid as long as possible. Besides you will never get the mind of any country from its dispatches and its interviews with the press. If you assume that any country in Europe is playing an evil game, surely the best thing is to ask it to come and talk matters over. If they are bad, they will be exposed; if they are good, they will be appreciated. If you yourself were, for one reason or another, to begin to believe evil things about me, the very first thing I should do would be to go and see you, or to get you to come and see me. I would not write you long letters; and that I think is how our international business must be done more and more. That is why (and I am sure, my good friend, you will never misunderstand me when I say this) I regretted so much that you started discussing this matter with Germany alone. I felt nothing would come out of it, but that Germany would draw out of the disarmament conference and leave all of us who are trying to get a friendly spirit abroad in Europe to face new troubles and more recondite situations. I want no pacts nor treaties to come out of these conversations. I just want such an understanding as will enable the ordinary machinery now set up at Geneva to go on using our work as an opportunity for itself to reach success.

I recapitulate one or two of the things that have greatly occupied my mind when I was away from Downing Street and supposed to be enjoying a holiday in Scotland:

1. What is to be done regarding Germany and the Versailles treaty?
2. How are we all to cooperate in finding solutions for the international problems, political and economic, which are now facing us under critical circumstances? It is possible to get the four big European powers – yourselves, Germany, Italy and ourselves – to understand each other so thoroughly that we shall not remain suspicious each of the other, but approach every international problem in which we are concerned in a spirit of goodwill and confidence?

You may shake your shaggy head at this, but it is the idealism which has carried us through this far, and which neither you nor I nor our countries dare abandon at this moment.

Within very recent times we here have had to face a development in press propaganda which threatens to make all agreements impossible and all confidence a mere dream. The press rapidly becomes one of the most serious international problems. Today, as I was coming up from Chequers, I saw a contents bill issued by a liberal paper which, since the liberal secessions from the Cabinet has become a mere partisan sheet – reckless as regards what it publishes, except that it must damage the national government. The bill announced that I had given a pledge to Berlin. It is quite untrue, but if I deny it for a month people will not cease to believe it. I suppose it will be used to give you trouble in France, and in Berlin it will be reproduced for the purpose of stirring up feeling there. There is no doubt but the finger of the devil is pretty prominent in this generation. I believe the news came from Geneva. Geneva is becoming more and more like what Riga has been as regards the russian revolution, and certain other places which you know were during the war.

Now, my dear Herriot, I have made bold just to think aloud and to put my passing thoughts on paper, because I want you to see what is in my mind generally. I am not writing as a Prime Minister, but as a friend concerned with you in all the big problems which this generation unfortunately has to face in a bunch. This is in no sense even remotely an official document; it is a letter from one who trusts another and whose desire will always be to retain friendship and confidence.

I am with kindest regards yours strong sincerely.

2. General Weygand reviews French defence policy, 16 January 1933

From Documents diplomatiques français, 1932–1939, *1st series, 1932–5, vol. II (Paris, 1966), no. 203. General Weygand was inspector general of the army, vice president of the Conseil Supérieur de la Guerre.*

At a time when reorganization of the military forces of France is on the agenda, as a result of estimates to be made because of the reduction in contingents during the years 1935 to 1940, and negotiations in Geneva regarding limitation of armaments, as well as budgetary difficulties of 1933, it is important to define what France requires of her national forces as a whole. If we do not settle what purpose they must serve, we run the risk of treating these serious problems, whose solution determines the future and independence of the country, from a purely subjective point of view, losing sight of the very purpose of these forces. We thus become involved in arrangements of detail, partial concessions and reductions decided without a thorough inquiry. Pared down in this manner by retrenchments, none of which seems vital to those who agree to them but whose total and incidence multiply the destructive effects, the military forces will eventually suffer very grave impairment. If such procedures continue, these forces, in spite of the admirable devotion of the cadres, will gradually become incapable of fulfilling their basic function.

. . . The old formula, 'We must have an army which corresponds to the needs of our policy', has lost none of its value. It means that an army can be organized according to just principles only if the policy, which she must see carried out, is clearly defined.

France is profoundly pacifist. This is true, this is simple, but it is just too simple to be sufficient to define her policy. The policy of a great country like ours, which through her possessions has spread over the whole surface of the globe, has to reckon with various and complex elements which are the results of her geographic and demographic situation, the nature of her frontiers and the inclinations of her neighbours, the treaties in force and the agreements made with other powers.

(1) France has land frontiers of more than 1,000 km, of which she shares about 300 km with Italy, and which are reinforced by the barrier of the Alps; she shares 300 km of frontier with Germany without natural protection to the west of the Rhine. She is the only European country to have maritime frontiers opening on the north, west and south, on three seas which are free of ice all the year round. Her eastern and south-eastern neighbours openly assert a policy of destruction of the state of things established by the treaties, and of aggressive intentions towards her. They do not even leave her ignorant of the terms and conditions of the future conflict, summed up in the newly fashionable term, 'sudden war', by land, sea and air.

The result is that the first duty of the military, air and naval forces of the national defence is to defend the territory while defending themselves against these attacks. However, the new conditions of sudden attack and barbarism which one is obliged to consider, force France, who refused to be the aggressor, to withstand the attack and consequently to have on her frontiers a defence system which is always in good order and easily alerted. This necessity creates obligations as far as the present manpower, equipment service and calling up of reserves are concerned.

On the other hand, it must be made clear that the often-used term, 'defensive army', has no meaning. Even in the defensive, especially in the defensive, an army which has neither the will nor the means to manoeuvre is doomed to defeat. Consequently, the defence system must include large manoeuvring units, in addition to the fortress units.

(2) The German frontier, however, is common to France and Belgium. They are linked by an agreement for their joint defence. Belgium does not have the means of protecting the 120 km which stretch from the south of

Luxembourg to the Dutch Limburg against invasion. France must go to her rescue without delay in order to stop the enemy on this line. . . . There she will have the advantages of having to block 120 km with the support of the Belgian army instead of 350 km with her own forces alone, and of keeping the enemy at a distance from the rich country of the north. The extent of territory to be covered by French strategic deployment is therefore increased by a substantial part of Belgian territory. Consequently, new large manoeuvring units, certain of which must be capable of special speed, are seen to be indispensable on this account.

(3) We have another ally, Poland. The invasion of Polish Pomerania by the Germans is a common topic of conversation. What will be the attitude of France if this manifestation of 'sudden war' surprises her in the midst of peace ? Will she immediately enter Germany to make the Germans respect the treaties and to take securities there ? What will her present military condition allow her to do without having recourse to any mobilization measures ? If what she can do is not sufficient, what preparations should she make ?

(4) Other agreements link us with the nations which form the Little *Entente*. In what obligations will they involve us, and involve themselves ? What instructions will the governments give to their General Staffs, in case of conflict, as to how to conduct the war ? Against which enemy will the initial effort be made ? What cooperation in the way of equipment would be useful to these countries ? . . .

(8) The study of these questions, all of which are important to the organization of our national defence forces, will necessarily lead to combinations of manpower from the home territory, North Africa or the colonies. Bearing in mind the moral and material disadvantages of an unplanned augmentation, what is the maximum manpower of these overseas contingents which could be stationed in France ? Also, taking into account the security of our colonies and protectorate countries, what is the minimum manpower of the forces of each nationality which must be maintained there ?

If we leave questions of this magnitude without examining or solving them, we shall be led inexorably day by day, under the pressure of budgetary necessities, political influences or international blackmail, to take measures which will gradually drain our national forces of their substance. They will become merely a façade and will not be in a condition to fulfil their mission at the hour of danger.

It therefore appears absolutely essential to begin this methodical and exhaustive study without delay. Its results will be the obligatory basis for all organization or reorganization of the national defence forces. It can only be done by responsible chiefs: ministers and military chiefs, that is, by a reduced and rationally formed council of national defence.

3. *Mein Kampf*, 1925

From Adolf Hitler, Mein Kampf, *trans. by Ralph Mannheim, intro. by D. C. Watt (London, Hutchinson, 1969), pp. 596–8.*

As opposed to this, we National Socialists must hold unflinchingly to our aim in foreign policy, namely, *to secure for the German people the land and soil to which they are entitled on this earth.* And this action is the only one which, before God and our German posterity, would make any sacrifice of blood seem justified: before God, since we have been put on this earth with the mission of eternal struggle for our daily bread, beings who receive nothing as a gift, and who owe their position as lords of the earth only to the genius and the courage with which they can conquer and defend it; and before our German posterity in so far as we have shed no citizen's blood out of which a thousand others are not bequeathed to posterity. The soil on which some day German generations of peasants can beget powerful sons will sanction the investment of the sons of today, and will some day acquit the responsible statesmen of blood-guilt and sacrifice of the people, even if they are persecuted by their contemporaries.

And I must sharply attack those folkish pen-pushers who claim to regard such an acquisition of soil as a 'breach of sacred human rights' and attack it as such in their scribblings. One never knows who stands behind these fellows. But one thing is certain, that the confusion they can create is desirable and convenient to our national enemies. By such an attitude they help to weaken and destroy from within our people's will for the only correct way of defending their vital needs. For no people on this earth possesses so much as a square yard of territory on the strength of a higher will or superior right. Just as Germany's frontiers are fortuitous frontiers, momentary frontiers in the current political struggle of any period, so are the boundaries of other nations' living space. And just as the shape of our earth's surface can seem immutable as granite only to the thoughtless soft-head, but in reality only represents at each period an apparent pause in a continuous development, created by the mighty forces of Nature in a process of continuous growth, only to be transformed or destroyed tomorrow by greater forces, likewise the boundaries of living spaces in the life of nations.

State boundaries are made by man and changed by man.

The fact that a nation has succeeded in acquiring an undue amount of soil constitutes no higher obligation that it should be recognised eternally. At most it proves the strength of the conquerors and the weakness of the nations. And in this case, right lies in this strength alone. If the German nation today, penned into an impossible area, faces a lamentable future, this is no more a commandment of Fate than revolt against this state of affairs constitutes an affront to Fate. No more than any higher power has promised another nation more territory than the German nation, or is offended by the fact of this unjust distribution of the soil. Just as our ancestors did not receive the soil on which we live today as a gift from Heaven, but had to fight for it at the risk of their lives, in the future no folkish grace will win soil for us and hence life for our people, but only the might of a victorious sword.

Much as all of us today recognise the necessity of a reckoning with France, it would remain ineffectual in the long run if it represented the whole of our aim in foreign policy. It can and will achieve meaning only if it offers the rear cover for an enlargement of our people's living space in Europe. For it is not in colonial acquisitions that we must see the solution of this problem, but exclusively in the acquisition of a territory for settlement, which will enhance the area of the mother country, and hence not only keep the new settlers in the most intimate community with the land of their origin, but secure for the total area those advantages which lie in its unified magnitude.

The folkish movement must not be the champion of other peoples, but the vanguard fighter of its own. Otherwise it is superfluous and above all has no right to sulk about the past. For in that case it is behaving in exactly the same way. The old German policy was wrongly determined by dynastic considerations, and the future policy must not be directed by cosmopolitan folkish drivel. In particular, we are not constables guarding the well-known 'poor little nations', but soldiers of our own nation.

But we National Socialists must go further. *The right to possess soil can become a duty if without extension of its soil a great nation seems doomed to destruction.* And most especially when not some little nigger nation or other is involved, but the Germanic mother of life, which has given the present-day world its cultural picture. *Germany will either be a world power or there will be no Germany.* And for world power she needs that magnitude which will give her the position she needs in the present period, and life to her citizens.

And so we National Socialists consciously draw a line beneath the foreign policy tendency of our pre-War period. We take up where we broke off six hundred years ago. We stop the endless German movement to the south and west, and turn our gaze towards the land in the east. At long last we break off the colonial and commercial policy of the pre-War period and shift to the soil policy of the future.

If we speak of soil in Europe today, we can primarily have in mind only *Russia* and her vassal border states.

Here Fate itself seems desirous of giving us a sign. By handing Russia to Bolshevism, it robbed the Russian nation of that intelligentsia which previously brought about and guaranteed its existence as a state. For the organisation of a Russian state formation was not the result of the political abilities of the Slavs in Russia, but only a wonderful example of the state-forming efficacity of the German element in an inferior race. Numerous mighty empires on earth have been created in this way. Lower nations led by Germanic organisers and overlords have more than once grown to be mighty state formations and have endured as long as the racial nucleus of the creative state race maintained itself. For centuries Russia drew nourishment from this Germanic nucleus of its upper leading strata. Today it can be regarded as almost totally exterminated and extinguished. It has been replaced by the Jew. Impossible as it is for the Russian by himself to shake off the yoke of the Jew by his own resources, it is equally impossible for the Jew to maintain the mighty empire forever. He himself is no element of organisation, but a ferment of decomposition. The Persian[1] empire in the east is ripe for collapse. And the end of Jewish rule in Russia will also be the end of Russia as a state. We have been chosen by Fate as witness of a catastrophe which will be the mightiest confirmation of the soundness of the folkish theory.

Our task, the mission of the National Socialist movement, is to bring our own people to such political insight that they will not see their goal for the future in the breath-taking sensation of a new Alexander's conquest, but in the industrious work of the German plough, to which the sword need only give soil.

4. Hitler's first speech to the generals, 3 February 1933

From Documents on Nazism, 1919–1945, *intro. and ed. by Jeremy Noakes and Geoffrey Pridham (London, Jonathan Cape, 1974), pp. 508–9.*

The sole aim of general policy: *the regaining of political power*. The whole State administration must be geared to this end (all departments!).

1. *Domestic policy:* Complete reversal of the present domestic political situation in Germany. Refusal to tolerate any attitude contrary to this aim (pacifism!). Those who will not be converted must be broken. Extermination of Marxism root and branch. Adjustment of youth and of the whole people to the idea that only a struggle can save us and that everything else must be subordinated to this idea. (Realized in the millions of the Nazi movement. It will grow.) Training of youth and strengthening of the will to fight with all means. Death penalty for high treason. Tightest authoritarian State leadership. Removal of the cancer of democracy!
2. *Foreign policy:* Battle against Versailles. Equality of rights in Geneva; but useless if people do not have the will to fight. Concern for allies.

---

[1] Second edition has 'giant' instead of 'Persian'.

3. *Economics:* The farmer must be saved! Settlement policy! Further increase of exports useless. The capacity of the world is limited and production is forced up everywhere. The only possibility of re-employing part of the army of unemployed lies in settlement. But time is needed and radical improvement not to be expected since living space too small for German people.

4. *Building up of the armed forces:* Most important prerequisite for achieving the goal of regaining political power. National Service must be reintroduced. But beforehand the State leadership must ensure that the men subject to military service are not, even before their entry, poisoned by pacifism, Marxism, Bolshevism or do not fall victim to this poison after their service.

How should political power be used when it has been gained? That is impossible to say yet. Perhaps fighting for new export possibilities, perhaps – and probably better – the conquest of new living space in the east and its ruthless Germanization. Certain that only through political power and struggle can the present economic circumstances be changed. The only things that can happen now – settlement – stopgap measures.

Armed forces most important and most Socialist institution of the State. It must stay unpolitical and impartial. The internal struggle not their affair but that of the Nazi organizations. As opposed to Italy no fusion of Army and SA intended – most dangerous time is during the reconstruction of the Army. It will show whether or not France has statesmen: if so, she will not leave us time but will attack us (presumably with eastern satellites).

5. Colonel Beck denies rumours that Poland is planning a preventive war against Germany, 4 May 1933

From Documents diplomatiques français, 1932–1939, *1st series, 1932–5, vol. III (Paris, 1967), no. 238. Telegram from Laroche, the French ambassador, to Paul-Boncour, the French foreign minister. Colonel Beck was the Polish foreign minister.*

Warsaw, 4 May 1933

The foreign minister asked me to see him this morning. He wished to tell me about the interview that M. Wysocki [Polish minister in Berlin] had with the German Chancellor yesterday.

M. Beck recalled to me the rumours circulating in the German press attributing to Poland plans for a preventive war. The Polish press has replied to them. . . . But the Polish government considered that in view of the conclusions that might be drawn from it the question was too serious to be left to the press alone and an official explanation was necessary. The Polish Minister in Berlin had therefore asked to be received by Chancellor Hitler. He had spoken to him about the anxieties aroused here by various manifestations on the German side and demanded to know the position of the government of the Reich. He explained that Poland had no aggressive intentions. . . .

The Chancellor replied in a moderate tone . . . he clearly expressed the intention of the German government to maintain peace and observe treaties. . . .

. . . the foreign minister this morning summoned the German Minister. . . . He spoke to him in similar terms to those used by M. Hitler. . . .

Colonel Beck told me that he wanted the French government to know the origins of these two interviews. He was not concerned with the kind of interpretation the government might give to the démarches, it was only the result that mattered, which is to put an end to the ambiguity caused by tendentious rumours, as harmful to Poland as they are to peace. It is however just as important that the French government should be accurately informed as to the motives of the Polish government. Those who accuse the Polish government of desiring a preventive war, an idea which it has never even contemplated, might just as well accuse it of throwing itself into the arms of Germany. . . .

6. Sir Horace Rumbold's last dispatch, 30 June 1933

From Documents on British Foreign Policy, 1919–1939, *ed. E. L. Woodward and Rohan Butler, 2nd series, vol. V (London, HMSO, 1956), no. 229.*

BERLIN, *June 30, 1933*

Sir,

I have reported in separate despatches on the recent measures taken by the German Government against the Social Democratic party, the German National party and the Evangelical Church. This despatch is an attempt at a general appreciation of the situation here on the eve of my departure from this post. . . .

2. I need not examine the genesis of the Hitler movement nor trace its development up to the time when the leader of the movement became Chancellor. In the foreign domain the Hitler regime has succeeded in a very brief space in antagonising practically the whole world. The present despatch deals mainly with the effects of the internal policy as hitherto

pursued by that regime. Before proceeding further, however, it seems only fair to recognise the good points in the Hitler ideology. Briefly, it is meant to develop a spirit of comradeship and of unselfish devotion to the State. The individual is to be subordinate to the welfare of the community, and the movement aims at restoring the self-respect of the citizen and, through him, of the State itself. Class warfare is to cease and labour to be ennobled. Convinced National Socialists such as Dr. Goebbels profess to believe that Hitler's ideals are bound eventually to be adopted by all countries, and that the mission of the Hitler creed is to regenerate nations which have been corrupted by democracy and by association with the Jews. Germany, they say, is now, or will be, the 'sittlich-moralischer Führer', i.e., the moral leader of Europe. Hitler himself has been credited with having an almost divine mission. He has also been compared with Mahomet, and more than one paper has accepted the comparison.

3. The average German does not appear to possess a true sense of proportion. Hitlerism *inter alia* is a reaction from what are alleged to be the criminal shortcomings and international outlook of all German Governments since 1919. It has, therefore, gone to the other extreme and produced an aggressive nationalism which is accompanied by a seemingly profound contempt for and disregard of foreign opinion. Soviet methods are being used, as exemplified by the arrest of prominent personalities, such as Dr. Löbe, without any indication of the reasons for those arrests, confiscation of the funds and property of the parties in opposition to the present regime and, generally, the continued execution of measures which are in direct conflict with the existence of what may be termed a 'Rechtsstaat'. . . .

5. Visitors from abroad usually ask where this policy is leading and who is the driving force in the Nazi party. Some competent observers doubt whether the Nazi party itself knows what its goal is. The leaders, when pressed, almost invariably take refuge in verbiage and generalities. The outside world is best acquainted with the three chiefs, Hitler, Göring and Goebbels. All three are notoriously pathological cases, Hitler and Göring as a result of wounds and hardships in the war, Goebbels as a result of a physical defect and neglect in childhood. His club-foot is a constant source of bitterness to him, and his friends attribute his peculiarly venomous tongue to a 'vanity complex' arising out of it. It is known that Göring and Goebbels cordially dislike each other, and that fact is an element of strength for Hitler. . . .

15. Unpleasant incidents and excesses are bound to occur during a revolution, but the deliberate ruthlessness and brutality which have been practised during the last five months seem both excessive and unnecessary. I have the impression that the persons directing the policy of the Hitler Government are not normal. Many of us, indeed, have a feeling that we are living in a country where fanatics, hooligans and eccentrics have got

the upper hand, and there is certainly an element of hysteria in the policy and actions of the Hitler regime. Two Nazis were shot in a house in Cöpenick three or four days ago. They were promptly accorded a State funeral, and flags flew at half-mast over the Reichstag and other public buildings. Asked by a member of my staff what they thought about their new duties, three members of the Prussian police force on duty at His Majesty's Consulate said that they had long since ceased to think. They had returned to the war mentality of 1916, when they obeyed any order without troubling about the sense or meaning of it. . . .

18. I am loth to conclude my last despatch from this post with a question mark, yet it would be idle for me to attempt to forecast the development of Germany during the next few years or even the next twelve months. I am confident that neither Hitler nor his Ministers have themselves any clear idea of the course which events will take, nor have I met anyone who is prepared to venture an opinion. Politically, the National Socialists can reduce this country to the drab uniformity which characterises Soviet Russia, but economically and socially the development is obscure. The Chancellor is concentrating his attention on the problem of reducing unemployment in the realisation that his stay in office depends to a great extent on the economic situation next winter. As yet his remedies have not differed in any important respect from the stereotyped remedies of other countries. So far as foreign policy is concerned, it will take him a long time to retrieve the ground lost since the resignation of Dr. Brüning, and it is a matter of regret to me that my departure should coincide with an undeniably serious coolness in Anglo–German relations. Not that there is any hostility to Great Britain on the German side, particularly in official circles – my visit to Neudeck and other indications have reassured me in that respect – but it is obvious that the Anglo–Saxon world regards the National Socialist experiment with deep-seated distrust, if not hostility.

I have, &c.,

HORACE RUMBOLD

7. Sir John Simon believes Italy is the key to peace, 7 September 1933

From Austen Chamberlain Papers (University of Birmingham Library), AC 40/5/85. Letter of 7 September 1933 from Sir John Simon, then foreign secretary, to Austen Chamberlain.

My Dear Chamberlain,

I have just been reading a telegram from Rome which gives some account of your talk with Mussolini and of the way in which you impressed upon him the importance of a genuine Franco–Italian rapprochement. May

I say how entirely I agree with you and how grateful I am to you for having the opportunity to urge this with the authority and experience which you (now that Grey has gone) alone possess. I also agree most profoundly with your reading of German psychology and with the Teutonic failing of misreading generosity and imagining that it betokens weakness rather than a warning of strength. More and more do I feel in these days that Italy is the real key to European peace. I believe that our visit to Rome and the Four Power Pact in its ultimate form were valuable influences in the right direction. . . . It seems to me that the prospect of Hitlerism becoming established on a more respectable basis in Germany is great, and there are strong signs that Nazi influence in Austria will, in the end, be too strong for poor Dollfuss. If so, Austria is becoming a focus of terrible anxiety, and everything depends on keeping Italy on the right path. . . .

> Yours ever sincerely
> John Simon

8. Sir Robert Vansittart on Germany, 7 April 1934

From Documents on British Foreign Policy, 1919–1939, *ed. E. L. Woodward and Rohan Butler, 2nd series, vol. VI (London, HMSO, 1957), app. III, pp. 975–90. Memorandum from Vansittart, then permanent under secretary of state for foreign affairs.*

FOREIGN OFFICE, *April 7, 1934*

It may perhaps be asked whether the Defence Requirements Committee, in its recent report, was justified in taking Germany as the ultimate potential enemy. It is possible that such doubt may be entertained, if no opportunity has been given to see as a whole the evidence on which such a conclusion is based; and this paper is written to supply that deficiency. . . .

Sir Horace Rumbold, early 1933: 'The present German Government have to rearm on land, and, as Herr Hitler explains in his memoirs, they have to lull their adversaries into such a state of coma that they will allow themselves to be engaged one by one. . . . Since he assumed office, Hitler has been as cautious and discreet as he was formerly blunt and frank. It would be misleading to base any hopes on a serious modification of the views of the Chancellor and his entourage. Hitler has, of course, sufficient meed of cunning to realise the necessity for camouflage. . . . Protestations of peace on the lines of the Chancellor's Potsdam speech are likely. . . . I have the definite impression that a deliberate policy is now being pursued. The aim of this policy is to bring Germany to a point of preparation, a jumping-off point from which she can reach solid ground before her adversaries can interfere'. . . .

In January 1934 Sir Eric Phipps wrote: 'Nazi Germany believes neither in the League nor in negotiation. . . . Germany's foreign policy may be said to comprise the following aims: (1) Fusion with Austria; (2) rectification of the eastern frontiers; (3) some outlet for German energy to south or east; (4) the recovery of some colonial foothold overseas. . . . When Germany is rearmed and feels secure from foreign intervention, it will be possible to take in hand the programme outlined above. . . . For the moment Germany desires peace, for the reason that she is not prepared for war. . . . Later she will presumably demand the territorial revision of the "unjust" peace treaties . . . as of right, and will hope to secure these *desiderata* by peaceful means or at all events by the threat of force. If these methods fail, and the "just" claims of Germany should lead to war, the blame will be laid on her enemies. . . .'

It is, therefore . . . difficult to see how, on such evidence, the Defence Requirements Committee could have come to any conclusion other than that whereby 'we take Germany as the ultimate potential enemy against whom our "long range" defence policy must be directed'. I submit that my colleagues made a fair statement of a situation created wholly by Nazi Germany herself. . . .

There is probably no *immediate* danger. As the Defence Requirements Committee put it: 'We have time, though not too much time, to make defensive preparations'. Opinion must necessarily vary and depart into the realms of prophecy in estimating the length of that first period. The Germans are too competent, and matters are now moving too fast, to make a long estimate a safe one. . . .

To many, including myself, it may indeed seem not unnatural that Germany should wish to recover part at least of what she had, and I have in the past made no secret of my view that a 'long-range' policy must aim at the reconciliation of revisionist ideas with anti-revisionist fears and obstinacy.

9. François Piétri criticises the French Note of 17 April 1934

From Piétri Papers. Typescript memorandum: 'Observations présentées par M. Piétri [minister for the navy] à la séance du conseil des ministres du 17 Avril 1934'.

I can only give my support to M. BARTHOU's [French foreign minister] note since he considers that it is the only acceptable position for France, nationally and internationally. But I give it unwillingly.

I do recognise that it is the most defensible position from a parliamentary point of view but regret strongly, with M. Flandin, that however good the motive (or the pretext) invoked in support of our negative reply, to wit the publication of the German budget . . . the initiative of closing the door comes from us. I would have preferred that this initiative should have come from England, confronted with German intransigence . . . she can henceforth claim that it is our intransigence which has ended negotiations.

And, in this respect, if we had asked for the inclusion of the naval problem in the debate, England would necessarily have become the defendant. . . .

I wish simply to point out that we must henceforth have the defence policy required by our diplomacy, and that the Government must expect the Ministers of National Defence . . . to present new demands. . . .

I will not say of the Navy what the Marshal [Pétain, minister of war] has said, perhaps a little harshly of the Army, namely that it is only 'a façade'. The Navy is strong, it is prepared. . . .

But it has two serious weaknesses: the lack of an effective fleet air arm and the lack until 1937 of really modern ships.

It is necessary, at all cost, that I should be given the means to meet this double deficiency, which will create in 1935 or 1936 – at a time when the Germans will have two 'DEUTSCHLAND' afloat – a very lean period. . . .

M. Tardieu [minister of state in the Doumergue Cabinet, February 1934] exaggerates when he says: 'What has happened to all the money spent ?'. Not so much money as all that has been spent. . . . Defence Budgets are hardly larger, in real terms, than in 1914, and that of the Navy is below. . . .

For several years France has spent her time feeling apprehensive, whilst she possessed a formidable war machine in face of a weak Germany.

Today at the precise moment when Germany rearms . . . France diminishes her military potential and practises massive economies. . . .

We are initiating today a policy of force. Let us know how to follow it logically and let us not be surprised that it must cost us dearly and be quickly pursued.

10. Sir Warren Fisher argues for *rapprochement* with Japan, 19 April 1934

From Documents on British Foreign Policy, 1919–1939, *ed. W. N. Medlicott and Douglas Dakin, 2nd series, vol. XIII (London, HMSO, 1973), app. I, pp. 924–30. Sir Warren Fisher was permanent under secretary for the Treasury.*

TREASURY CHAMBERS, *April 19, 1934*

The 1935 Naval Conference

. . . The Naval Staff and the Treasury are in complete agreement on the fundamental point of ensuring to the utmost limit possible the safety of our Country and Empire. But one of the principal ingredients in successful insurance is a wise disposition of our resources. The Naval Staff most pertinently observe that if 'a two-Power standard' is beyond our capacity 'we cannot simultaneously fight Japan and the strongest European naval Power'. . . . It will be common ground to the Admiralty and the Treasury that the British Empire, whether in Asia or elsewhere, would become defenceless if England herself were knocked out. It will probably be agreed that even at the extreme limit of her endeavour Japan by herself could not knock out England or deprive her of the essentials in food-stuffs and raw materials. . . .

While this is no argument for ignoring all reasonable measures to bring home to the Japanese that we are not a negligible factor, it is certainly not a reason for basing our war preparations on an encounter with Japan. For the risk which really could involve us in disaster is much nearer home; and it is highly dangerous to limit our estimate of a future German menace merely to the consideration of our present relative position vis à vis Germany in naval strength. . . .

Given the consistency of the attitude of these Teutonic tribes, who century after century have been inspired by the philosophy of brute force, we should be more than usually stupid if we assumed that the sweet reasonableness of the Treaty of Versailles had converted them to the tenets of the Sermon on the Mount; and if we want to survive we had better think most carefully how so to economise our resources as to meet the danger at its maximum point . . . we have everything to gain and nothing to lose by coming, as I believe we most easily could, to an accommodation with Japan, in substance though not in form, similar to our agreement of thirty years ago. . . . It is common ground that we cannot successfully fight both Japan and Germany at the same time. The first essential therefore to our own safety is that we must be free to concentrate our strength where it is most needed. . . . . What, then, is the prime condition for attaining this essential object of definitely relieving ourselves of any danger of being involved in a war with Japan? I suggest that the first, and, indeed, cardinal requirement for this end is the disentanglement of ourselves from the United States of America. . . . To secure our national and imperial safety my advice therefore is (1) that we should regain our freedom to make such preparations and dispositions in regard to our Fleet as are necessitated by our own needs; (2) that we should effect a thorough and lasting accommodation with the Japanese . . . ; (3) that we should make it evident so that the Germans can be under no illusion – that we intend to have available for immediate concentration our maximum force in the event of their engineering any future cataclysm in Europe.

N. F. W. F.

11. State Secretary Bülow on Germany's international position, August 1934

From Documents on German Foreign Policy, 1918–1945, *series C, vol. III*, (*London, HMSO, 1959*), *no. 162.*

In judging the situation we should never overlook the fact that no kind of rearmament in the next few years could give us military security. Even apart from our isolation, we shall for a long time yet be hopelessly inferior to France in the military sphere. A particularly dangerous period will be 1934–35 on account of the reorganization of the Reichswehr. Our only security lies in a skilful foreign policy and in avoiding all provocation.

In so doing we must, of course, not only prevent the taking of military measures against Germany such as are being quite openly discussed in military circles abroad. . . . In view of our isolation and our present weakness, economically and as regards foreign currency, our opponents need not even expose themselves to the hazards, the odium and the dangers of military measures. Without mobilizing a single man or firing a single shot, they can place us in the most difficult situation by setting up a financial and economic blockade against us, either covert or overt. In a few of the most important countries 'mobilization measures' for this purpose, within the framework of the economic sanctions in Article 16, have been in readiness for years. Nevertheless, in my view, we need not at the moment fear a preventive war. For France, Britain and others will first wait to see whether, and how, we shall deal with our economic and other difficulties. Their present restraint, however, must not make us think that they would still remain passive if they had nothing more to expect from German domestic difficulties and if we rearmed intensively.

France and Britain also would then intervene, the more so as they could not permit an unlimited unilateral German rearmament. It would be wishful thinking to expect them to wait until we are strong enough to be a serious danger to them. They would probably demand guarantees regarding the extent and purpose of our armaments even before we had recovered economically.

12. Mussolini on Abyssinia, 10 August 1934

From G. Rochat, Militari e politici nella preparazione della Campagna d'Etiopia: Studio e documenti, 1932–1936 *(Milan, 1971), no. 21, pp. 356–7.*

Mussolini, Chief of Government to De Bono, Minister of Colonies, Baistroochi, Cavagnari and Valle, Under-Secretaries for War, for the Navy, and the Air Force, and Badoglio, Chief of the General Staff.

Rome, 10 August 1934

I confirm precisely and peremptorily my aim on the Abyssinian question, so that each action of yours and of your subordinates as well, must strictly conform to my directives.

1) Because the Disarmament Conference has now broken down, and because of conflicts in the Far East, the present situation in Europe is so uncertain that all the Italian Armed Forces must be kept in constant efficiency and on their guard to confront, in the best conditions of all, any events that might suddenly break out, as happened at the end of last July.
2) Any action which at this moment might result in a considerable decrease of military forces from the European, as well as in a reduction of our war potential as a whole, must be regarded as highly dangerous.
3) As a consequence the line to be adopted with regard to Abyssinia must be such as to create the general impression that we still continue to adhere faithfully to the Treaty of Friendship. Every means must be adopted to put an end to the rumours recurring in Italy and in the colonies which make out the aggressive nature of our aims towards Abyssinia. These rumours could require of us the heaviest sacrifices tomorrow.
4) It is the job of the Minister of Colonies to make use of all stratagems to accelerate the rhythm of the defensive preparations, which are to be set in motion in our colonies, according to the programme decided on at the interdepartmental meeting held at Palazzo Venezia, following upon the

decisions reached in the preceding meetings. Priority must be given to the following requirements. . . .

6) I repeat and most firmly maintain that in the event of an Abyssinian aggression against us the line to be followed is:

> To resist behind our defensive positions, and only after having inflicted a decisive defeat on the enemy, to pass over to the counter-offensive in whichever direction and towards whatever objectives that the situation at the time will require.

13. Sir John Simon on German rearmament, 29 November 1934

From Documents on British Foreign Policy, 1919–1939, *ed. W. N. Medlicott and Douglas Dakin, 2nd series, vol. XII (London, HMSO, 1972), no. 235. Sir John Simon was foreign secretary.*

FOREIGN OFFICE, *November 29, 1934*

Now that the House of Commons' debate of Wednesday, November 28th is successfully over, we are left face to face with a fundamental question of policy which will compel us both to act, and to announce our action, very shortly in accordance with the way in which the question is decided. It is therefore very necessary to face the question and decide it in our own minds without delay. Temporising methods will not help us at all, and indeed, a failure to come to grips with the problem now will very quickly lose for the Government the improved position resulting from Wednesday's debate, and will, in the end, fasten upon us a well-founded charge that the direction of our foreign policy in this respect is not clear and definite. . . .

2. The question is that which I formulated in Cabinet some weeks ago, viz.: –

(a) Are we prepared to contemplate the legalisation of German armaments ? and

(b) If we are not prepared to do so, what is our line going to be when Germany either demands their legalisation or announces that she has armed in violation of the Treaty of Versailles, and intends to continue to disregard the Treaty ?

To this might be added –

(c) If we are prepared to legalise German re-armament, what are we to say to the French and when and how are we to say it ? . . .

I tentatively advance the following propositions: –

(i) Apart from the enormous difficulty raised by its effect on Anglo–French relations, the best course would be to recognise that Germany's re-armament in breach of the Treaty is a fact which cannot be altered and to reach the conclusion that this had better be recognised without delay in the hope that we can still get, in return for legalisation, some valuable terms from Germany. Germany would prefer, it appears, to be 'made an honest woman'; but if she is left too long to indulge in illegitimate practices and to find by experience that she does not suffer for it, this laudable ambition may wear off.

(ii) The main condition would be that Germany would return to Geneva both for the Disarmament Conference and for League purposes. I do not think it would be possible to get Germany to return on the basis that she was still bound by Part V of the Treaty of Versailles, but that release would come as soon as a new agreement was negotiated. Germany is certain, I consider, to require the release to take place concurrently with her return. Equality of rights will then be an established and admitted fact. It may be possible for us in the course of negotiations for bringing this about to get certain understandings with Germany, *e.g.*, the limit she will accept for her navy, but broadly speaking she will want to be free first and to negotiate afterwards.

(iii) To all this the French will reply 'security'. (They will also protest that wrongdoers and blackmailers should not be given the fruit of their wrongdoing, but all this must be rejected on the two grounds that British opinion will not stand for it and that the practical results of continuing to take this line are disastrous.) As to security, is it possible to get Germany to look more favourably on the Eastern Pact? I doubt it, for Chancellor Hitler likes bilateral agreements on the model of the German–Polish Pact, but he suspects multilateral pacts. We might perhaps do what we could in discussion with Germany to get her to make this contribution as a way of reaching equality of rights, but if it fails, it looks as though the Franco–Russian agreement (which Herr Hitler asserts and Sir Eric Phipps denies), may be the form of security which France will be left with.

(iv) The grouping of other European Powers, if the above line were pursued with the French, is not difficult to imagine. It must, I think, be admitted that there would be a tendency to increase the division into different camps, and the difficulties and obstacles accumulate as one reflects. But what is the alternative? I cannot think that British public opinion will remain satisfied with the futility of ignoring the facts that German armaments are in breach of the Treaty. Once that it is avowed that they are and admitted on all hands that this cannot be prevented, there will be an increasing demand to get rid of the lumber while it may still fetch a price. And the retribution if we do not adopt a definite policy in regard to this, whatever that policy should be, will be severe.

J. S.

14. Mussolini on Abyssinia, 30 December 1934

From G. Rochat, Militari e politici nella preparazione della Campagna d'Etiopia: Studio e documenti, 1932–1936 (*Milan, 1971*), *no. 29, pp. 376–9.*

Memorandum by Mussolini for Marshal Badoglio, Chief of the General Staff. Directive and Plan of Action to solve the Abyssinian question.

Rome, 30 December 1934

1. The problem of Italian–Abyssinian relations has very recently shifted from a diplomatic plane to one which can be solved by force only: like all 'historical' problems of this kind it admits of one solution: a resort to arms.
2. The development of the Abyssinian situation poses these incontrovertible facts. The tendency of the Negus has aimed at centralising the Imperial authority and reducing to a nominal level, through continuous violence, intrigue and bribery, the power of the *Rases* (Chieftains) living in the peripheral areas. A long period will be needed before Abyssinia can be described as a state in the European sense of the word; still, it is necessary to bear in mind that in modern history this process can be speeded up, in particular since the missions of some European countries have come to her assistance. This enables us to foresee that the trend towards centralisation and unification can be crowned with success within a reasonably short time, provided it is not interrupted by external events.
3. This 'political' development constitutes a powerful factor to increase the military potentiality and efficiency of the Abyssinian Empire.
4. Moreover, all information indicates a similar progress towards the centralisation of military power, as well as a general tendency to transform – on a European pattern – both Abyssinia's internal organisation for war and, above all, her armaments. It might not be long before such a transformation is complete, especially because it is speeded up by European instructors, provided that it is not interrupted

by external events. With regard to those arms carried by hand (machine guns, rifles, automatic weapons . . .) Abyssinia is equipped with really modern arms, the number of which is beginning to be considerable.

5. Taking into account what is said above, one logical conclusion can be drawn: *time is working against us.* The longer we delay the solution of this problem, the more difficult the task will be and the greater the sacrifices. . . .

6. I decide on this war, the object of which is nothing *more nor less than the complete destruction of the Abyssinian army and the total conquest of Abyssinia.* In no other way can we build the Empire. . . .

8. One essential condition, which is in no way prejudicial to our action, is having a peaceful Europe on our hands, certainly for the period of two years 1935–36 and for 1936–37, by the latter period the solution must be completed. An examination of the position, emerging at the beginning of 1935, leads to the conclusion that in the next two years war will be averted in Europe. . . . Elements making for stability are: the agreements between Italy and France. These agreements remove the danger of a renewed German attack on Austria. On the other hand, the inevitable result of the Italian–French agreements is an improvement of Italian–Yugoslav relations. . . . Moreover it can be said of Germany that her military machine has not even approximately reached that level of efficiency which would enable her to take the initiative in starting war. . . . Poland which had previously seemed to be a pawn in Germany's game, is now making a noticeable move in the direction of France. . . .

9. For our arms to achieve a rapid and decisive victory, we must deploy on a vast scale the mechanised forces, which are now at our disposal, and which the Abyssinians either do not possess at all or do so only in an insufficient degree, but which they will possess within a few years. . . .

10. . . . The speedier our action the less likely will be the danger of diplomatic complications. In the Japanese fashion there will be no need whatever officially for a declaration of war and in any case we must always emphasize the purely defensive character of operations. *No one in Europe would raise any difficulties provided the prosecution of operations resulted rapidly in an accomplished fact. If would suffice to declare to England and France that their interests would be recognised.* . . .

12. Since our preparations will be partly or fully completed only in the autumn of 1935 it must be a matter of policy to prevent all incidents which might anticipate the conflict. . . .

15. Anglo–German conversations, Berlin, 25–6 March 1935

From Documents on British Foreign Policy, 1919–1939, *ed. W. N. Medlicott and Douglas Dakin, 2nd series, vol. XII (London, HMSO, 1972), no. 651.*

Sir John Simon [British foreign secretary] said that he wished to present to the Chancellor on behalf of His Majesty's Government the view which His Majesty's Government and the British people took of the present situation, and to describe the anxiety that occupied their minds. The object of British policy was to preserve general peace by helping to secure co-operation amongst all European countries. His Majesty's Government most earnestly wished that Germany should work with all countries for that object. They felt that the future of Europe would take one of two forms. It would either take the form of general co-operation for securing continued peace – and this was the form which His Majesty's Government earnestly desired. Or it would take the form of a division into two camps – isolation on the one side, and combination (which might look like encirclement) on the other. The message which he had to deliver on behalf of His Majesty's Government was that they were convinced that the future would develop in one of these two ways.

Herr Hitler then produced a diagram on which the colonial possessions of the various Powers were illustrated, together with the corresponding size of their territories in Europe. Herr Hitler said that this diagram would give the British Ministers a clear idea of what he meant. It was a position of inequality and inferiority under which Germany, with a population of 68 millions and 460,000 square kilometres of territory – with 137 inhabitants to each square kilometre – had no colonies.

This question of Germany's equality could not be solved by some solution which might be regretted on the following day by the Powers who were parties to the settlement. It could only be solved by absolute satisfaction on every side. No temporary solution was possible; the solution must take account of all the aspects of the question to which Herr Hitler had referred.

If a satisfactory solution of this question was found, then Britain would have engaged Germany; and Germany would blindly and loyally fulfil her undertakings.

Herr Hitler was not asking the impossible, because he knew that certain things were impossible now. But he was asking the absolute minimum; and if they looked into the distant future, the British Government might ask themselves whether British interests would be served by allowing

Germany to become a pariah when she might have allowed Germany to take part with her.

The moment would come when the European nations must stand together. For the time being they were engaged in preventing their own controversies from exploding. But the moment might come when the European nations must stand together, in particular, when Germany and Britain must stand together.

In times of peace there had never been hatred against Britain in Germany; and in the National Socialist movement there was no anti-British feeling.

The German Government wanted agreement with Britain and also with France, but in the case of the latter it was very difficult to dissipate certain misunderstandings; and an understanding with Britain would be a valuable asset.

Herr Hitler's proposal was a very bold one, but as Germany knew that she could never defend alone her colonial possessions, so it might be that even the British Empire might one day be glad to have Germany's help and Germany's forces at her disposal. If they could find such a solution and give satisfaction to Germany's most urgent and primitive demands, they would lead Germany back to co-operation and friendly relations with Great Britain.

He had outlined a bold idea, but he had wished to put it forward.

SIR JOHN SIMON said that there had been frank speech on both sides; and he must now make two observations.

First, Herr Hitler had been sketching out a thought in his mind which would seem to involve on the part of Britain some willingness to separate herself from general co-operation in Europe and which might almost seem an invitation to Britain to regard France as less associated with her than Germany. The British Government wished to have the closest association with Germany, but they wanted that without prejudice to their relations with France. They did not wish to substitute one friend for another, because they wanted to be loyal friends to all. He must say that at once. Otherwise he would not be acting faithfully to those who were not present that day.

Britain had no special engagements. She was free and wished to remain free and to give friendship to all. But she was not open to the solicitation that she would not be faithful to her old relationships when seeking to improve relationships elsewhere.

Secondly, as to the question of colonies, he took note of and would report what had been said, but he must point out that as regards mandated territories they were not at the sole disposal of Britain. Other Powers were concerned. It was right to point that out.

Then as regards that large area which had represented British colonial territory on Herr Hitler's diagram, Herr Hitler must remember that that area included not only colonies comparable with the colonial possessions of other Powers, but the great Dominions of Canada, of the Union of South Africa, of the Commonwealth of Australia, and of New Zealand.

There had no doubt been a time when those great Dominions had been dependent on Britain; but that had long since passed, and to-day they were in no sense whatever in a relationship to Britain comparable in any way to the colonies of other Powers. The matter was very important. He did not wish to leave the Chancellor under any misapprehension that he held out any hope whatever that the British Government could do anything about the colonial question. He took note of what had been said and he would report. But he did not wish to leave the Chancellor under any mistaken impression. It was best to be frank.

16. The British Cabinet considers its policy for the Stresa Conference, 8 April 1935

From Cabinet Papers (Public Record Office, London), CAB 23/81.

The Cabinet held a special Meeting to consider the policy to be adopted at, and the arrangements to be made for, the Stresa Conference. . . .
. . . A suggestion was very generally supported that, if asked by France and Italy to put an end to conversations with Germany and to do nothing more than indicate our intention to stand firm with France and Italy, we should not agree to it. . . . Our line, therefore, it was suggested, should be that we could not agree to make a complete breach with Germany, and to take no action except to threaten her. . . . At the same time it was suggested that we ought to reaffirm our commitments under Locarno with all possible emphasis, and express emphatically our intention to carry out the Treaty without entering into more specific undertakings for implementing the Treaty. . . . It was pointed out that if France or Italy asked us to join them in a statement that we would not stand a breach of the peace anywhere, that meant in effect an undertaking that we would be prepared to take forcible action anywhere. Germany was in a volcanic mood and not inclined to yield to threats. We ought not to agree to such a proposition unless we were prepared to take action anywhere, e.g., in the event of trouble in Memel. There was general agreement that we ought not to accept further commitments. . . .

17. Vansittart's views on Abyssinia, 8 June 1935

From Documents on British Foreign Policy, 1919–1939, *ed. W. N. Medlicott and Douglas Dakin, 2nd series, vol. XIV (London, HMSO, 1976), no. 301. Minute from Sir Robert Vansittart, permanent under secretary of state for foreign affairs, to Sir Samuel Hoare, foreign secretary, and Mr Eden, minister for League of Nations affairs.*

FOREIGN OFFICE, *June 8, 1935*

. . . The position is as plain as a pikestaff. Italy will have to be bought off – let us use and face ugly words – in some form or other, or Abyssinia will eventually perish. That might in itself matter less, if it did not mean that the League would also perish (and that Italy would simultaneously perform *another* volte-face into the arms of Germany, a combination of haute politique and haute cocotterie that we can ill afford just now).

I agree that we cannot trade Abyssinia. The price that would now satisfy Italy would be too high for Abyssinia even to contemplate.

If we are all clear and in unison about that, it follows clearly that either there has got to be a disastrous explosion – that will wreck the League and very possibly His Majesty's Government too, if the League is destroyed on the eve of an election – or else that we have got to pay the price . . . with British Somaliland, though payment would clearly have to be deferred, even if promised.

Personally I opt unhesitatingly for the latter. I have long thought the distribution of this limited globe quite untenable, and quite unjustifiable. Like fools we made it far worse at Versailles. What *has* happened in regard to Japan; what is happening in regard to Italy, and what is about to happen in regard to Germany, should surely confirm this view to anyone with political antennae. We are grossly over-landed (and British Somaliland is a real debit). Indeed, looking a little further ahead – say a couple of generations at most – who can for a moment imagine that Canada and Australia will really be allowed to continue their present policies of shut doors and shut eyes?

I should like to see the question of Somaliland considered at least, while we can still get something for less than nothing. If this cock won't fight, let some one else produce another that will. But whence? Failing these, we may prepare for a horrid autumn – and beyond.

18. Sir Eric Phipps on Hitler, 12 June 1935

From Documents on British Foreign Policy, 1919–1939, *ed. W. N. Medlicott and Douglas Dakin, 2nd series, vol. XIII (London, HMSO, 1973), no. 327. Sir Eric Phipps was British ambassador in Berlin, 1933–7.*

. . .

6. I have just sent over to your Department a list of instances when Herr Hitler broke faith in the past. The list is by no means exhaustive, but I trust that I shall not be required to expand it and that, even as it stands, it may not weigh too heavily in any final decision. By rummaging Herr Hitler's actions or writings in a past of greater freedom and less responsibility, we can doubtless find events and tendencies alike disquieting. To conclude therefrom that no faith can be attached to his signature in the future would condemn us to a policy of sterility.

7. His Majesty's Government may decide that it is now undesirable to conclude any convention with this country; they may prefer to maintain their liberty of action. If, however, they feel that advantage should be taken of the presence of M. Laval at the head of the French Government and of his notorious desire to come to some reasonable understanding with Germany, I earnestly hope that they will not allow themselves to be deterred by the mere contemplation of Herr Hitler's past misdeeds or breaches of faith. After all, he now leads nearly 70 millions of industrious, efficient and courageous, not to say pugnacious, people. He is, like most men, an amalgam, and he may, like many men have evolved since the old, somewhat gangsterlike days at Munich. His signature, once given, will bind his people as no other could. It need not bind Great Britain to any state of undue weakness: it need not blind her to the undoubted dangers lying ahead. And if the worst befall, and Hitler decide to break his freely-given, solemn pledge, surely our battle-ground would be all the firmer for having put him to the test?

I have, &c.,
ERIC PHIPPS

19. The Peace Ballot, July 1935

From Dame Adelaide Livingstone, The Peace Ballot: The Official History (*London, Gollancz, 1935*), *pp. 49–51*.

The Peace Ballot, 1935

Question 1   *Should Great Britain remain a member of the League of Nations?*

Total *Yes* answers:	10,642,560
Total *No* Answers:	337,964
Percentage of *Yes* answers in relation to total *Yes* and *No* answers:	97·0
Percentage of *Yes* answers in relation to total *Yes*, *No* and *Doubtful* answers and *Abstentions*:	96·0

In many districts, both large and small, the percentage of *Yes* answers in relation to the total *Yes* and *No* answers was even higher, amounting in some cases to 100%, as the following figures illustrate:

	YES	No	YES Percentage
Porthleven (Cornwall)	892	0	100
Melbost and Branahuie (Hebrides)	107	0	100
Ceres (Fife)	243	1	99·6
Shetland Islands	10,478	48	99·5
Essendon (Hertfordshire)	196	1	99·5
Kirkconnel (Dumfries)	1,374	8	99·4
Forest of Dean (Gloucestershire)	12,326	102	99·2
Barnard Castle (Durham)	10,695	81	99·2
Castleford (Yorkshire)	12,738	109	99·2
Colne Valley (Yorkshire)	34,452	309	99·1
Durham (Durham)	21,560	224	99·0

Question 2   *Are you in favour of an all-round reduction of armaments by international agreement?*

Total *Yes* answers:	10,058,026
Total *No* answers:	815,365
Percentage of *Yes* answers in relation to total *Yes* and *No* answers:	92·5
Percentage of *Yes* answers in relation to total *Yes*, *No* and *Doubtful* answers and *Abstentions*:	90·7

Question 3 *Are you in favour of the all-round abolition of national military and naval aircraft by international agreement?*

Total *Yes* answers:	9,157,145
Total *No* answers:	1,614,159
Percentage of *Yes* answers in relation to total *Yes* and *No* answers:	85·0
Percentage of *Yes* answers in relation to total *Yes*, *No* and *Doubtful* answers and *Abstentions*:	82·6

Question 4 *Should the manufacture and sale of arms for private profit be prohibited by international agreement?*

Total *Yes* answers:	10,002,849
Total *No* answers:	740,354
Percentage of *Yes* answers in relation to total *Yes* and *No* answers:	93·1
Percentage of *Yes* answers in relation to total *Yes*, *No* and *Doubtful* answers and *Abstentions*:	90·2

The voting on this Question is of particular interest in view of the enquiry now in progress by the Royal Commission on the Manufacture of and Trading in Arms.

Even in those towns where a considerable number of the working population is dependent on armaments-manufacture for its living, the proportion of affirmative answers to this Question was very high. Here are the figures for some of the districts:

	YES	NO
Coventry	56,473	4,197
Sheffield	126,268	16,525
Portsmouth	36,804	4,705
Birmingham	242,418	26,429
Barrow-in-Furness	8,269	956

Question 5a *Do you consider that, if a nation insists on attacking another, the other nations should combine to compel it to stop by economic and non-military measures?*

Total *Yes* answers:	9,627,606
Total *No* answers:	607,165
Percentage of *Yes* answers in relation to total *Yes* and *No* answers:	94·1
Percentage of *Yes* answers in relation to total *Yes*, *No*, *Doubtful* and *Christian Pacifist* answers and *Abstentions*:	86·8

Question 5b   *Do you consider that, if a nation insists on attacking another, the other nations should combine to compel it to stop by, if necessary, military measures?*

Total *Yes* answers:	6,506,777
Total *No* answers:	2,262,261
Percentage of *Yes* answers in relation to total *Yes* and *No* answers:	74·2
Percentage of *Yes* answers in relation to total *Yes, No, Doubtful* and *Christian Pacifist* answers and *Abstentions*:	58·6

20. Chatfield stresses the unreadiness of the three services for war with Italy, 8 August 1935

From Documents on British Foreign Policy, 1919–1939, *ed. W. N. Medlicott and Douglas Dakin, 2nd series, vol. XIV (London, HMSO, 1976), no. 431. Letter from Admiral Sir A. Ernle Chatfield, first sea lord and chairman of the chiefs of staff committee, to Sir Robert Vansittart, permanent under secretary of state for foreign affairs.*

Secret and Personal.   ADMIRALTY, *August 8, 1935*

My dear Van,

We had an important meeting of the Chiefs of Staff this afternoon to draw up our report as to the measures to be taken at once, and other measures that require Cabinet approval, in view of the Mediterranean situation. I was surprised to find how very unready the other two Services were and how long it would take them before they could give any effective resistance to Italian action by land or air. The Naval situation is bad enough, as you are well aware, and consequently we have put an important covering letter to our Report which it is most necessary that the Secretary of State, Eden and yourself should see before you go to Paris. We also think that the Prime Minister should receive a copy, if possible. Cabinet secretaries will arrange this I think.

Apart from our proposals as to steps to be taken the sense of our feeling is that everything possible should be done to avoid precipitated hostilities with Italy until we are more ready. It would be a serious business if the great League of Nations, having at last agreed to act together, was able to be flouted militarily by the nation whom it was trying to coerce. The Navy will, of course, do its best provided you give us time and enough warning, but it would be a dangerous prospect for us to go to war with Italy with the British Fleet unmobilised and the Home Fleet on leave and scattered.

It would indeed be the greatest foolishness if anything of the sort happened. Further, we are exceedingly anxious lest you should obtain the moral support of France without a definite assurance of her military support also *and some knowledge of what that military support would be*, which indeed ought to be concerted beforehand in London or Paris. War is not a light measure which we can go into blindfold trusting to luck.

I only want to be sure that the Foreign Office are fully apprised of the military situation and they do all they can to delay the danger of hostilities, meanwhile authorising us to prepare. When the meeting at Geneva takes place and if all this is going to happen it would be equally important to obtain the military support of all the Mediterranean Powers as we shall want to use their harbours and to have the assistance of their naval forces. Further, it must not be forgotten that the United States and Germany can completely frustrate Article 16 of the Covenant if they are not approached beforehand and their benevolent neutrality obtained.

I am sure you realise all I have written in this letter but I only do it to relieve my conscience before going off on leave and to make sure that you do see and carefully measure the Chiefs of Staff Report. Little [Deputy Chief of Naval Staff] has seen this letter.

Yours ever,
ERNLE CHATFIELD

21. Hoare explains British policy on Abyssinia, 24 August 1935

From Documents on British Foreign Policy, 1919–1939, *ed. W. N. Medlicott and Douglas Dakin, 2nd series, vol. XIV (London, HMSO, 1976), no. 493. Letter from Sir Samuel Hoare, foreign secretary, to Sir George Clerk, ambassador in France.*

Private & Personal   FOREIGN OFFICE, *August 24, 1935*

It may help you in your dealings with the French Government if I give you very confidentially the background of our present position. I have already sent you the accounts of my meetings with the various party leaders and you will have received from the Office the main conclusions of Thursday's Cabinet. To these papers I will add the following comments.

The general feeling of the country, fully reflected in the Cabinet, can, I think, be summarised as one of determination to stick to the Covenant and of anxiety to keep out of war. You will say that these feelings are self-contradictory. At present at least the country believes that they can be reconciled. Most people are still convinced that if we stick to the Covenant and apply collective sanctions, Italy must give in and there will be no war.

You and I know that the position is not as simple as this and that the presumptions that, firstly, there will be collective action including full collective action by the French, and secondly, that economic sanctions will be effective are, to say the least, very bold and sanguine. None the less, whatever may develop it is essential that we should play out the League hand in September. If it is then found that there is no collective basis for sanctions, that is to say in particular that the French are not prepared to give their full co-operation, or that the action of the non-member States, for example Germany, the United States and Japan, is so unhelpful as to make economic sanctions futile, the world will have to face the fact that sanctions are impracticable. We must, however, on no account assume the impracticability of sanctions until the League has made this investigation. It must be the League and not the British Government that declares that sanctions are impracticable and the British Government must on no account lay itself open to the charge that we have not done our utmost to make them practicable. . . .

This is the position. Would you think it over and give me your advice as to how best to deal with the French Government between now and the meeting at Geneva ? It seems to me most essential that we should not drift into Geneva, neither side fully understanding the position of the other. At the same time I am most anxious to avoid implying either too much or too little to the French, too much in suggesting that we are determined to apply sanctions however futile the investigation may prove them to be, too little by implying to them that we have come to the view that sanctions are impracticable. I am particularly anxious to continue to impress upon them the gravity of the situation and the great strength of British public opinion behind the Covenant.

22. France asks if Britain will enforce collective security in Europe, 10 September 1935

From Documents on British Foreign Policy, 1919–1939, *ed. W. N. Medlicott and Douglas Dakin, 2nd series, vol. XIV (London, HMSO, 1976), no. 547. Telegram from Sir Robert Vansittart, permanent under secretary of state for foreign affairs, to Sir Samuel Hoare, foreign secretary, then in Geneva.*

Immediate   FOREIGN OFFICE, *September 10, 1935, 6.45 pm*

Following from Sir R. Vansittart for Sir S. Hoare.

The French Ambassador came to see me this afternoon urgently. He said he had a most important question to put to His Majesty's Government on behalf of the French Government, and it was one to which the latter would be grateful for a very early reply, as the answer to it would naturally enter into their estimate of the present situation. Moreover the nature of the answer to the question might be raised soon in a very concrete form of which he would give me an illustration later.

He said that I would remember that during the last conversation which Mr. Eden and I had had with M. Laval [French Prime Minister] in Paris he had asked us a question in regard to the future attitude of this country which he had not pressed at the time and had only asked tentatively and unofficially. M. Corbin said that he had now instructions to ask that question officially and in concrete terms. The French Government in fact wanted to know up to what point and in what conditions would His Majesty's Government be prepared to apply sanctions and join in effective solidarity if the Covenant were violated by a recourse to force in Europe. M. Corbin said that this question arose directly out of a conversation he had had with the Secretary of State in which the question had emerged of the situation which would arise in this country if in the Italo–Abyssinian dispute negotiations broke down and the question of sanctions arose. M. Corbin said that the French Government had necessarily to take stock of the whole situation and in doing so must realise that the attitude of England had not hitherto, i.e. before the Italo–Abyssinian dispute, been strongly in favour of sanctions. It was essential for the French Government to know whether this attitude had changed and if so how far. Could the French Government in deciding their course in the present great difficulty, which might be pregnant with consequences for them, be sure that His Majesty's Government would be henceforth prepared to execute effectively its obligations under the Covenant if it was aggressively violated in Europe ? He said he would give me the illustration to which I have referred above. Germany, said M. Corbin, might perhaps be encouraged by Italy's example to attack Austria. Would His Majesty's Government in that case take the same attitude as regards sanctions as they were doing in the case of Abyssinia ?

23. Britain reserves her liberty of action as to how Article 16 of the Covenant should be applied, 24 September 1935

From Cabinet Papers (Public Record Office, London), CAB 23/82.

1. The Cabinet had before them the following documents:–

A Memorandum by the Secretary of State for Foreign Affairs on the French request for an assurance regarding the future British attitude

in the event of a resort to force in Europe or of an infraction of the
Covenant by another European Power (C.P.–177 (35)):
A draft Note in reply to the above French request, circulated by the
Secretary of State for Foreign Affairs (C.P.–179 (35)).

. . . As an introduction to the discussion of the French Note the Secretary
of State for Foreign Affairs gave the Cabinet a brief account of developments in the political field since their last Meeting on August 22nd, and
an appreciation of the present position in the dispute between Italy and
Abyssinia. . . .
Turning to the Question of the French Note, he recalled that M. Laval
had given notice of his intention to raise this question in his talks with the
Minister for League of Nations Affairs [Anthony Eden] in Paris some
weeks ago. Knowing that the question was to be raised, the Secretary of
State for Foreign Affairs had addressed part of his remarks in the Assembly
[League of Nations Assembly, Geneva] to this issue, and the draft now
before the Cabinet was really a re-statement, only slightly embroidered,
of what he had then said. He thought it imperative to give an answer,
and to give it soon; otherwise there would be criticisms from two direc-
tions, namely, from the French Government on the ground that we were
interested only in Abyssinia, and from Mr. Lloyd George that we were
undertaking new commitments to France. He had discussed the draft
reply with one or two of his colleagues. He asked for liberty of action as
to the time when he should give it to France: but he also asked for
authority, in connection with the answer, to put to the French Government
the question as to what France would do supposing, *per impossible*, Italy
were to make an attack on our forces or interests in the Mediterranean. . . .
Summarising, he asked the Cabinet, first, to approve the action he had
taken: second, to approve the Note, subject to a small alteration so as to
make it clear . . . that we reserved liberty of action as to how Article 16
of the Covenant should be applied. . . .
The Cabinet agreed – . . .
That on the French request for an assurance regarding the future British
attitude in the event of a resort to force in Europe or of an infraction of
the Covenant by another European Power, the draft reply contained in
C.P.–179 (35) should be approved, subject to an amendment to make it
clear that we reserved our attitude on the form in which Article 16 should
be applied. . . .

24. Edouard Herriot on French reactions to the Abyssinian crisis, 19 October 1935

From Austen Chamberlain Papers (University of Birmingham Library), AC 41/1/63. Letter of 19 October 1935 to Sir Austen Chamberlain. Herriot was leader of the radical-socialists, and a former prime minister and foreign minister.

. . . We have just witnessed in France an imbecile and almost criminal right wing action. I am ashamed of it for my country. I am proud of having deserved the worst threats. But do not worry: this artificial frenzy is only momentary. It is noisy because those who are making most noise have plenty of money, at home and abroad. But the mass of the French people, faithful to its memories, to its good sense, and loyal, rejects the provocation with horror. More than ever we must remain united. We are at a great turning point in history. . . . England and France have received a great historic mandate, that of safeguarding all that can give some value to human life, the introduction and maintenance of moral elements in politics. . . .

25. General Gamelin's notes on a meeting of the Haut Comité Militaire, 21 November 1935

From General M. G. Gamelin, Servir, vol. II: Le Prologue du drame (1930–1939) (Paris, Plon, 1946), pp. 177–81. Gamelin was chief of the French general staff.

Friday, 22 November 1935: 6 o'clock in the morning

Impossible to close my eyes. Last night I experienced one of the most painful moments of my life. After leaving the meeting of the Haut Comité Militaire, chaired by M. Laval [prime minister and foreign minister], which had begun at 5 p.m., at the foreign ministry . . . I came straight home about 8 p.m. And something happened to me which has not occurred since the death of my dear mother, I wept. . . .

I wept for the destiny of my Country, which until now has found the men it needed: not only a Joffre, a Foch, but a Poincaré and a Clemenceau. . . .

After having discussed the problems on the agenda . . . which will be considered today at the Conseil Supérieur de la Défense Nationale . . . he (*Laval*) explained to us his general policy. . . .

'I could not do otherwise than commit myself to England. I was tied by article 16 of the Pact . . . but all the same we have exchanged some very stiff notes which must never come out of the archives. I did not want my country to be treated like a Portugal. . . .

'Mussolini remains grateful to me. . . . He knows of my efforts for a conciliatory settlement. . . . But I must say that I have not encountered on the English side the same desire for conciliation, the same goodwill to accept the conditions which Italy needs. . . .

'I told the English: You will always be the same. Tomorrow you will accept the fait accompli and you will cede to the Italians much more than you could give them today. . . .

'It would be best to conclude as quickly as possible. . . . I have in effect a secret agreement with Mussolini. . . .'

But then comes the most serious news. Laval tells us of the opening of new negotiations with Germany.

'M. François-Poncet [French ambassador in Berlin] is to see Hitler today. I have also informed him (*Hitler*) of my point of view by a special emissary. . . . (How, apart from our ambassador ?)

'Hitler has shown his desire on several occasions for an entente with France. At the funeral of Marshal Pilsudski, Marshal Pétain had a long talk with Göring. . . .

'Tomorrow, doubtless, Parliament will ratify our convention with the Soviets [the Franco–Soviet pact of 2 May 1935, which was not ratified until February 1936]. I have purged it of the most dangerous elements. But none the less I distrust them. I do not want them to drag France into a war. . . .

'The French are always pleased with alliances because they anticipate help coming to them but they do not see the obligations. . . .

'So we wish to live in peace with Germany but only if she declares her acceptance of present frontiers. . . . Nothing must be done without England's knowledge. Hitler must explain *Mein Kampf* . . . there could be a common declaration of a desire for good relations and we could reopen disarmament talks with Germany. . . .'

I no longer understand.

At the same time as Parliament is to ratify the treaty with the Soviets it is cancelled by an entente with Germany ? What are Czechoslovakia, and Romania whom we are pushing to negotiate with Russia, going to say ? And Poland, where sympathy for us has shown itself since Pilsudski's death ? And Italy, if we abandon her in the Austrian question ? And what is Germany's promise not to modify her frontiers worth ? . . .

Is this policy without grandeur, of continual bargaining, worthy of France ? Can we think of going to war without allies ? And by trifling with all do we not risk finding ourselves alone ? . . .

26. Paul Reynaud supports sanctions against Italy, 31 December 1935

From Paul Reynaud Papers (Archives de France, Paris), 74AP.2. Letter of 31 December 1935 to André Tardieu. Reynaud was a leading right-wing deputy who became prime minister in 1940. Tardieu, a former prime minister, was also a right-wing deputy.

. . . In face of the growing peril, it is our only chance of peace . . . you complain about England. I do not. . . . Thus at the very moment when England commits herself to the course which for fifteen years we have asked her to follow, at the precise moment when 50 nations are assembled in Geneva to enforce collective security, at the moment when the French thesis triumphs at last, you wish to stop this effort, to break this zeal. . . .

It is precisely our hesitant attitude over several months which has created a split between world opinion and France. Our own public knows nothing of it.

I do not accept this break in the straight line which French policy has followed until now, and with which we have both been associated. This is the reproach I have against the government. . . .

You object to my speech being applauded mainly by the left. The new fact is the silence of a part of the assembly. We have known a time when the French Chamber was unanimous in acclaiming this same policy of collective security which is our chance of peace. . . .

27. Pierre Laval and Mussolini exchange letters on Abyssinia, December 1935 – January 1936

From Hubert Lagardelle, Mission à Rome (Paris, 1955), pp. 275–7.

LAVAL TO MUSSOLINI

Paris, 22 December 1935

My dear President,

The present situation obliges me to send you this letter. You will excuse its terms, but I would be failing for the first time in the duties of friendship towards you if I did not express myself with complete frankness. As you have recalled, I was fortunate in being able to complete an often interrupted negotiation which had lasted for several years, in Rome on 7 January last, and it seems to me to be useful to point out in what spirit we made our agreements. In a general declaration we affirmed our wish to develop the traditional friendship which unites our two nations and to co-operate in upholding peace in a spirit of mutual confidence.

I have not hesitated to sacrifice important economic advantages which long and costly efforts had produced for my country in East Africa. I agreed to limit these interests in Ethiopia to the zone necessary to supply the railway traffic from Djibouti to Addis Ababa. . . .

There is no need to add that the rich future prospects laid open by this agreement did not extend beyond the economic field. They could not have gone beyond this limit without coming up against the guarantees set up around the sovereign independence and territorial integrity of Ethiopia by international acts in which Italy and France had participated. . . .

During our talks, I did not omit to stress all the advantages which you could obtain from our agreements for the development of your peaceful action in Ethiopia. You have shown me your wish to make use of our agreements only for peaceful purposes. Last February, at the time when large Italian military forces were sent to Eritrea and Somaliland, I did not omit to point out to you in a friendly manner the danger of measures which appeared to exceed the requirements of the immediate defence of your two colonies. . . .

MUSSOLINI TO LAVAL

Rome, 25 December 1935

My dear President,

I appreciate the frankness with which you spoke to me, and in my reply I would not wish to have recourse to any other method or style. . . .

You told me that your concessions relating to Abyssinia were concerned only with the recognition of an economic superiority of Italy in this country and that I had undertaken to develop a peace policy. I cannot agree with your argument; I venture to remind you, if only to affirm the spirit of these agreements, that the interview we had in Rome was also determined by the necessity for a verbal understanding, since it was understood that as far as the question of 'desisting' was concerned, it would not have been possible to say everything in written records. So it was that in our conversations there was occasion to mention several times the 'free hand' which had been allowed to me in Abyssinia, except for the reservations for your rights which were expressly specified in the document. . . . Moreover, even an examination of the specific clauses of the document is sufficient to show that something which went beyond mere economic achievements in favour of Italy was under consideration.

It is furthermore obvious that none of Italy's requirements would have found satisfaction in Ethiopia if it had not been based on the guarantee of a political control.

Naturally, I do not hereby mean to say that you have given your approval to this war which ensuing circumstances made inevitable. . . .

LAVAL TO MUSSOLINI

Paris, 23 January 1936

My dear President,

I do not wish to leave the ministry without replying to your letter of 25 December last.

. . . You remind me that the expression 'free hand' came up again during our talks. You interpret these words as an extending of the scope of the agreements of 7 January.

I was able to use this colloquialism, with the freedom of tone justified by the friendly nature of a conversation at the Farnese Palace on the evening of 6 January.

I believe that it is even more useless to cavil at the meaning of these words since your letter of 25 December gave what was to me the essential evidence, that is, that I had never given my approval to the war which you subsequently believed yourself obliged to undertake. . . .

28. Mussolini abandons Austria, 7 January 1936

From Documents on German Foreign Policy, 1918–1945, *series C, vol. IV*
(London, HMSO, 1962), no. 485. Telegram from Ulrich von Hassell,
German ambassador in Italy.

Mussolini received me this afternoon, after I had let him know that I
would be in Berlin in the middle of next week. . . .

As far as Germany was concerned, he fully appreciated her neutrality,
which he described as benevolent. This being so, he thought it would
now be possible to achieve a fundamental improvement in German–Italian
relations and to dispose of the only dispute, namely, the Austrian problem.
Since we had always declared that we did not wish to infringe Austria's
independence, the simplest method would be for Berlin and Vienna
themselves to settle their relations on the basis of Austrian independence,
e.g., in the form of a treaty of friendship with a non-aggression pact,
which would in practice bring Austria into Germany's wake, so that she
could pursue no other foreign policy than one parallel with that of
Germany. If Austria, as a formally quite independent State, were thus in
practice to become a German satellite, he would have no objection. He
saw in this great advantages for Germany as well as for Italy, in that
Germany, as already stated, would acquire a reliable satellite, while at the
same time German–Italian mistrust would be eliminated and all Danubian
Pact machinations frustrated. Should this not come about, then it was to
be feared that Austria, who was beginning to doubt Italy's ability to help
her at the decisive moment, would be driven to side with Czechoslovakia
and thus with France. I replied that these remarks were of very great
interest to me; had I rightly understood him to mean that Italy would not
oppose, either directly or indirectly, a settlement of German–Austrian
relations on the basis of formal independence and close German–Austrian
co-operation in foreign policy? Mussolini expressly confirmed this. . . .

29. Report of a meeting of the Haut Comité Militaire, 18 January 1936

From Documents diplomatiques français, 1932–1939, *2nd series, 1936–9,*
vol. I (Paris, 1963), no. 83.

The War Minister pointed out that the reversal of our policy with regard
to Italy compels us to maintain on the Alps and in the Mediterranean

basin nearly a fifth of the total of our forces, whereas after the Rome Agreements it was possible for us to have them intervene in the north-east almost in their entirety. He then drew attention to the importance of the results already obtained in Germany in completing the military programme decreed by the Hitler government. The French programme of April 1935 is thus notoriously inadequate, particularly as far as armaments are concerned: an effort is imperative especially for artillery and armoured equipment. . . .

[General Gamelin] then pointed out the aims which our enemies seemed to be pursuing by creating powerful armoured units. It is to be feared that certain of our allies cannot ward off the attacks of such divisions which are intended, it would seem, for action on free or slightly built up terrain. The delay shown by the Belgians in improving the measures already taken for the defence of their territory creates in this respect a situation which is particularly favourable to an enemy attempting to outflank our fortified regions through the plains of the North (Belgium and the Netherlands). This constitutes a problem for France which deserves our attention from three angles: manpower, equipment and fortifications.

In conclusion General Gamelin again pointed out the considerable advantage which France has at present in her system of fortifications which, by making our north-eastern frontier particularly strong, compels our possible enemy to seek yet again the decision of invading Belgium, and probably even the Netherlands, using costly equipment which takes a relatively long time to prepare.

The War Minister concluded by indicating that the plan of April 1935 which covered a relatively favourable situation no longer enabled us to face a singularly aggravated state of affairs. The million men which Germany could have in arms in peacetime from 1936 was matched in France by effectives which were indeed considerable, but which unless some new measure were introduced in this connection, ran the risk of again finding themselves even more clearly inferior in numbers. As regards equipment, Germany is on the point of overtaking us outright. Our superiority therefore remains in our fortifications alone, and to this day, in the ability of our High Command, the number and training of our officers, and finally in the undeniable advance which we owe to a military organization whose function and development nothing has so far impeded. . . .

General Gamelin estimates that, if it is impossible for us to equal Germany in the fight for manpower, this does not apply to equipment. . . .

General Gamelin then showed how the military action of the Reich seemed to be able to develop against the powers of the Little *Entente*. First of all, it would no doubt be a matter of neutralizing the French army by establishing a fortified barrier similar to ours on the western frontiers (the demilitarized zone would be reoccupied as soon as possible for this purpose). Thus freed from any fear of an offensive on our part, Germany would be completely at liberty to settle the fate of the powers of the Little *Entente*, in whose favour only Russia and Poland would be able to intervene directly. The intervention of Russian forces against Germany can be achieved only by crossing Polish or Rumanian territories; it is doubtful whether either of these two powers would accept this possibility.

. . .

The Air Minister pointed out the narrow rear zone which the Russian aviation called upon to operate in Czechoslovakia would have available; the slightest German advance would risk compromising the security of the airfields. The question of providing spares or repair of equipment based in this manner outside the national territory, moreover presents problems which are often difficult to solve.

The War Minister considers that Britain and Poland remain with France the only powers around which resistance to an aggression from the Reich could be organized.

30. French military leaders discuss Germany's reoccupation of the Rhineland, 8 March 1936

From Documents diplomatiques français, 1932–1939, *2nd series, 1936–9, vol. I (Paris, 1963), no. 334.*

Present: General Gamelin, Admiral Durand-Viel, General Pujo [respectively chiefs of army, navy and air staffs], [5 other serving officers].

General Gamelin: The government has asked me, 'Are you prepared to hold them?' I replied that, if a conflict between Germany and France were limited to the land front on the Franco–German border, forces on each side would be so large that saturation point would be quickly reached. The fronts would become stabilised. Only the air forces would be able to carry out offensive action on enemy territory.

If the theatre of operations extends into Belgium, what will England do ?

Admiral Durand-Viel: According to the discussions which took place last night at the Foreign Ministry (MM. Sarraut, Flandin, Piétri, General Maurin, Déat [respectively prime minister, foreign minister and service ministers], General Gamelin, Admiral Durand-Viel, General Pujo . . .) the French government, after bringing the question before the Council of the League in accordance with Article 4 of the Locarno Treaty, will ask that the League should send a Commission of Enquiry to the Rhineland. Germany would be declared an aggressor. So that it can examine what our attitude will be then, the government has asked the military, 'Are you prepared to drive the Germans out of the zone ?'

General Gamelin: By the fact of our entry into the zone, war would be unleashed. Such action would thus require general mobilisation. Before the Franco-Soviet pact was ratified General Gamelin gave his written opinion on the probable consequences of this ratification (German occupation of the demilitarised zone). He had a conversation on this subject with M. Léger [secretary general of the foreign ministry] and M. Sarraut, and told them, 'If we oppose this occupation by force, it means war.' M. Léger replied that everything had been done to eliminate from this treaty all that might be dangerous, that the debate on ratification had been delayed as long as possible, but that it was now no longer possible to delay it further.

General Gamelin thinks that we can only enter the Rhineland zone . . . at the same time as the guarantor powers of Locarno (England, Italy). . . . British and Italian contingents must be with us and the Belgians. . . .[1]

Admiral Durand-Viel: At the moment England could give us nothing but moral support. Before anything more the Ethiopian affair would need to be liquidated. It is impossible to see how to envisage common action with two powers (England, Italy) which are themselves in a state of reciprocal hostility. When this hostility is ended, at least a fortnight will be needed before English naval forces are ready to act in the North Sea and the Channel. At present the British Isles are deprived of any naval protection.

General Pujo: At present there are 150 fighter aircraft in England, and 150 modern bombers. The 150 fighters would probably be assigned to the defence of London. But England might still send us a few of them, and some of the 150 bombers.

The Belgians have 18 squadrons: 6 of fighter, 6 of bombers, 6 for reconnaissance. The Italians have completely reorganised their home air force. They have at present about 900 aircraft in Italy, mostly of recent construction. They might send us 100 bombers. Employment of the air force of the U.S.S.R. would involve sending munitions and spares into Czechoslovakia. It is said that airfields with underground shelters have been prepared for Russian aircraft in Czechoslovakia.

General Gamelin wonders whether the Germans would not compromise if faced by a very firm attitude. He has asked that a General should go to Geneva, where important technical problems are to be discussed. In particular it would be most important that English and Italian troops should immediately be sent to France, and that our own troops should be able to enter Belgium. . . .

---

[1] Original document defective.

31. An American assessment of European affairs, 9 March 1936

From Foreign Relations of the United States: Diplomatic Papers 1936, vol. I (*Washington, 1953*), *pp. 219–27. Memorandum from the minister in Austria to the secretary of state.*

VIENNA, March 9, 1936.

Perhaps the most important single basic factor disturbing Europe today is that facts are not being generally faced and given the interpretation which common sense dictates and met with the action which elementary prudence obviously requires. This applies whether the facts be political, economic or fiscal.

The greatest danger and the one which threatens to destroy Europe is not facing the facts with respect to Germany and Italy, particularly with respect to Germany, in which the situation is essentially more dangerous, because of its nature and the potential power of the forces behind it.

The facts with respect to Germany are known but they have not been consistently faced. In some countries there has been an effort through press control, entire or partial, to keep the facts from the people, and Europe is now hampered in facing facts through an unprepared public opinion. Even in some of the best informed foreign offices and in some well informed financial and industrial circles there is a tendency to hold to illusions and to hopes which the facts and any common sense interpretation show are without foundation. The fundamental fact which Europe has to face today is that the National Socialist regime in Germany is based on a program of ruthless force, which program has for its aim, first, the enslavement of the German population to a National Socialist social and political program, and then to use the force of these 67 million people for the extension of German political and economic sovereignty over South-Eastern Europe – thus putting it into a position to dominate Europe completely and to place France and England definitely in the position of secondary powers. From this position of vantage the National Socialist program contemplates that Germany will be able to dictate its policies to the rest of the world. Fantastic as this program may seem, it has been and is the program of National Socialist Germany, and the action of Europe in not facing the facts and meeting them with the necessary decision has so far facilitated the various steps in the German program, which has up to now proceeded according to plan. . . .

Certain factors within Germany are making her weaker, but these continued successes give new life to the party, which feverishly hopes that by these successful steps it may be able to sufficiently lengthen its life until it is able to itself strike the decisive blow. A determined stand by the powers now is almost certain not to lead to war, and it is the only thing which will bring to an end the series of *faits accomplis* which the German program provides for.

It is up to Europe now to decide whether it will face the facts, and there is still time. It is perhaps too much to say that this will be the last chance which Europe has to save itself from the ultimate catastrophe of a great war but there are many indications that this is the turning point on which the future course towards war or peace will be determined

G. S. Messersmith.

32. André François-Poncet on the Franco–Soviet Pact, 25 March 1936

From Documents diplomatiques français, 1932–1939, *2nd series, 1936–9, vol. I (Paris, 1963), no. 503. François-Poncet was French ambassador in Germany, 1931–8.*

Nobody recalls . . . that the agreement of 2 May is only the residue of a more far-reaching operation, of which Germany had been informed and which it had repeatedly been invited to join. Even before the project for an Eastern pact had been made public, M. Louis Barthou [French foreign minister, 1934] had taken care to communicate its terms to the government of the Reich.

On his instructions, I had paid a visit to Herr von Bülow on 7 June 1934. I had urged the Secretary of State not to adopt a negative attitude prematurely, with respect to the proposals which had been made to his country. I entreated him to examine favourably a combination which was in no way directed against the Reich but on the contrary offered Germany pledges of security and provided it with the means of emerging from its isolation. I had set out before my interlocutor the advantage of a multi-lateral agreement which was inspired solely by the concern to organize the peace of Europe rationally and methodically.

I had not omitted to add that if Germany met our suggestions with a categorical refusal, it would perhaps succeed in destroying the work to which we had applied ourselves; but that it must expect that we would then achieve a bilateral *entente* with Moscow, after a private meeting about which the government of the Reich would not be in a position to complain, since it would have caused it and made it inevitable.

On 12 July 1934 the British Ambassador had approached Baron von Neurath [German foreign minister] in a similar manner.

During the months that followed we did not let slip any opportunity of reminding Germany that the Eastern pact was still accessible to it and that we hoped to see it departing from its dilatory attitude. We insisted to this effect shortly after the London Conference in February 1935. We renewed our entreaties and Germany even seemed for a moment ready to yield, at the time of the Stresa Conference. Later, while our meetings with the Russians were developing, we again endeavoured to point out to Hitler's government that the contemplated pact was, in a way, of a provisional nature and would change its character when the Reich agreed to join, and that in this case a much wider and more effective system of security could emerge from a limited arrangement.

33. General Badoglio warns Gamelin of the consequences of sanctions, 10 June 1936

From Archives of the Ministry of Foreign Affairs, Paris. Letter of 10 June 1936 from Badoglio, Italian chief of staff, to Gamelin, chief of the French general staff.

Rome, 10 June 1936

... It was not without surprise that after the reconciliation of January 1935 the Italian people saw France among the sanctionist countries – that is to say among the countries which sought to asphyxiate us. . . . In spite of that our relations with France have remained correct and cordial and we on our side have pointed out that the military accords [Gamelin–Badoglio convention of 27 June 1935] were still effective.

Now the war is over but sanctions continue and it is said that our effort will not be recognised, which is – after all – an effort of peace and of civilisation. . . .

Since October the French government has not made a single friendly gesture towards us. So, after having consulted the head of my government, I have the duty to tell you that if France maintains her sanctionist attitude ... our accords have no justification and Italy will consider them forfeit....

34. The Quai d'Orsay takes stock of France's alliances, 30 June 1936

From Documents diplomatiques français, 1932–1939, 2nd series, 1936–9, vol. II (Paris, 1964), no. 372.

Putting aside the Rhineland pact denounced by Germany, the treaties concluded by France in view of the consolidation of peace and the safeguard of her own security, are as follows:

A number of treaties concluded with Poland in 1921, with Czechoslovakia in 1924, with Rumania in 1926 and with Yugoslavia in 1927, described in current language as treaties of alliance, but in fact consisting only of an undertaking to act together within the framework of the League of Nations with a view to safeguarding common interests. They are consequently of limited scope with regard to the assistance to be given, but on the other hand, of unlimited scope with regard to the countries which could threaten the aforesaid interests. However, although they have these two features in common, these four treaties are not identical in form, and the intention with which some of them were concluded could make their operation very difficult. Hence, from the beginning, the Polish treaty has been considered as applying to a Russian threat at least as much as to a German threat.

Two other treaties were concluded by France with Poland and with Czechoslovakia in Locarno, which were unlimited as far as the assistance to be given was concerned, but limited on the other hand as to the countries against which assistance would be due. These commitments were undertaken without appearing to be directed against a third-party country, for it was a matter not of an alliance but of a guarantee given for carrying out the commitment, which occurred the same day, and by the consent of all, between France and Germany, Germany and Poland and Germany and Czechoslovakia not to have recourse to arms and to settle by peaceful means all differences which could arise between two countries.

Finally, France has concluded a treaty of assistance with the USSR whose functions have been even more precisely stipulated than the preceding ones, with the exception, it is true, of the functions of the Rhineland pact and Locarno. This is a treaty which in principle was not a bilateral treaty, nor is it a treaty guaranteeing undertakings made by a third party. It is a treaty which remains open to Germany in particular, without the latter having entered into it.

There is a disparity among these various treaties – one has only to read the texts to be convinced of this – which makes their application very difficult and which, from now onwards, would be enough to put us in an embarrassing situation if one of our 'allies' took it into its head to benefit from an agreement which was as strict as any other made by friendly countries.

Politically, our system of alliances is even less coherent. Among the five countries of which each has a treaty known as an 'alliance' with France, there are few who regard themselves as allies of one another. There is no need to dwell on the relations between the USSR and Poland, between Poland and Czechoslovakia, on the mutual distrust of Poland and Rumania, born of Polish–Russian hostility, and which makes the Polish–Rumanian alliance a figment of the imagination, the absence of an undertaking of assistance between the three states of the Little *Entente*, except against

Hungary, the situation of Yugoslavia, who is hypnotized by fear of Italy and continues to ignore the Soviet Union, without mentioning less apparent but persistent rivalries and differences.

These facts lead one to think that – if there were no other motive for ruling out a 'policy of alliances' – such a policy is not practicable, for it assumes first of all that the participants are, in fact, all allied among themselves. The result of the present situation is not only weakness. It also results in the concentration on France of any attempt made against peace, France being – and how inadequately – the only link between countries which would be inclined to oppose such an attempt.

35. The American ambassador in France on the reasons why the Blum government refuses to supply arms to the Spanish Republic, 27 July 1936

From Foreign Relations of the United States: Diplomatic Papers 1936, *vol. II (Washington, 1954), pp. 447–8.*

PARIS, July 27, 1936 – 8 p.m.
[Received July 27 – 3:30 p.m.]

668. Following upon a series of revelations and bitter criticism in the French Right press during the last week, the intricate matter of alleged attempted supply by the Blum government of arms and munitions to the Madrid Government was brought to a focus over the weekend.

While no mention is made of it in the laconic communiqué issued after a Cabinet Council hastily summoned on July 25th, an inspired press statement made it known that the Blum government had unanimously decided against supplying arms to the Madrid Government and against intervention in the domestic affairs of another nation.

The reasons which led to the decision were communicated to the Embassy by a reliable press contact who obtained his information from a member of the French Supreme War Council. According to his informant certain members of the Blum Cabinet particularly Cot, Air Minister, decided on July 21 to accede to a request from Spain and to send arms and ammunition urgently required by the Madrid Government. To this decision it is understood that Blum gave his tacit approval.

On July 22 Corbin, French Ambassador in London, telephoned Blum personally and called to his attention that the British Government was extremely worried about this contingency. Corbin urged Blum to come over and discuss the situation with Baldwin [British prime minister] and Eden [foreign secretary] as soon as possible. Thus Corbin's request was the chief reason for Blum's sudden decision to proceed to London and not as is generally believed to join in the tripartite conversations which were then taking place.

In London Eden drew Blum's attention to the grave international consequences which might result from French active support of the Madrid Government. The fears of the British Government were strengthened by a report from the French Military Intelligence which indicated a certain movement of German troops on the French eastern border. Eden furthermore made it quite clear that he considered that any assistance lent by the French Government to the Spanish Government might conceivably develop a most critical international situation in view of the Italian and German attitude in the matter.

Blum returned to Paris on the 25th and immediately called the Cabinet Council meeting mentioned above in the course of which the British point of view was brought forcibly to the attention of his extremist colleagues particularly Cot. After a lengthy debate the more moderate elements Blum, Daladier [war minister] and Delbos [foreign minister] who advocated a policy of strict neutrality won out and the decision mentioned above was taken.

36. Sir George Clerk warns Yvon Delbos of the dangers of French intervention in the Spanish Civil War, 7 August 1936

From Foreign Office Papers (Public Record Office, London), FO 371/20528/ 5628. Telegram of 7 August 1936.

Paris, August 7, 1936.

I asked Minister for Foreign Affairs to see me this afternoon. I told him that my visit was a personal one and made because I was profoundly disturbed about the situation in Spain and hoped that he might possibly have some comfort to give me. What was his latest information from Rome, Berlin, Lisbon and Moscow in regard to the French proposal for non-intervention? M. Delbos said that the Soviet Government was favourable, that from Rome he had had nothing since the Italian communiqué of 6th August, in regard to which he said that he was not going to be drawn into a polemical discussion on point 2; Herr von Neurath had expressed a personal agreement in principle, but M. Delbos had had no official reply of any sort; and Lisbon had included in its answer the conditions that the Soviet Government should also accept fully the French proposal and that the French and British Governments should guarantee the safety of Portugal if that safety was threatened by the conflict in Spain. M. Delbos continued that he would be very grateful for any support that His Majesty's

Government could give the French proposal in Berlin, where he felt that at the moment we carried more weight than the French Government. As regards the Portuguese request, he presumed that our treaty with Portugal was a sufficient answer so far as we were concerned and France would, of course, act up to her obligations under the Covenant.

Turning to another aspect of the question, I said that I understood that the French Government, though they were still maintaining their refusal to deliver ammunition or war material to the Madrid Government, had felt that they could not refuse to allow five Dewoitine aircraft, which it was said had been ordered before the troubles began, to be delivered, and the departure of the five machines had accordingly been authorised. M. Delbos admitted that that was so. He said that, in face of the already known provision of Italian aircraft to the insurgents and of the despatch of twenty-eight German aeroplanes from Hamburg to the same destination, of which information had reached the French Government, though it was not known whether the machines had yet arrived, the French Government considered that it was not possible for them to maintain their embargo. But this showed the urgent need for agreement on the French proposal. I said that, while I could understand the reasoning of the French Government, there were two points that occurred to me: One was, how could he hope to reconcile the despatch of French aircraft to Spain with the holding up in France of British aircraft designed for Portugal? The other point was, was he sure that the Government in Madrid was the real Government, and not the screen behind which the most extreme anarchist elements in Spain were directing events? M. Delbos made no attempt to reply to my first question, though he made a note of it. As regards my second point, he said that it might be so in Catalonia, but law and order ruled in Madrid, and the Government was functioning unhampered by Extremists. I asked him if he considered that the forcible entry into a foreign Legation and the dragging out and shooting of two Spanish gentlemen was an instance of law and order. He had no reply. (This incident was reported to the Embassy this morning by Captain Charles, formerly commercial secretary in Madrid and manager of Rio Tinto, who has just returned from the Spanish frontier. The victims were the two sons of the Conde de Casa Valencia, at one time Spanish Ambassador in London.)

I concluded the interview by expressing the hope that the French Government, even though, pending an agreement of non-intervention, they might feel themselves precluded from stopping private commercial transactions with Spain, would do what it could to limit and retard such transactions as much as possible. I asked M. Delbos to forgive me for speaking so frankly, and I repeated that all I had said was entirely personal and on my own responsibility, but I felt that in so critical a situation I must put before him the danger of any action which might definitely commit the French Government to one side of the conflict and make more difficult the close co-operation between our two countries which was called for by this crisis. M. Delbos said that, on the contrary, he thanked me for speaking so openly and that he and his colleagues wished for nothing more than that the two Governments should act together as closely as possible. He viewed the situation with the gravest anxiety. He had every reason to fear that General Franco had offered the bait of the Balearic Islands to Italy and the Canaries to Germany, and if that materialised, good-bye to French independence.

I realise my responsibility in speaking to the Minister for Foreign Affairs as I did without instructions, but I had reason to believe that the Extremists in the Government were putting increasing pressure on M. Blum and I felt sure what I said might strengthen the hands of the moderate and sober elements.

37. Hitler on the Four Year Plan, August 1936

From Documents on Nazism, 1919–1945, *intro. and ed. by Jeremy Noakes and Geoffrey Pridham (London, Jonathan Cape, 1974), pp. 401–10.*

The development of our military capacity is to be effected through the new Army. *The extent of the military development of our resources cannot be too large, nor its pace too swift.* It is a major error to believe that there can be any argument on these points or any comparison with other vital necessities. However well-balanced the general pattern of a nation's life ought to be, there must at particular times be certain disturbances of the balance at the expense of other less vital tasks. *If we do not succeed in bringing the German Army as rapidly as possible to the rank of premier army in the world so far as its training, raising of units, armaments, and, above all, its spiritual education also is concerned, then Germany will be lost!* In this the basic principle applies that omissions during the months of peace cannot be made good in centuries.

Hence all other desires without exception must come second to this task. For this task involves life and the preservation of life, and all other desires – however understandable at other junctures – are unimportant or even mortally dangerous and are therefore to be rejected. Posterity will ask us one day, not what were the means, the reasons or the convictions by which we thought fit today to achieve the salvation of the nation, but *whether* in fact we achieved it. And on that day it will be no excuse for our downfall for us to describe the means which were infallible, but, alas, brought about our ruin. . . .

(c) It is, however, impossible to use foreign exchange allocated for the purchase of raw materials to import foodstuffs without inflicting a heavy and perhaps even fatal blow on the rest. *But above all it is absolutely impossible to do this at the expense of national rearmament.* I must at this point sharply reject the view that by restricting national rearmament, that is to say, the manufacture of arms and ammunition, we could bring about an 'enrichment' in raw materials which might then benefit Germany in the event of war. Such a view is based on a complete misconception, to put it mildly, of the tasks and military requirements that lie before us. For even a successful saving of raw materials by reducing, for instance, the production of munitions would merely mean that we should stockpile these raw materials in time of peace so as to manufacture them only in the event of war, that is to say, we should be depriving ourselves during the most critical months of munitions in exchange for raw copper, lead, or possibly iron. . . .

Nearly four precious years have now gone by. There is no doubt that by now we could have been completely independent of foreign countries in the spheres of fuel supplies, rubber supplies, and partly also iron ore supplies. Just as we are now producing 700,000 or 800,000 tons of petroleum, we could be producing 3 million tons. Just as we are today manufacturing a few thousand tons of rubber, we could already be producing 70,000 or 80,000 tons per annum. Just as we have stepped up the production of iron ore from $2\frac{1}{2}$ million tons to 7 million tons, we could process 20 or 25 million tons of German iron ore and even 30 millions if necessary. There has been time enough in four years to find out what we cannot do. Now we have to carry out what we can do.

I thus set the following tasks:

I. The German armed forces must be operational within four years.
II. The German economy must be fit for war within four years. . . .

Politics are the conduct and the course of the historical struggle of nations for life. The aim of these struggles is survival. Even ideological struggles have their ultimate cause and are most deeply motivated by nationally determined purposes and aims of life. But religions and ideologies are always able to impart particular bitterness to such struggles, and therefore also to give them great historical impressiveness. They leave their imprint on centuries of history. Nations and States living within the sphere of such ideological or religious conflicts cannot opt out of or dissociate themselves from these events. Christianity and the barbarian invasions determined the course of history for centuries. Mohammedanism convulsed the Orient as well as the Western world for half a millennium. The consequences of the Reformation have affected the whole of central Europe. Nor were individual countries – either by skill or by deliberate non-participation – able to steer clear of events. Since the outbreak of the French Revolution the world has been moving with ever-increasing speed towards a new conflict, the most extreme solution of which is Bolshevism; and the essence and goal of Bolshevism is the elimination of those strata of mankind which have hitherto provided the leadership and their replacement by world-wide Jewry. . . .

No nation will be able to avoid or abstain from this historical conflict. *Since Marxism, through its victory in Russia, has established one of the greatest empires as a forward base for its future operations, this question has become a menacing one. Against a democratic world which is ideologically split stands a unified aggressive will, based on an authoritarian ideology.*

The military resources of this aggressive will are in the meantime rapidly increasing from year to year. One has only to compare the Red Army as it actually exists today with the assumptions of military men of ten or fifteen years ago to realize the menacing extent of this development. Only consider the results of a further development over ten, fifteen or twenty years and think what conditions will be like then.

Germany

Germany will as always have to be regarded as the focus of the Western world against the attacks of Bolshevism. I do not regard this as an agreeable mission but as a serious handicap and burden for our national life, regrettably resulting from our disadvantageous position in Europe. We cannot, however, escape this destiny. Our political position results from the following:

At the moment there are only two countries in Europe which can be regarded as standing firm against Bolshevism – Germany and Italy. The other nations are either corrupted by their democratic way of life, infected by Marxism and therefore likely to collapse in the foreseeable future, or ruled by authoritarian Governments, whose sole strength lies in their military resources; this means, however, that being obliged to protect their leadership against their own peoples by the armed hand of the Executive, they are unable to use this armed hand for the protection of their countries against external enemies. None of these countries would ever be capable of waging war against Soviet Russia with any prospects of success. In fact, apart from Germany and Italy, only Japan can be considered as a Power standing firm in the face of the world peril.

It is not the aim of this memorandum to prophesy the moment when the untenable situation in Europe will reach the stage of an open crisis. I only want, in these lines, to express my conviction that this crisis cannot and will not fail to occur, and that Germany has the duty of securing her existence by every means in the face of this catastrophe, and to protect herself against it, and that this obligation has a number of implications involving the most important tasks that our people have ever been set. *For a victory of Bolshevism over Germany would lead not to a Versailles Treaty but to the final destruction, indeed to the annihilation, of the German people.*

The extent of such a catastrophe cannot be estimated. How, indeed, would the whole of densely populated Western Europe (including Germany), after a collapse into Bolshevism, live through probably the most gruesome catastrophe which has been visited on mankind since the downfall of the states of antiquity. *In face of the necessity of warding off this danger, all other considerations must recede into the background as completely irrelevant.*

38. Edouard Daladier advises against Franco–Soviet staff talks, 13 October 1936

From Documents diplomatiques français, 1932–1939, *2nd series, 1936–9, vol. III (Paris, 1966), no. 343. Letter of 13 October 1936 from Daladier, minister of national defence and war, to Yvon Delbos, foreign minister.*

Following the desire expressed by M. Léger, Secretary General of the foreign ministry, during an interview with General Schweisguth [deputy chief of the French general staff], I have the honour to send you . . . a copy of the report prepared by this officer . . . on the recent army manoeuvres in the USSR.

You will note on page 33 of this report Marshal Tukhachevskii's [first deputy commissar for defence] invitation . . . for the opening of talks between the French and Soviet general staffs.

This invitation follows similar ones repeated for over a year and of which the first was the subject of my letter no. 1365/SAE of 29 May 1935.

I believe I should recall to you on this occasion the new fact of a declaration which President Beneš [president of Czechoslovakia, 1935–8, 1940–8] made to General Schweisguth during a mission . . . to the Czechoslovak manoeuvres, which I reported to you in memorandum no. 1236/SAE of the 29 August last. The terms of this memorandum are as follows:

'I then asked M. Beneš whether he did not think that the day when our two governments considered military contacts with the Soviets to be opportune they should be preceded by a semi-official understanding between the general staffs of Prague and Paris in order to decide together on the nature and methods of the co-operation to be requested from the Soviets. The President replied that such a prior entente seemed to him indispensable.'

I entirely share the opinion of President Beneš on the necessity of an agreement between the French and Czechoslovak general staffs preceding any military contacts with the Soviet general staff.

I would add that, in the present circumstances, these staff talks, which may well alarm certain friendly powers and provide Germany with the ready pretext of an attempt at encirclement, would present, in my view, serious disadvantages, of which you are in a better position to judge the significance than myself.

39. Anthony Eden opposes Franco–Soviet staff talks, 15 May 1937

From Documents diplomatiques français, 1932–1939, *2nd series, 1936–9, vol. V (Paris, 1968), no. 429. Memorandum of conversation with Yvon Delbos, French foreign minister. Eden was then secretary of state for foreign affairs.*

. . . Without contesting the political and military considerations which obliged the French government to consider . . . the proper establishment of technical studies between French and Russian general staffs allowing for the eventual application of the Franco–Soviet pact, the British Minister maintained insistently his reservations . . . on the inopportuneness at this time of any apparent improvement in Franco–Soviet solidarity. Personally M. Eden accepted the analysis which had been given to him of the situation and conclusions facing the French government, concerned for its responsibilities regarding the external security of France, as well as for the general interest of Europe: but he believed he should out of loyalty express his apprehension about the reactions of public opinion in England . . . which his government could be forced to take into account.

40. The Hossbach Memorandum, 10 November 1937

From Documents on German Foreign Policy, 1918–1945, *series D, vol. I (London, HMSO, 1949), no. 19.*

MINUTES OF THE CONFERENCE IN THE REICH CHANCELLERY, BERLIN, NOVEMBER 5, 1937, FROM 4:15 to 8:30 P.M.

Present: The Führer and Chancellor,

Field Marshal von Blomberg, War Minister,
Colonel General Baron von Fritsch, Commander in Chief, Army,
Admiral Dr. h. c. Raeder, Commander in Chief, Navy,
Colonel General Göring, Commander in Chief, *Luftwaffe*,
Baron von Neurath, Foreign Minister,
Colonel Hossbach.

The Führer began by stating that the subject of the present conference was of such importance that its discussion would, in other countries, certainly be a matter for a full Cabinet Meeting, but he – the Führer – had rejected the idea of making it a subject of discussion before the wider circle of the Reich Cabinet just because of the importance of the matter. His exposition to follow was the fruit of thorough deliberation and the experiences of his $4\frac{1}{2}$ years of power. He wished to explain to the gentlemen present his basic ideas concerning the opportunities for the development of our position in the field of foreign affairs and its requirements, and he asked, in the interests of a long-term German policy, that his exposition be regarded, in the event of his death, as his last will and testament.

The Führer then continued:

The aim of German policy was to make secure and to preserve the racial community [*Volksmasse*] and to enlarge it. It was therefore a question of space. . . .

German policy had to reckon with two hate-inspired antagonists, Britain and France, to whom a German colossus in the centre of Europe was a thorn in the flesh, and both countries were opposed to any further strengthening of Germany's position either in Europe or overseas; in support of this opposition they were able to count on the agreement of all their political parties. Both countries saw in the establishment of German military bases overseas a threat to their own communications, a safeguarding of German commerce, and, as a consequence, a strengthening of Germany's position in Europe. . . .

Germany's problem could only be solved by means of force and this was never without attendant risk. The campaigns of Frederick the Great for Silesia and Bismarck's wars against Austria and France had involved unheard-of risk, and the swiftness of the Prussian action in 1870 had kept Austria from entering the war. If one accepts as the basis of the following exposition the resort to force with its attendant risks, then there remain still to be answered the questions 'when' and 'how'. In this matter there were three cases [*Fälle*] to be dealt with:

Case 1: Period 1943–1945
After this date only a change for the worse, from our point of view, could be expected.

The equipment of the army, navy, and *Luftwaffe*, as well as the formation of the officer corps, was nearly completed. Equipment and armament were modern; in further delay there lay the danger of their obsolescence. In particular, the secrecy of 'special weapons' could not be preserved forever. The recruiting of reserves was limited to current age groups; further drafts from older untrained age groups were no longer available.

Our relative strength would decrease in relation to the rearmament which would by then have been carried out by the rest of the world. If we did not act by 1943-45, any year could, in consequence of a lack of reserves, produce the food crisis, to cope with which the necessary foreign exchange was not available, and this must be regarded as a 'waning point of the regime.' Besides, the world was expecting our attack and was increasing its countermeasures from year to year. It was while the rest of the world was still preparing its defenses [*sich abriegele*] that we were obliged to take the offensive.

Nobody knew today what the situation would be in the years 1943-45. One thing only was certain, that we could not wait longer.

On the one hand there was the great *Wehrmacht*, and the necessity of maintaining it at its present level, the aging of the movement and of its leaders; and on the other, the prospect of a lowering of the standard of living and of a limitation of the birth rate, which left no choice but to act. If the Führer was still living, it was his unalterable resolve to solve Germany's problem of space at the latest by 1943-45. The necessity for action before 1943-45 would arise in cases 2 and 3.

Case 2:
If internal strife in France should develop into such a domestic crisis as to absorb the French Army completely and render it incapable of use for war against Germany, then the time for action against the Czechs had come.

Case 3:
If France is so embroiled by a war with another state that she cannot 'proceed' against Germany.

For the improvement of our politico-military position our first objective, in the event of our being embroiled in war, must be to overthrow Czechoslovakia and Austria simultaneously in order to remove the threat to our flank in any possible operation against the West. In a conflict with France it was hardly to be regarded as likely that the Czechs would declare war on us on the very same day as France. The desire to join in the war would, however, increase among the Czechs in proportion to any weakening on our part and then her participation could clearly take the form of an attack toward Silesia, toward the north or toward the west.

If the Czechs were overthrown and a common German-Hungarian frontier achieved, a neutral attitude on the part of Poland could be the more certainly counted on in the event of a Franco-German conflict. Our agreements with Poland only retained their force as long as Germany's strength remained unshaken. In the event of German setbacks a Polish action against East Prussia, and possibly against Pomerania and Silesia as well, had to be reckoned with.

On the assumption of a development of the situation leading to action on our part as planned, in the years 1943-45, the attitude of France,

Britain, Italy, Poland, and Russia could probably be estimated as follows:

Actually, the Führer believed that almost certainly Britain, and probably France as well, had already tacitly written off the Czechs and were reconciled to the fact that this question would be cleared up in due course by Germany. Difficulties connected with the Empire, and the prospect of being once more entangled in a protracted European war, were decisive considerations for Britain against participation in a war against Germany. Britain's attitude would certainly not be without influence on that of France. An attack by France without British support, and with the prospect of the offensive being brought to a standstill on our western fortifications, was hardly probable. Nor was a French march through Belgium and Holland without British support to be expected; this also was a course not to be contemplated by us in the event of a conflict with France, because it would certainly entail the hostility of Britain. It would of course be necessary to maintain a strong defense [*eine Abriegelung*] on our western frontier during the prosecution of our attack on the Czechs and Austria. And in this connection it had to be remembered that the defense measures of the Czechs were growing in strength from year to year, and that the actual worth of the Austrian Army also was increasing in the course of time. Even though the populations concerned, especially of Czechoslovakia, were not sparse, the annexation of Czechoslovakia and Austria would mean an acquisition of foodstuffs for 5 to 6 million people, on the assumption that the compulsory emigration of 2 million people from Czechoslovakia and 1 million people from Austria was practicable. The incorporation of these two States with Germany meant, from the politico-military point of view, a substantial advantage because it would mean shorter and better frontiers, the freeing of forces for other purposes, and the possibility of creating new units up to a level of about 12 divisions, that is, 1 new division per million inhabitants.

Italy was not expected to object to the elimination of the Czechs, but it was impossible at the moment to estimate what her attitude on the Austrian question would be; that depended essentially upon whether the Duce were still alive.

The degree of surprise and the swiftness of our action were decisive factors for Poland's attitude. Poland – with Russia at her rear – will have little inclination to engage in war against a victorious Germany.

Military intervention by Russia must be countered by the swiftness of our operations; however, whether such an intervention was a practical contingency at all was, in view of Japan's attitude, more than doubtful.

Should case 2 arise – the crippling of France by civil war – the situation thus created by the elimination of the most dangerous opponent must be seized upon whenever it occurs for the blow against the Czechs.

The Führer saw case 3 coming definitely nearer; it might emerge from the present tensions in the Mediterranean, and he was resolved to take advantage of it whenever it happened, even as early as 1938. . . .

If Germany made use of this war to settle the Czech and Austrian questions, it was to be assumed that Britain – herself at war with Italy – would decide not to act against Germany. Without British support, a warlike action by France against Germany was not to be expected. . . .

In appraising the situation, Field Marshal von Blomberg and Colonel General von Fritsch repeatedly emphasized the necessity that Britain and France must not appear in the role of our enemies, and stated that the French Army would not be so committed by the war with Italy that France could not at the same time enter the field with forces superior to ours on our western frontier. General von Fritsch estimated the probable French forces available for use on the Alpine frontier at approximately twenty divisions, so that a strong French superiority would still remain on the western frontier, with the role, according to the German view, of invading the Rhineland. In this matter, moreover, the advanced state of French defense preparations [*Mobilmachung*] must be taken into particular account, and it must be remembered apart from the insignificant value of our present fortifications – on which Field Marshal von Blomberg laid special emphasis – that the four motorized divisions intended for the West were still more or less incapable of movement. In regard to our offensive toward the southeast, Field Marshal von Blomberg drew particular attention to the strength of the Czech fortifications, which had acquired by now a structure like a Maginot Line and which would gravely hamper our attack.

General von Fritsch mentioned that this was the very purpose of a study which he had ordered made this winter, namely, to examine the possibility of conducting operations against the Czechs with special reference to overcoming the Czech fortification system; the General further expressed his opinion that under existing circumstances he must give up his plan to go abroad on his leave, which was due to begin on November 10. The Führer dismissed this idea on the ground that the possibility of a conflict need not yet be regarded as so imminent. To the Foreign Minister's objection that an Anglo–French–Italian conflict was not yet within such a measurable distance as the Führer seemed to assume, the Führer put the summer of 1938 as the date which seemed to him possible for this. In reply to considerations offered by Field Marshal von Blomberg and General von Fritsch regarding the attitude of Britain and France, the Führer repeated his previous statements that he was convinced of Britain's nonparticipation, and therefore he did not believe in the probability of belligerent action by France against Germany. Should the Mediterranean conflict under discussion lead to a general mobilization in Europe, then we must immediately begin action against the Czechs. On the other hand, should the powers not engaged in the war declare themselves disinterested, then Germany would have to adopt a similar attitude to this for the time being.

Colonel General Göring thought that, in view of the Führer's statement, we should consider liquidating our military undertakings in Spain. The Führer agrees to this with the limitation that he thinks he should reserve a decision for a proper moment.

The second part of the conference was concerned with concrete questions of armament.

CERTIFIED CORRECT: HOSSBACH
Colonel (General Staff)

41. Neville Chamberlain on Lord Halifax's visit to Germany, 26 November 1937

From Keith Feiling, The Life of Neville Chamberlain (*London, Macmillan, 1946*), *pp. 332–3. Chamberlain was prime minister at this time, and Halifax lord president of the council.*

26 November 1937
. . . the German visit was from my point of view a great success, because it achieved its object, that of creating an atmosphere in which it is possible to discuss with Germany the practical questions involved in a European settlement. . . . Both Hitler and Goering said separately, and emphatically, that they had no desire or intention of making war, and I think we may take this as correct, at any rate for the present. Of course, they want to dominate Eastern Europe; they want as close a union with Austria as they can get without incorporating her in the Reich, and they want much the same things for the Sudetendeutsche as we did for the Uitlanders in the Transvaal.

They want Togoland and Kameruns. I am not quite sure where they stand about S.W. Africa; but they do not insist on Tanganyika, if they can be given some reasonably equivalent territory on the West Coast, possibly to be carved out of Belgian Congo and Angola. I think they would be prepared to come back to the League, if it were shorn of its compulsory powers, now clearly shown to be ineffective, and though Hitler was rather non-committal about disarmament, he did declare himself in favour of the abolition of bombing aeroplanes.

Now here, it seems to me, is a fair basis of discussion, though no doubt all these points bristle with difficulties. But I don't see why we shouldn't say to Germany, 'give us satisfactory assurances that you won't use force to deal with the Austrians and Czechoslovakians, and we will give you similar assurances that we won't use force to prevent the changes you want, if you can get them by peaceful means'

42. Anglo–French conversations, London, 29–30 November 1937

From Documents diplomatiques français, 1932–1939, *2nd series, 1936–9, vol. VII (Paris, 1972), no. 287.*

. . . M. Delbos [French foreign minister] . . . as for the methods by which the Reich hoped to realise its ambitions, it seemed that for Austria these would consist of the introduction of national socialist ministers into the government, leading to a plebiscite; for Czechoslovakia . . . a federal constitution, then quasi-autonomy, ending in attachment to Germany.

Mr Neville Chamberlain [British prime minister] asked what were the consequences for the Franco–Czech treaty.

M. Delbos replied that the treaty committed France in the event of Czechoslovakia being the victim of aggression. If risings occurred among the German population, supported by the armed intervention of Germany, France was committed in a measure to be defined according to the gravity of the facts.

Mr Eden [British foreign secretary] thought that this was the nub of the matter and that if one wished to establish a connection between the colonial question and that of European appeasement it was necessary to know in advance how the two governments envisaged the possibilities which had just been mentioned. . . .

Mr Neville Chamberlain wondered how short of using force Germany could be prevented from carrying out the aims which M. Delbos had mentioned earlier.

M. Delbos thought this depended to a great extent on the respect that Britain and France together might impose, the agreement of the two powers could make Germany more reasonable.

There were two possible methods: to let things slide, and the result of that was obvious: or to take an interest in central Europe in a firm and conciliatory spirit. If this latter method was followed, the situation did not seem altogether desperate.

Mr Neville Chamberlain thought that there was much of value in M. Delbos's second suggestion. The Germans obviously would hesitate before using force. . . . If they opted for peaceful methods, there was a chance of rendering less dangerous each of their actions . . . and of being able to count on Italian sympathy in the Austrian question.

M. Delbos feared that Italy, in the hope of saving Austria, might encourage still more German designs on Czechoslovakia. . . .

Mr Neville Chamberlain drew the attention of French ministers to the state of opinion in England. There was a strong current against Great Britain running the risk at any price of being involved in a war for

Czechoslovakia, a distant country, with whom England had little in common. . . . As for the difficulties between Berlin and Prague, the public considered that the Sudeten Germans had not been fairly treated by the Czechoslovak government. . . .

M. Delbos considered that the concern of the Prime Minister was perfectly justified. France had repeatedly advised Czechoslovakia to deprive the Germans of any pretext for complaint; yet it was necessary to give the same advice to the Germans. . . . The Czechs certainly needed to carry out certain reforms. . . . But if in reality Germany aimed at the absorption of Austria and Czechoslovakia the European order would be overturned and German hegemony established. . . .

Mr Eden . . . hoped that M. Delbos during his stay in Prague would not limit himself only to saying to the Czechs: 'Do nothing which might provide the Germans with a pretext' but that he would go further and say to them: 'Do what you can for the Sudeten Germans'. . . .

Mr Neville Chamberlain summed up the morning's discussion by saying that it seemed desirable to try to realise an accord with Germany on Central Europe. Whatever Germany's aims, even if she wanted to absorb some of her neighbours, one might hope to postpone the execution of German plans . . . the further the Czech government believed it could go, the longer it would be possible to act on Germany.

M. Chautemps [French prime minister] remarked that M. Delbos's task would be easier if he could say that he spoke both in the name of France and of Great Britain and could tell the Czechs that once they had done their utmost to satisfy the legitimate grievances of the Sudeten Germans they would be entitled to count on the sympathy of Great Britain and France, if in spite of everything they were victims of aggression. . . .

Mr Eden observed that the British government had already made its views known in Prague. . . . But M. Delbos would be fully justified in saying that the more the Czechs could demonstrate their goodwill, the stronger they would be towards German claims.

Mr Neville Chamberlain thought that the British government could hardly go further, nor could it give any assurance in the event of aggression. . . .

43. General Jodl's amendment to 'Operation Green', 7 December 1937

From Documents on German Foreign Policy, 1918–1945, *series D, vol. VII* (*London, HMSO, 1956*), *app. III (K), pp. 635–7. Jodl was chief of the national defence section in the high command of the armed forces.*

. . .

(1) The further development of the diplomatic situation makes 'Operation Red' increasingly less likely than 'Operation Green'. . . .

(3) The political preconditions for the activation of 'Operation Green' have changed, following the directives of the Führer and Reich Chancellor, and the objectives of such a war have been expanded.

The previous Section II of Part 2 of the directive of the High Command of the Armed Forces of 24 June 1937 is therefore to be deleted and replaced by the enclosed new version. . . .

The main emphasis of all mobilization planning is now to be placed on 'Operation Green'. . . .

II. *War on two fronts with main effort in south-east ('Operation Green')*

1. *Prerequisites*

When Germany has achieved complete preparedness for war in all spheres, then the military conditions will have been created for carrying out an offensive war against Czechoslovakia, so that the solution of the German problem of living space can be carried to a victorious conclusion even if one or another of the Great Powers intervene against us.

Apart from many other considerations, there is in the first place the defensive capacity of our western fortifications, which will permit the western frontier of the German Reich to be held with weak forces for a long time against greatly superior strength.

But even so the Government [*Staatsführung*] will do what is politically feasible to avoid the risk for Germany of a war on two fronts and will try to avoid any situation with which, as far as can be judged, Germany could not cope militarily or economically.

Should the political situation not develop, or develop only slowly, in our favour, then the execution of 'Operation Green' from our side will have to be postponed for years. If, however, a situation arises which, owing to Britain's aversion to a general European War, through her lack of interest in the Central European problem and because of a conflict breaking out between Italy and France in the Mediterranean, creates the probability that Germany will face no other opponent than Russia on Czechoslovakia's side, then 'Operation Green' will start before the completion of Germany's full preparedness for war.

2. The military objective of 'Operation Green' is still the speedy occupation of Bohemia and Moravia with the simultaneous solution of the Austrian question in the sense of incorporating Austria into the German Reich. In order to achieve the latter aim, military force will be required only if other means do not lead or have not led to success.

In accordance with this military objective it is the task of the German Wehrmacht to make preparations so that:

(a) the bulk of all forces can invade Czechoslovakia with speed, surprise and the maximum impetus;

(b) reserves, mainly the armed units of the SS, are kept ready in order, if necessary, to march into Austria;

(c) in the west, security can be maintained with only a minimum of forces for rearguard protection of the eastern operations. . . .

44. The British Cabinet reviews its foreign and defence policies, 8 December 1937

From Cabinet Papers (Public Record Office, London), CAB 23/90A.

10   The Cabinet had before them a Memorandum by the Minister for Co-ordination of Defence (C.P.–295 (37)) covering a Most Secret Report by the Chiefs of Staff Sub-Committee (C.I.D. Paper No. 1366–B) on the Comparison of the Strength of Great Britain with that of certain other Nations as at January, 1938. The *draft* Conclusions reached by the Committee of Imperial Defence (303rd Meeting, Minute 3) after consideration of the above Report were as follows:

F.R.10(38)10

' (i) To take note of:

(a) The warnings contained in the Report of the Chiefs of Staff Sub-Committee (C.I.D. Paper No. 1366–B):

F.R.1.(38)1.

(b) The statement on foreign policy made at this meeting by the Secretary of State for Foreign Affairs, which, it was agreed, takes proper account of the facts of the situation, including those mentioned in the Report by the Chiefs of Staff:

(c) The Prime Minister's observations as summarised in the above Minutes.

(ii) That the Report by the Chiefs of Staff Sub-Committee (C.I.D. Paper No. 1366–B) together with the above conclusions (but not the full

Minutes) should be circulated to the Cabinet; it being left to the
Prime Minister to explain the gist of the discussion to the Cabinet.'

In compliance with the second of the conclusions quoted above, the
Prime Minister made a statement to the Cabinet.

He pointed out that in paragraph 41 of their memorandum, the Chiefs
of Staff Sub-Committee had summarised their conclusions. In paragraph
42 they had expressed the warnings referred to in conclusion (i)(a) above.
From this paragraph, he quoted the following extracts:

'From the above Report it will be seen that our Naval, Military and Air
Forces, in their present stage of development are still far from sufficient
to meet our defensive commitments, which now extend from Western
Europe through the Mediterranean to the Far East. . . . Without over-
looking the assistance which we should hope to obtain from France, and
possibly other allies, we cannot foresee the time when our defence
forces will be strong enough to safeguard our territory, trade and vital
interests against Germany, Italy and Japan simultaneously. We cannot,
therefore, exaggerate the importance, from the point of view of Imperial
defence, of any political or international action that can be taken to
reduce the numbers of our potential enemies and to gain the support
of potential allies.'

The Foreign Secretary, the Prime Minister continued, had circulated
a short paper to the Committee of Imperial Defence dealing with certain
aspects of the Chiefs of Staff paper but not pretending to give any general
account of our foreign policy. At the meeting of the Committee, however,
the Foreign Secretary had made a verbal statement, the general effect of
which had been summarised in conclusion (i)(b). He then summarised the
main considerations that had been brought to the notice of the Committee.
It was true, as the Chiefs of Staff had pointed out, that we could not hope
to confront satisfactorily Germany, Italy and Japan simultaneously and,
when we looked round as to what help we could get from other nations,
the results were not very encouraging. France was our most important
friend. Though she was strong defensively and possessed a powerful army,
the French Air Force was far from satisfactory. During the Anglo–French
visit, M. Chautemps had admitted to an output of aircraft that was only
about one-fifth (60–300) of our own. A long time must elapse before
France would be able to give us much help in the air. The Power that
had the greatest strength was the United States of America, but he would
be a rash man who based his calculations on help from that quarter. Our
position in relation to the smaller Powers was much better than formerly,
but he did not think that they would add much to our offensive or defensive
strength. In time of peace their support was useful, but in war less so.

The Chiefs of Staff, as he had mentioned, said they could not foresee the time when our defence forces would be strong enough to safeguard our territory, trade and vital interests against Germany, Italy and Japan simultaneously. They had urged that our foreign policy must be governed by this consideration, and they had made rather a strong appeal to this effect. Of course, it would be possible to make an effort to detach one of the three Powers from the other two and it might even succeed. This, however, could only be done at the cost of concessions which would involve humiliations and disadvantages to this country by destroying the confidence of other nations. No-one would suppose, therefore, that we should try and bribe one of the three nations to leave the other two. What the Foreign Secretary was doing was to try and prevent a situation arising in which the three Powers mentioned would ever be at war with us. He recalled that before the trouble had arisen in the Far East, we had been making great efforts to improve our relations with Japan and that considerable progress had been made. Owing to recent events, we had been compelled to break off these negotiations, but we had tried to keep open the position of resuming them later on. We had avoided threats ourselves and had restrained others from making them. The improvement in relations with Italy was not easy, but we had made some efforts to get on better terms, in spite of the difficult attitude of Mussolini and we were about to make a further effort at that end of the Berlin–Rome Axis. As he himself had pointed out before, however, Germany was the real key to the question. In view of the recent consideration given by the Cabinet to the question of improving relations with Germany, it was unnecessary to develop that theme any further. He thought, however, that he had said enough to show that the strategic considerations urged by the Chiefs of Staff were fully taken into account in our foreign policy and that was what underlay the taking note by the Committee of Imperial Defence of conclusion (i)(b) quoted above, namely –

'(b) The statement on foreign policy made at this meeting by the Secretary of State for Foreign Affairs, which, it was agreed, takes proper account of the facts of the situation, including those mentioned in the Report by the Chiefs of Staff.'

In the course of a short discussion, attention was drawn to the late Prime Minister's undertaking as to the maintenance of parity between the Air Force of the United Kingdom and that of Germany.

The Minister for Co-Ordination of Defence pointed out that Lord Baldwin's statement required interpretation. He had never taken it to mean that we must have exactly the same number of fighters and bombers as Germany in order to carry out the contemplated equality.

The Prime Minister said he did not intend to repeat Lord Baldwin's words and, if the question were raised, he would make it clear that the Government did not consider it necessary to have precise equality in every class of aircraft. It might be necessary to make a statement on this subject before very long.

After some further discussion, the Cabinet agreed:

To take note of the Report contained in C.P. 296(37), together with the Prime Minister's remarks thereon and summarised above.

45. Eden instructs Sir Nevile Henderson on the terms of a new approach to Germany, 12 February 1938

From Cabinet Papers (Public Record Office, London), CAB 24/275. Eden was then foreign secretary, and Henderson ambassador in Germany.

Foreign Office, February 12, 1938

Sir,

IN the present despatch I send you instructions as to the terms in which you are to approach the German Government on the matters which His Majesty's Ministers discussed with you during your recent visit to London. In making your communication, you should emphasise its absolutely secret character. I shall send you supplementary instructions by telegram regarding the moment at which your approach to the German Government should be made. Pending the receipt of those telegraphic instructions, you should not take any action on the present despatch.

2. You should inform the German Chancellor and the German Foreign Minister that during your recent visit to London you have had discussions with His Majesty's Government in the United Kingdom on all the issues arising out of the conversations held during Lord Halifax's recent visit to Germany. These issues naturally cover the contributions towards appeasement which, as the bases of a possible agreement, each country might be able to make in Europe and elsewhere.

3. In order not to create misunderstanding, which might give rise to greater difficulties at a later stage, you should remind the German Government of the observations you made recently as to the importance that would be attached, not only by His Majesty's Government, but by other Governments, to German collaboration in appeasement. Mention should be made of Czechoslovakia and Austria as illustrative of the general principle of collaboration.

4. You should refer to the question of limitation of armaments, and say that while His Majesty's Government recognise the difficulty of making progress on this subject if treated as a general question, they have taken

note of the German Chancellor's references to bombing, a subject which they agree with him in regarding as of great importance. They attach still greater importance – and they believe the German Government do the same – to a limitation of bombing aircraft. You should say that the suggestions made by Herr Hitler in the past are being carefully considered, and that His Majesty's Government themselves are making a study of the whole question. They earnestly hope that it may be possible to reach agreement on practical proposals that will command general assent.

5. As regards the colonial question, you might say that you had found a real disposition to study this question carefully in all its bearings and to make progress if possible. The question, of course, was full of difficulties, as the German Government were well aware, and, as the German Government were also aware, public opinion in this country was extremely sensitive on the subject. You could say that every aspect of the problem had been under close examination by His Majesty's Government. A solution which seemed to them to have many attractions might be found in a scheme based upon the idea of a new régime of colonial administration in a given area of Africa, roughly corresponding to the conventional zone of the Congo Basin Treaties, acceptable and applicable to all the Powers concerned on exactly equal terms. Each Power, while solely concerned for the administration of its own territories, would be invited to subscribe to certain principles designed to promote the well-being of all. Some indication of the régime might be given, starting perhaps from the conception of the Berlin Act of 1883. For instance, there would be the question of demilitarisation; also perhaps a commission consisting of representatives of all the Powers having territory in the area covered by the new arrangements, as well as stipulations for the welfare and progress of the natives, and for freedom of trade and communications. You should endeavour to ascertain in general terms how the German Government are disposed to view this suggestion. You should not at this stage discuss what particular territories might be transferred.

6. If this suggestion meets generally with a favourable reaction on the part of the German Government, fuller instructions will be sent to you later.

7. I am instructing His Majesty's Ambassador in Paris to make a communication to the French Government in the terms shown in the following paragraph, and you are authorised to use the same terms in acquainting your French colleague with your approach to the German Government. In both cases the absolutely secret character of the communication is to be emphasised. You should not make this communication to your French colleague until after you have made your communication to the German Government.

46. The Blum government considers ways and means of helping Czechoslovakia and Republican Spain, 15 March 1938

From Documents diplomatiques français, 1932–1939, *2nd series, 1936–9, vol. VIII (Paris, 1973), no. 446.*

The Comité Permanent de la Défense Nationale [permanent committee of national defence] held its eleventh session, on Tuesday 15 March 1938, at the Hôtel Matignon, under the presidency of M. Edouard Daladier, Minister of National Defence and of War.

The Prime Minister and the Foreign Minister were present.
The subject of the session was the study of the following questions:

1. Aid for Czechoslovakia in the event of German aggression
2. Intervention in Spain. . . .

M. Paul-Boncour, Foreign Minister indicated the initial purpose of this meeting:
In talks with Great Britain we have been trying for several days to obtain from the English a declaration on the subject of their attitude towards the Czechoslovak problem.
In reply to our representations the English . . . are saying: 'You say that you will help Czechoslovakia but in practical terms what will you do?'
It was this question that he was putting to the competent military body . . . as much as to be able to reply to the English question as to support the declarations that the government intended to make on this subject. . . .
M. E. Daladier, Minister of National Defence and War pointed out that France could not initially give Czechoslovakia any direct help.
The only aid she might give was indirect . . . by mobilising so as to keep German troops on our frontiers.
The problem was to know whether, given these conditions, Germany would have sufficient strength left to attempt an attack on Czechoslovakia.
General Gamelin, Chief of National Defence Staff remarked that France could reinforce this action . . . by attacking, but as these attacks would take place in a fortified zone they would involve us in lengthy operations.
M. Léon Blum, Prime Minister declared that Russia would intervene.
General Gamelin, Chief of National Defence Staff replied that he could not see what effective aid Russia could give initially. . . . In any case the effectiveness of Russian aid was conditioned by the attitude of Poland and Rumania.

General Vuillemin, Chief of Air Staff explained that from the point of view of air power, Russian intervention in aid of Czechoslovakia was very difficult.

. . . It would be necessary to cross Poland and Rumania, which assumed that they had decided their attitude.

Besides there were very few airfields in Czechoslovakia: 40, which the German air force would quickly render unusable.

M. Léon Blum, Prime Minister . . . summed up the explanations that had just been given:

1 We can pin down, at the price of our mobilisation, German forces. . . .
2 But we cannot prevent an attack on Czechoslovakia. . . .

M. Léon Blum, Prime Minister introduced the second question that he wanted to put to the Comité Permanent:

How can we intervene in Spain? How can we support an ultimatum to General Franco of this kind: 'If within 24 hours you have not renounced the help of foreign troops France . . . will take whatever measures . . . she judges necessary. . .'. It would, he observed, be a manoeuvre of the same kind as that which Chancellor Hitler had just tried . . . in Austria and carried out.

General Gamelin, Chief of National Defence Staff remarked that the conditions were not the same.

We normally had an active army of 400,000 men in France while the Germans had 900,000 men.

If we wanted to play a similar game we needed a million men. . . .

M. Campinchi, Minister for the Navy asked what in view of the weakness of our air force would be the effect on the war of Germany's air supremacy?

General Vuillemin, Chief of Air Staff considered that in 15 days our air force would be crushed. . . .

M. Guy La Chambre, Air Minister explained . . . that the present production was only 40, it would soon be 60 a month.

Marshal Pétain compared this figure with the production of our main adversary which modest estimates put at 250 a month. . . .

M. E. Daladier, Minister of National Defence and War declared that one would have to be blind not to see that intervention in Spain would unleash a general war. It did not seem possible to intervene except in the event of a new factor: important foreign reinforcements. . . .

M. E. Daladier asked what would be the reactions of Germany and Italy in the event of our intervention in Spain.

Would it be, asked *M. Léon Blum, Prime Minister*, a *casus belli*?

Without any doubt, replied *M. Léger, Secretary General of the Foreign Ministry*. . . .

47. Chamberlain decides against a British guarantee for Czechoslovakia, 20 March 1938

From Keith Feiling, The Life of Neville Chamberlain (*London, Macmillan, 1946*), *pp. 347–8.*

20 March

. . . with Franco winning in Spain by the aid of German guns and Italian planes, with a French government in which one cannot have the slightest confidence, and which I suspect to be in closish touch with our Opposition, with the Russians stealthily and cunningly pulling all the strings behind the scenes to get us involved in war with Germany (our Secret Service doesn't spend all its time looking out of the window), and finally with a Germany flushed with triumph, and all too conscious of her power, the prospect looked black indeed. In face of such problems, to be badgered and pressed to come out and give a clear, decided, bold, and unmistakable lead, show 'ordinary courage', and all the rest of the twaddle, is calculated to vex the man who has to take the responsibility for the consequences. As a matter of fact, the plan of the 'Grand Alliance', as Winston calls it, had occurred to me long before he mentioned it. . . . I talked about it to Halifax, and we submitted it to the chiefs of the Staff and the F.O. experts. It is a very attractive idea; indeed, there is almost everything to be said for it until you come to examine its practicability. From that moment its attraction vanishes. You have only to look at the map to see that nothing that France or we could do could possibly save Czechoslovakia from being overrun by the Germans, if they wanted to do it. The Austrian frontier is practically open; the great Skoda munitions works are within easy bombing distance of the German aerodromes, the railways all pass through German territory, Russia is 100 miles away. Therefore we could not help Czechoslovakia – she would simply be a pretext for going to war with Germany. That we could not think of unless we had a reasonable prospect of being able to beat her to her knees in a reasonable time, and of that I see no sign. I have therefore abandoned any idea of giving guarantees to Czechoslovakia, or the French in connection with her obligations to that country.

48. Hitler's instructions to the Sudeten German leaders, 28 March 1938

From Documents on German Foreign Policy, 1918–1945, *series D, vol. II (London, HMSO, 1949), no. 106.*

. . . The Führer stated that he intended to settle the Sudeten German problem in the not-too-distant future. He could no longer tolerate Germans being oppressed or fired upon. He told Henlein [leader of the Sudeten German Party] that he knew how popular he, Henlein, was and that he was the rightful leader of the Sudeten German element, and as a result of his popularity and attractiveness he would triumph over circumstances. To Henlein's objection that he, Henlein, could only be a substitute, Hitler replied: I will stand by you; from tomorrow you will be my Viceroy [*Statthalter*]. I will not tolerate difficulties being made for you by any department whatsoever within the Reich.

The purport of the instructions which the Führer has given to Henlein is that demands should be made by the Sudeten German Party which are unacceptable to the Czech Government. Despite the favourable situation created by the events in Austria, Henlein does not intend to drive things to the limit, but merely to put forward the old demands for self-administration and reparation at the Party Rally (23–24 April 1938). He wishes to reserve for later on a suggestion of the Führer's that he should demand German regiments with German officers, and military commands to be given in German. The Reich will not intervene of its own accord. Henlein himself will be responsible for events for the time being. However, there must be close cooperation. Henlein summarized his view to the Führer as follows: We must always demand so much that we can never be satisfied. The Führer approved this view. . . .

49. Halifax warns France not to count on British help in the event of a war over Czechoslovakia, 22 May 1938

From Documents on British Foreign Policy, 1919–1939, *ed. E. L. Woodward and Rohan Butler, 3rd series, vol. I (London, HMSO, 1949), no. 285. Telegram from Halifax, foreign secretary, to Paris, 22 May 1938.*

FOREIGN OFFICE, *May 22, 1938*

Sir,

The French Ambassador came to see me this afternoon, and told me that, from information that the French Government had received, Prague was quiet and it was raining, and that the Czechoslovak Government thought the military measures which they had taken had exercised a good effect. The German press also, he understood, had been more moderate this morning. This was all to the good.

2. I told the Ambassador of the representations we had made in Berlin, in which a warning on the line of the Prime Minister's speech had, as the French Government knew, been associated with an appeal for patience. I was, however, very much concerned to ensure that the French Government did not in any way fall into the danger of reading more into the Prime Minister's speech of the 24th March than it, in fact, contained. It was, in my view, right that we should have used the strong language in Berlin that we had, in fact, employed, but it was no less important that the French Government should realise the view that we took of the military situation in the case of the worst developments. I fully appreciated the position in which the French Government were placed, but the fact of their obligations, taken with the facts of the military situation, made it essential that they should leave nothing undone to avoid being confronted with the dilemma of choice between war and failure to honour their obligations. I felt I ought again to make it plain, although I had no doubt that it was much in the mind of the French Government, that, while we were bound to assist France to the utmost of our power in the case of unprovoked aggression by Germany, we were not so bound to join forces with her in the event of her going to the assistance of Czechoslovakia.

3. His Excellency said that I need be under no misapprehension as to the realisation of this distinction by the French Government, and that they were doing all they could to avoid an emergence of the dilemma of which I had spoken. On the other hand, they were very sensible of the damage that would be wrought upon the European situation as a whole if the German Government did, in fact, carry out a successful attack on Czechoslovakia. I said that, of course, I fully realised this, but that kind of argument might, though this was not in his mind, be employed to justify what was commonly known as a preventive war – an idea that I had been glad to hear M. Daladier [prime minister and war minister], when he was in London, repudiate in strong terms. His Excellency expressed his agreement in condemnation of the idea of a preventive war, and repeated the determination of his Government to do everything in their power to assist in finding a peaceful issue to our present anxieties.

I am, &c.

HALIFAX

50. Hitler's directive for the destruction of Czechoslovakia, 20 May 1938

From Documents on German Foreign Policy, 1918–1945, *series D, vol. II (London, HMSO, 1949), no. 221.*

TOP SECRET, MILITARY   BERLIN, May 30, 1938.
Supreme Commander of the *Wehrmacht*.
O.K.W. No. 42/38 Top Secret, Military. L I
ONLY TO BE HANDLED BY AN OFFICER
WRITTEN BY AN OFFICER

By order of the Supreme Commander of the *Wehrmacht*, part 2, section II of the directive on the combined preparations for war of the *Wehrmacht* of June 24, 1937 (Supreme Headquarters No. 55/37, Top Secret, Mil. L I a). (War on Two Fronts With Main Effort in the Southeast, Strategic Concentration 'Green') is to be replaced by the attached version. Its execution must be assured by October 1, 1938, at the latest.

Alterations to the other parts of the directive are to be expected during the next few weeks.

KEITEL
Chief of the Supreme Headquarters
of the Wehrmacht

To: C.-in-C. Army
  „ „ „ Navy
  „ „ „ Air Force
  O.K.W. Section L

Certified true copy,
ZEITZLER
Lieut. Colonel, General Staff

[Enclosure]

TOP SECRET, MILITARY   Copy of 4th version.
Appendix to: Supreme Commander of the *Wehrmacht* O.K.W. No. 42/38, Top Secret, Military, L I a, dated May 30, 1938.
ONLY TO BE HANDLED BY AN OFFICER
WRITTEN BY AN OFFICER

II. WAR ON TWO FRONTS WITH MAIN EFFORT IN SOUTHEAST
(STRATEGIC CONCENTRATION 'GREEN')

1) *Political Assumptions.*
  It is my unalterable decision to smash Czechoslovakia by military action

in the near future. It is the business of the political leadership to await or bring about the suitable moment from a political and military point of view.

An unavoidable development of events within Czechoslovakia, or other political events in Europe providing a suddenly favorable opportunity which may never recur, may cause me to take early action.

The proper choice and determined exploitation of a favorable moment is the surest guarantee of success. To this end preparations are to be made immediately.

2) *Political Possibilities for Commencing the Operation.*

The following are necessary prerequisites for the intended attack:

a) A convenient apparent excuse and, with it,

b) Adequate political justification,

c) Action not expected by the enemy which will find him in the least possible state of readiness.

Most favorable from a military as well as a political point of view would be lightning action as the result of an incident which would subject Germany to unbearable provocation, and which, in the eyes of at least a part of world opinion, affords the moral justification for military measures.

Moreover, any period of diplomatic tension prior to war must be terminated by sudden action on our part, unexpected in both timing and extent, before the enemy is so far advanced in his state of military readiness that he cannot be overtaken.

3) *Conclusions for the Preparation of Operation 'Green'.*

a) For the military operations it is essential to make the fullest use of the surprise element as the most important factor contributing to victory, by means of appropriate preparatory measures, already in peacetime, and an unexpected swiftness of action.

Thus it is essential to create a situation within the first two or three days which demonstrates to enemy states which wish to intervene the hopelessness of the Czech military position, and also provides an incentive to those states which have territorial claims upon Czechoslovakia to join in immediately against her. In this case the intervention of Hungary and Poland against Czechoslovakia can be expected, particularly if France, as a result of Italy's unequivocal attitude on our side, fears, or at least hesitates, to unleash a European war by intervening against Germany. In all probability attempts by Russia to give Czechoslovakia military support, particularly with her air force, are to be expected.

If concrete successes are not achieved in the first few days by land operations, a European crisis will certainly arise. Realization of this ought to give commanders of all ranks an incentive to resolute and bold action. . . .

4) *Tasks of the Wehrmacht.*

Wehrmacht preparations are to be carried out on the following principles:

a) The whole weight of all forces must be employed against Czechoslovakia.

b) In the West, a minimum strength is to be provided as cover for our rear, as may become necessary; the other frontiers in the East against Poland and Lithuania are only to be held defensively; the southern frontier to remain under observation.

c) The army formations capable of rapid employment must force the frontier fortifications with speed and energy, and must break very boldly into Czechoslovakia in the certainty that the bulk of the mobile army will be brought up with all possible speed.

Preparations for this are to be made and timed in such a way that the army formations most capable of rapid movement cross the frontier at the appointed time *simultaneously* with the penetration by the *Luftwaffe*, before the enemy can become aware of our mobilization.

To this end a timetable is to be drawn up by the Army and *Luftwaffe* in conjunction with O.K.W. and submitted to me for approval.

51. Georges Bonnet tells Czechoslovakia that France will not fight, 20 July 1938

From Archives of the Ministry of Foreign Affairs, Paris. Bonnet's note of conversation of 20 July 1938 (he was foreign minister at the time).

I have had a talk with M. Osusky [Czechoslovak envoy to France]. It was a question of explaining clearly once again to M. Osusky the French position.

I read to him again the key passages of the British memorandum of 22 May 1938. The British government was not willing to support France in the Sudeten affair. . . . It considered moreover that the outcome of a conflict would be 'doubtful' at the present time.

The Czechoslovak government must fully understand our position: France will not go to war for the Sudeten affair. Certainly, publicly we will affirm our solidarity, as the Czechoslovak government desires, – but this affirmation of solidarity is to allow the Czechoslovak government to reach a peaceful and honourable solution. In no case must the Czechoslovak government think that if war breaks out we will be at her side, especially since in this matter our diplomatic isolation is almost total. . . .

I told him that, of course, if I had to speak publicly I would recall the bonds that united us to Czechoslovakia. But the Czechoslovak government had to be fully convinced that France, like England, would not go to war.

It is painful for me to have conversations of this kind with M. Osusky, with whom I am on friendly terms. But above all it is essential for things to be clear. . . .

52. France asks the Soviet Union what aid it can give to Czechoslovakia, 2 September 1938

From V. F. Klochko et al. (*eds*), New Documents on the History of Munich (*Prague, Orbis, 1958*), *no. 26.*

September 2, 1938

The French Chargé d'Affaires, Payart, on the instructions of Bonnet, today asked me officially what aid from the U.S.S.R. Czechoslovakia could count on, taking into consideration the difficulties raised by Poland and Rumania. I reminded Payart that France was under an obligation to assist Czechoslovakia irrespective of our help, while our help is conditional on that of France and for this reason we have a greater right to be interested in France's help. To this I added that with the proviso that France renders help we were determined to fulfil all our obligations under the Soviet–Czechoslovak Pact, using all available means to this end. Although Poland and Rumania are now putting obstacles in the way, their behaviour, especially that of Rumania, may be different if the League of Nations takes a decision on aggression. This is envisaged by the Soviet–Czechoslovak Pact. In any case, such a decision by the League would facilitate our actions. In view of the fact that the apparatus of the League of Nations can only be set in motion very slowly it would, in our opinion, be necessary now to take the necessary measures for which Article II of the League Covenant provides in the event of a threat of war. Payart expressed doubts as to the possibility of a unanimous decision and I said that even a decision of the majority would have a great moral effect, especially if Rumania herself were to come to agree with the majority.

As far as a definition of concrete help is concerned, we consider that for this it would be necessary to call a conference of representatives of the Soviet, French and Czechoslovak armies. It would be difficult to imagine the defence of Czechoslovakia by the three states without a preliminary discussion on practical measures by their military experts. We are prepared to participate in such a conference.

It is essential, however, to employ all means of preventing an armed conflict and for this reason, immediately after the Anschluss of Austria, we recommended that a conference of representatives of States interested in peace be called. We consider that at the present moment, such a conference with the participation of Britain, France and the U.S.S.R.

and the adoption of a common declaration that would no doubt receive the moral support of Roosevelt, would have greater chance of holding Hitler back from military adventures than any other measures. It is, however, essential to act promptly, before Hitler is finally involved.

Inform Krofta [Czechoslovak foreign minister] of the above.

M. Litvinov
[commissar for foreign affairs]

53. The American ambassador reports on the British government's handling of the dominions, 6 September 1938

From Foreign Relations of the United States: Diplomatic Papers 1938, vol. I (Washington, 1955), pp. 577–8. Telegram from the ambassador, Joseph P. Kennedy, to the state department.

LONDON, September 6, 1938 – 2 p.m.
[Received September 6 – 10:32 a.m.]
869. From a thoroughly reliable official source the following strictly confidential information has been obtained which may supplement information from other sources in the Department's hands. . . .

2. The British Dominions have been kept currently informed of the course of recent developments. The only Dominion that has thus far officially defined its attitude is Australia. In a long telegram received on Saturday it expressed disapproval of Beneš' [Czechoslovak president] machinations and in effect advised the British Government that if the Czechs did not satisfy the Sudeten Germans they should be told where to get off.

This will no doubt prove a useful lever in the hands of the British both internationally and in due course nationally vis-à-vis the opposition. It may be of interest to note how these things are worked here. For example the same source states that prior to Simon's [Sir John Simon, chancellor of the exchequer] Lanark speech the French Chargé d'Affaires was instructed to ask whether it would be possible for Simon to go beyond Chamberlain's May 24 [23] statement and likewise that Halifax's memorandum of his conversation showed that he told Cambon [French chargé d'affaires] that this would not be possible because of public opinion in this country and in certain of the Dominions. The telegraphic report of this conversation which was sent to the several Dominions omits the reference to public opinion in certain of the Dominions.

54. State department officials discuss the Czechoslovak crisis, 17 September 1938

From Nancy Harvison Hooker (ed.), The Moffat Papers: Selections from the Diplomatic Journals of Jay Pierrepont Moffat, 1919–1943 (Cambridge, Mass., Harvard University Press, 1956), pp. 205–6. Moffat was head of the Western European division in the state department.

Saturday, September 17, 1938.

. . . We then had a small conference, just six of us, the Secretary, Norman Davis, Messersmith, Berle, Jimmy Dunn, and myself, to talk over what should be done. One and all agreed that nothing could be done until we knew the extent of the sell-out which the British and presumably the French were about to approve. Our general impression was that despite the sell-out, Czechoslovakia would fight. We would be faced with a German–Czech war and wondered whether despite all their resolutions England and France could stay out. This was the period when, if any, a United States contribution might be made, but as to what such a contribution could be there were no clear-cut opinions. Berle views the present troubles as the birth pains of a new eastern empire, a German succession to the old, Austro–Hungarian Empire. Others see it merely as strengthening the domination of the Fascists over the democracies. Both British and French are trying their hardest to bring us into the picture now so that we share responsibility for the 'sell-out,' but on this score I believe their hopes are vain. . . .

55. Bonnet again warns Czechoslovakia not to rely on the French alliance, 19 September 1938

From Archives of the Ministry of Foreign Affairs, Paris.

After the meeting of the Cabinet I handed M. Osusky the Franco–British plan. I reminded him of our previous talks in June and in July. If I had continued, as the Czechoslovak government wanted, to affirm publicly our solidarity with Prague, Prague knew very well that it was not with a view to war – England and ourselves did not want to go to war – but in order to allow Prague to reach a peaceful settlement; he had been warned of that for a long time. I regretted that a solution had not been reached sooner. In any case the Franco–British plan represented for Czechoslovakia the least unpleasant solution at the present hour.

M. Osusky replied that he was going to telegraph the plan and our conversation to Prague. On leaving me he did not hide an emotion that I well understood.

56. Bonnet begs Daladier not to go to war for Czechoslovakia, 24 September 1938

From Archives Léon Blum (Fondation Nationale des Sciences Politiques, Paris), 3 BL Dr.10. Letter.

Paris, 24 September 1938

My dear President,

We have reached a decisive hour when each must speak their mind clearly. . . .

At no time in our diplomatic history since 1918 will France's position have been weaker if she declares war on Germany. . . .

In effect France . . . will have to sustain, alone, on land, the shock of the German and Italian armies combined, without counting Japan who, in the Far East, will doubtless attack French Indo-China.

On the first day you will have against France, Germany and Italy. You will have two frontiers to defend and perhaps three, with Spain.

On what help could France count?

She cannot count on Poland . . . now completely committed to Germany. . . .

She cannot count any more on . . . the *Petite Entente*. Neither Rumania nor Yugoslavia are willing to stand by us.

There remains the Soviet Union. Questioned by us, the Soviet government has said that it could only help Czechoslovakia if we ourselves begin to apply the pact. Moreover it . . . would consult the Council of the League of Nations and it would only be after a Council opinion recommending Rumania to allow the transit of aircraft that this assistance could be considered. . . .

The United States government has told us that it can give us neither a man nor a *sou*. And I warn you that the Neutrality Law will prevent us . . . from receiving the necessary armaments.

Great Britain's help, so important at sea, will however be almost non-existent on land during the first months. . . .

I do not think that France is in a state to commit herself voluntarily to such a difficult struggle. I think that France who did not fight for the demilitarised Rhineland zone, nor for German rearmament, nor for Austria . . . must wait . . . until she has rebuilt her strength, her alliances . . . her air force. On this point General Vuillemin's opinion is significant. . . .

The idea of a war freely entered into by us or even of general mobilisation leading to war has never been touched on in any discussion either with the British government or with the Czechoslovak government.

For five months, night and day, in the course of our affectionate collaboration, we have struggled for peace. I beg you to continue on this course.

It is the only one which can save the country.

Very affectionately,

Georges Bonnet

57. Halifax has second thoughts on Hitler's Godesberg proposals, 24–5 September 1938

From David Dilks (ed.), The Diaries of Sir Alexander Cadogan, 1938–1945 *(London, Cassell, 1971), pp. 103–5.*

Saturday, 24 September

Hitler's memo, now in. It's awful. A week ago when we moved (or were pushed) from 'autonomy' to cession, many of us found great difficulty in the idea of ceding people to Nazi Germany. We salved our consciences (at least I did) by stipulating it must be an 'orderly' cession – i.e. under international supervision, with safeguards for exchange of populations, compensation, &c. Now Hitler says he must march into the whole area *at once* (to keep order!) and the safeguards – and plebiscites! can be held *after!* This is throwing away every last safeguard that we had. P.M. is transmitting this 'proposal' to Prague. Thank God he hasn't yet recommended it for acceptance. He returned by lunch time. I dropped H. [foreign secretary] at the Palace at 10. He then went to meet P.M. and lunched with him, so I hardly saw H. in the morning. . . .

Meeting of 'Inner Cabinet' at 3.30 and P.M. made his report to us. I was completely horrified – he was quite calmly for total surrender. More horrified still to find that Hitler has evidently hypnotised him to a point. Still more horrified to find P.M. has hypnotised H. who capitulates totally. P.M. took nearly an hour to make his report, and there was practically no discussion. J.S. [Sir John Simon, chancellor of the exchequer] – seeing which way the cat was jumping – said that after all it was a question of 'modalities', whether the Germans went in now or later! Ye Gods! And during Thursday and Friday J.S. was as bellicose as the Duke of Plaza Toro. At times he almost went berserk. I gave H. a note of what I thought, but it had no effect. P.M. left at 5.10 to rest. I told J.S. and Sam Hoare [home secretary] what I thought: I think the latter shares my view, but he's a puny creature. Cabinet at 5.30 and H. got back at 8 completely and quite happily défaitiste-pacifist. He seemed to think the Cabinet were all right. I *wonder!* They don't yet understand and they haven't seen the map. (They're going round after dinner to have it explained to them by

Horace [Wilson, chief industrial adviser]!) Pray God there will be a revolt. Back to F.O. after dinner. H. got back from No. 10 talk with Labour about 10.30. Drove him home and gave him a bit of my mind, but didn't shake him. I've never before known him make up his mind so quickly and firmly on anything. I wish he hadn't chosen this occasion!

Sunday, 25 September
   Cabinet in morning, so I didn't go to F.O. till 11.30. Nothing doing. . . . Cabinet again at 3. . . . Monteiro [Portuguese ambassador in London] came in to say Franco had offered neutrality in European War. Even crumbs of good news are good! Cabinet up about 6. H. sent for me. He said 'Alec, I'm very angry with you. You gave me a sleepless night. I woke at 1 and never got to sleep again. But I came to the conclusion you were right, and at the Cabinet, when P.M. asked me to lead off, I plumped for refusal of Hitler's terms.' He *is* a frank and brave man. I apologised. He asked me whether I *knew* I was giving him an awful night. I said 'Yes' but had slept very well myself. Seems Cabinet anyhow wouldn't allow P.M. to make any further concessions (and I'm sure country wouldn't). We now have to look forward to frightful ordeal, but we face it with clean hands. I'm *relieved*. French arrived for discussion at 9 p.m. We agreed that we can't accept Hitler's proposals. J.S. was turned on in his best manner, to cross-examine French as to what they would *do*. Awful. But French kept their tempers and they agreed to send for Gamelin. Cabinet about 11.30. Short meeting with French again. Home about 1.30. Record of 3 Cabinets in one day!

58. A British Foreign Office official on the need to avoid Anglo–French recriminations, 28 September 1938

From Foreign Office Papers (Public Record Office, London), FO 371/21592. 11450/13/17. Memorandum.

On the assumption that the conference at Munich succeeds in reaching agreement on the disputed points and the crisis comes to an end there is sure to be a considerable tendency to recrimination between certain quarters in France and in this country. The French Government probably possess a certain amount of evidence of what will be described as a defeatist attitude on the part of certain important sections of British public opinion, and we certainly here in the Foreign Office have sufficient evidence to make the position of certain members of the French Government extremely unpleasant. Any washing of dirty Anglo–French linen in public in the near future would of course be very gratifying to the

German Government and might do us a very great deal of harm in the U.S.A.

In these circumstances might it not be worth while trying to conclude some kind of self-defending ordinance with the French designed to let bygones be bygones so far as this kind of evidence is concerned? It might perhaps be best if a member of H.M.G. spoke to a member of the French Government on the subject.

P. Nichols
28th September 1938

59. Pierre Comert's assessment of Bonnet's Munich diplomacy, 2 October 1938

From 'Lettres d'il y a trente ans', Politique aujourd'hui (Paris, January 1969), pp. 109–13. Letter of 2 October 1938. Comert was head of the press department of the French foreign ministry, 1935–8.

. . . To understand the attitude of Georges Bonnet during the crisis it must always be borne in mind that he was resolved not to allow war because war would have meant the disappearance of the privileged class. Perhaps this conviction came spontaneously to him. Perhaps his friends from the banking world inspired it. . . .

During the first period of the crisis G.B. adopted an attitude which, outwardly, was rather firm. . . . However in his private talks with the German and British ambassadors he did not conceal his softness. . . .

The calculation which inspired G.B.'s attitude was the following: England will certainly remain neutral; France, at the last moment, will shelter behind English neutrality; there is therefore no harm in declaring in public that we will maintain our obligations; but it would be dangerous to maintain this firmness in conversations with the British ambassador since that might perhaps dissuade him from his inclination towards neutrality. . . .

On Sunday 11 September came the English communiqué announcing that Great Britain could not 'remain aloof from a war which menaced the integrity of France'. [See *Documents on British Foreign Policy, 1919–1939*, ed. E. L. Woodward and Rohan Butler, 3rd series, vol. II (London, HMSO, 1949), app. III, pp. 680–2.]

This was the collapse of all the calculations built up by G.B. England would go to war.

Thenceforward a desperate struggle, resorting to all methods, . . . was organised in certain Parisian circles. G.B. was at the head of the movement. . . .

G.B. was then in Geneva. He learnt in the evening that the press office of the Quai d'Orsay had given journalists an interpretation of the communiqué representing it as an English engagement in the event of war in central Europe. He telephoned M. Jules Henry, [*chef de cabinet* to the foreign minister] explaining that it was necessary to tell the press that the word 'integrity' signified that England would only act if the Germans threatened French territory. . . . Jules Henry telephoned in this sense at 11 p.m. Louis Levy of the *Populaire.* . . .

However the crisis grew rapidly worse. The opposition to war became exasperated.

All M. Coulondre's telegrams announcing the certain participation of Russia were ignored. No mention of them was made to the press. Moreover G.B. went so far as to say in certain talks that the U.S.S.R. would remain neutral. All right wing circles spread the same rumour.

Then panic rumours began to circulate on the inferiority of France's defences, on the impossibility of attacking Germany. . . . A whole faction at the war ministry seconded this propaganda.

First it was the Siegfried line. It was impregnable. French regiments would be crushed in it. . . .

Then it was the air force. . . . On this point the campaign succeeded. M. Guy la Chambre [air minister] announced that Germany's monthly production of aircraft was two thousand against 45 on the French side. . . .

On the political front much play was made of the thesis of the absurdity of the Treaty of Versailles, the legitimate grievances of the Sudetens etc. . . .

On the other hand, certain Parisian circles informed Berlin very accurately on the results of this campaign. . . .

The French press, largely nourished by G.B. (the secret funds are exhausted) orchestrated each day its different themes.

The article of Stéphane Lauzanne [editor of *Le Matin*] on the plebiscite was written at G.B.'s request. Guimier [editor of *Petit Parisien*] has said that Flandin's article on mobilisation was approved by G.B. . . .

On the 26 September Hitler delivered a speech. . . .

The same evening the Foreign Office press department gave journalists . . . the famous note declaring that if France came to the aid of Czechoslovakia, Great Britain and Russia would be certainly at her side. . . . [See *Documents on British Foreign Policy*, op. cit., no. 1111, n. 1.]

Immediately it was rumoured that this communiqué was false . . . it was said to be a manoeuvre of the war faction in Paris. . . .

60. The Soviet response to Munich, 16 October 1938

From Ministry for Foreign Affairs of the USSR, Soviet Peace Efforts on the Eve of World War II (September 1938–August 1939): Documents and Records, *ed. V. M. Falin* et al., *part 1 (Moscow, 1973), no. 21.*

October 16, 1938

Coulondre [French ambassador in the Soviet Union] had evidently come to pay a farewell visit. He informed me with sadness of his forthcoming departure, expressed regret on this score and emphasized that he had come here intending to promote better relations but had to admit that after two years in Moscow he had not succeeded in this. He remained, however, an advocate of improvement and clarification of those relations. Coulondre expressed regret over the recent events. I told him that at Geneva the English, including even members of the Cabinet, had complained that, in resisting Chamberlain's policy and his plans, they had been disappointed in their hopes of obtaining the support of Daladier and Bonnet. It was my impression that this time Chamberlain did not have to drag the French Ministers after him, but that the latter had themselves been pushing Chamberlain towards the abyss into which they fell. I said that in the light of the recent events it became easier to explain the strange phenomenon that the French, having concluded with us a Pact of Mutual Assistance, had systematically evaded discussing military matters concerning methods of carrying out that assistance. They had evaded this even when Czechoslovakia was in need of that assistance. It now had to be concluded that the French Government had never intended to render the assistance envisaged by the pacts and that therefore it had seen no need to go into a detailed discussion about methods.

Coulondre replied that my assumption was too categoric and that the English had done their utmost to discourage the French from reaching a military agreement with us.

To Coulondre's question as to what could be done now, I replied that the important positions that had been lost could not be recovered or compensated for. We regarded what had happened as a disaster for the whole world. Only two things now could happen: either England and France continued to meet all of Hitler's demands with the result that the latter would gain domination over the whole of Europe, and over the colonies, after which he would calm down for some time so as to digest what he had swallowed, or else England and France realized the danger and began seeking ways to counter Hitler's further drive. In the latter case they would inevitably turn to us and speak with us in a different language. In the first case only three great powers would remain in Europe: England, Germany and the Soviet Union. Germany would, most likely, want to destroy the British Empire and become its heir. Less likely was an attack upon us, which would be more of a risk for Hitler.

Coulondre believed that the present French Ambassador to China, Naggiar, would be his successor in Moscow. Coulondre felt that he would probably have to leave some time next week and asked whether I would accept an invitation for dinner. I replied that, as he knew, I never attended any dinners and was ready to come and lunch with him, but that I would like first to arrange a farewell luncheon for him. We agreed that he would lunch with me on the 23rd and I with him on the 25th.

Litvinov

61. Chamberlain's continuing confidence in appeasement, 31 October 1938

From Cabinet Papers (Public Record Office, London), CAB 23/96.

3   *THE PRIME MINISTER* said that he would speak next day when the House re-assembled and he would have to deal with foreign policy, both generally and in relation to our rearmament programme.

Our Foreign policy was one of appeasement: We must aim at establishing relations with the Dictator Powers which will lead to a settlement in Europe and to a sense of stability.

There had been a good deal of talk in the country and in the Press about the need for rearmament by this country. In Germany and Italy it was suspected that this rearmament was directed against them, and it was important that we should not encourage these suspicions.

The Prime Minister said that he proposed to make it clear that our rearmament was directed to securing our own safety and not for purposes of aggression against other countries.

A good deal of false emphasis had been placed on rearmament, as though one result of the Munich Agreement had been that it would be necessary for us to add to our rearmament programmes. Acceleration of existing programmes was one thing, but increases in the scope of our programme which would lead to a new arms race was a different proposition.

The Prime Minister hoped that it might be possible to take active steps and to follow up the Munich Agreement by other measures, aimed at securing better relations. The putting into effect of the Anglo–Italian Agreement would be one step in this direction. He also hoped that some day we should be able to secure a measure of limitation of armaments, but it was too soon to say when this would prove possible. An improvement in confidence was first necessary. He proposed, therefore to make a reassuring statement on the morrow.

THE SECRETARY OF STATE FOR AIR referred in this connection to proposals which he had recently submitted in regard to the air programme. He thought that in presenting the decision to be reached on these proposals, it would be necessary to emphasise their defensive aspect. At the present time we were seriously deficient as compared with Germany. Indeed, our weakness might be said to be likely to provoke aggression by others.

THE SECRETARY OF STATE FOR FOREIGN AFFAIRS thought it was necessary to balance two factors in foreign policy. First, that our diplomacy was dependent upon our strength, and secondly that at the present time the Dictators were in a jumpy frame of mind. The Secretary of State referred to a conversation which had taken place between M. François Poncet, the French Ambassador in Berlin, and Herr Hitler. The account of this conversation which he (the Secretary of State) had received from Sir Eric Phipps, had been encouraging. The American Ambassador, however, had reported that Herr Hitler was obviously suspicious of our attitude, and had said that if Britain were getting ready to fight, this might have some adverse reaction on the Naval Agreement. He was trying to find out whether in fact this last remark had been made.

62. Hitler's secret speech to the German press, 10 November 1938

From Vierteljahrshefte für Zeitgeschichte, *vol. VI (October 1958), pp. 175ff.*

The achievements of this year 1938 were admittedly first of all due to the immense efforts of national socialism to educate the German people. These efforts are now gradually beginning to show results. . . .

There were a great number of measures which were taken this spring; they were all bound to take effect at a certain time. . . . The huge fortifications in the west came first on this list. That we took advantage of the prevailing circumstances was, finally, perhaps the most decisive factor to bring about these achievements. The world situation in general appeared to me more than ever favourable to asserting our demands. All this should, however, not make us forget what was no less decisive, namely our propaganda and . . . not only the propaganda at home (aimed at our own people) but also that abroad (aimed at foreign countries). The German people adopted on this occasion . . . an attitude entirely different from that of many other people and, indeed, also different from that adopted only recently by our people; this is I dare say, only the result of our continuous propagandist activities. . . .

Our first aim is to prepare the German people. It has been the pressure of circumstances that has made me talk of peace for decades on end. For only by repeatedly emphasizing the German wish for peace and its peaceful intentions could I hope gradually to secure freedom for the German people and to provide it with the right kind of armament which has always been the indispensable prerequisite for any further move. Such a peace propaganda lasting over a decade has necessarily also its questionable side effects. For many people may thereby easily be led to think that the existing regime is actually identical with the resolution and the wish to preserve peace at any cost. . . .

It was furthermore necessary to influence, through the press and other means of propaganda, the enemy we had to deal with first, namely Czechoslovakia. . . .

I have frequently been asked: 'Do you think this right? For months now shooting has been going on continuously day and night . . . along the Czech border. Czech bunkers are being shelled incessantly . . . you are, indeed, drawing everybody's attention to it.' I was convinced that through this I might slowly but surely wreck the nerves of those gentlemen in Prague; and to this end the press, too, had to contribute its share. It had to help slowly to destroy the nerves of these people and their nerves did, indeed, not stand up to it. At the moment of ultimate and decisive pressure the nerves of the others cracked and collapsed without our having finally to take to arms. . . .

63. Franco–German conversations, Paris, 6 December 1938

From Archives of the Ministry of Foreign Affairs, Paris. Memorandum. 'Entretiens de M Georges Bonnet et de M von Ribbentrop en présence de M Léger et du Comte Welczeck' (respectively French foreign minister, German foreign minister, secretary general of the Quai d'Orsay, and German ambassador to France). This is not a full and formal record of the conversation but a summary which M. Léger dictated immediately afterwards.

FRANCO–GERMAN RELATIONS

M Georges Bonnet reviewed the different aspects of Franco–German relations, notably those concerning commercial, press and tourist exchanges.

M von Ribbentrop replied that he wanted to bring about better psychological relations . . . the problem, however, was not as easy to resolve as was believed. On the German side, efforts had been made to foster the visits of ex-servicemen and youth contacts; although the results did not correspond to the efforts, the German authorities remained open to new initiatives. . . .

ITALY

M Georges Bonnet spoke of Franco–Italian relations which he wished to see harmonised within the framework of the improved general relations between the Powers.

M von Ribbentrop replied by confirming the perfect solidarity which united Germany and Italy, a solidarity which corresponded to Franco–British political action. Nothing, however, in the existence of these two groupings, in his opinion, prevented a harmonisation of the relations of the four Powers. . . .

As regards the recent anti-French demonstration in the Italian Chamber of Deputies, M von Ribbentrop affected not to have closely studied the question, which he claimed had not particularly attracted the attention of the German government. . . .

M Georges Bonnet replied that the Italian government had made no attempt to correct the impression created by the demonstration which had been public and that it had not even expressed its disapproval.

SPAIN

Concerning Spain, *M Georges Bonnet* explained how French policy was motivated solely by the desire to see Spain in the hands of the Spaniards.

M von Ribbentrop declared that it was the struggle against Bolshevism which had led Germany to play an active role in Spain. . . . It went without saying that he wanted the victory of General Franco. Moreover, he did not believe in the possibility of a truce. . . .

M Georges Bonnet replied that the French government was not complaisant towards Bolshevism, it was hostile to any seed of disorder, even in Spain. It remained faithful to the formula of Spain for the Spaniards and would have no objection to the victory of General Franco, or of anyone else, provided that this victory was not the result of foreign aid.

USSR

M von Ribbentrop raised the question of Franco–Russian relations. French policy towards the USSR seemed to him an illustration and a survival of the Versailles policy aimed at the encirclement of Germany.

M Léger remarked to the German minister that he was forgetting the genesis of the Franco–Soviet Pact which had its origin in a plan which was in no way bilateral. The conception of the accord was that of a general entente with which Germany and other Powers would be associated. The

Franco–Russian Pact was definitely only a foundation stone and it was not France's fault, or that of the USSR, that it had remained isolated.

M von Ribbentrop replied that in fact the Franco–Russian Pact had none the less fulfilled the role of a scheme tending towards the encirclement of Germany. . . .

CZECHOSLOVAKIA

As regards Czechoslovakia, *M von Ribbentrop* reproached French policy with the same goal of encirclement as the Franco–Russian accords implied. Germany had found herself face to face with the danger that Pierre Cot [former air minister and leading French socialist] had encapsulated in the phrase 'aircraft carrier'.

M Georges Bonnet having raised the question of the new guarantee promised to Czechoslovakia, *M von Ribbentrop* replied in a very ambiguous manner that he would examine this very question on his return to Berlin. The German minister gave it to be understood that he in no way intended to help bring about the realisation of this guarantee, for in general terms the idea of a guarantee had many disadvantages. If the Czechoslovak government contemplated returning to a Beneš-like policy, a very serious situation would be created.

M Léger stressed the contradictory features in such an outlook since the collective guarantee necessarily required neutrality. The giving of this guarantee, therefore, could not encourage an active Czechoslovak policy against any state.

M von Ribbentrop did not directly dispute this observation, but insisted on the need to allow the development of the natural friendship which now showed itself in Czechoslovakia towards Germany.

Following a further comment from M Georges Bonnet, M von Ribbentrop said without conviction that he would examine the matter on his return.

COLONIES

M von Ribbentrop raised the colonial question by asking for the views of the French government on this subject.

M Georges Bonnet referred to the governmental declarations in France on the colonial question which did not allow the matter to be discussed.

The Jewish question was not mentioned in the conversation.

Appearing to allude to central Europe, M von Ribbentrop pointed out that it was not understood in Berlin why certain Powers wished to meddle in Germany's own interests in Europe. He had already said so in London, but that had not prevented Lord Runciman [British mediator in Czechoslovakia in August 1938] from busying himself in Czechoslovakia with questions that did not concern him. . . .

64. Wladimir d'Ormesson on France's post-Munich policy, 27 December 1938

From Archives of the Ministry of Foreign Affairs, Paris. Letter of 27 December 1938 from d'Ormesson, editor of Figaro, *to Lord Winterton, chancellor of the Duchy of Lancaster.*

. . . I was absolutely opposed to going to war. . . . I criticised, and I still criticise the manner in which the whole operation was conducted in diplomatic terms. . . .

I would add that at the present time and given the *faits accomplis* and the general circumstances, I believe it would be senseless to oppose German expansion in the east. I even believe that this expansion is rather desirable. I also think that it does not involve a major disadvantage for the future of the European balance of power, for Germany . . . loses her strength – like Antaeus – once she is with others. . . . But there is no concealing the fact that this policy which has been forced on us by events upsets the European situation and drives us back upon ourselves. It makes us no more than a strictly Western and colonial power. This evolution can certainly be defended. On one clear condition however, namely that on this ground, at least, we must be absolutely firm and our position must not be battered down. . . .

What is certain is that we French can retreat no further, we have reached the extreme limit beyond which the least hesitation, the least weakness would entail disasters. . . .

65. Britain informs the United States of the possibility of a sudden German attack in the west, 24 January 1939

From Documents on British Foreign Policy, 1919–1939, *ed. E. L. Woodward and Rohan Butler, 3rd series, vol. IV (London, HMSO, 1951), no. 5.*

FOREIGN OFFICE, *January 24, 1939, 10.0 p.m.*
Please communicate following to the State Department for the personal and secret information of the President.

2. I have received a large number of reports from various reliable sources which throw a most disquieting light on Hitler's mood and intentions. According to these reports Hitler is bitterly resentful at the Munich Agreement which baulked him of a localised war against Czecho-

Slovakia and demonstrated the will to peace of the German masses in opposition to the war-mongering of the Nazi Party. He feels personally humiliated by this demonstration. He regards Great Britain as primarily responsible for this humiliation and his rage is therefore directed principally against this country which he holds to be the chief obstacle now to the fulfilment of his further ambitions.

3. As early as November there were indications which gradually became more definite that Hitler was planning a further foreign adventure for the spring of 1939. At first it appeared – and this was confirmed by persons in Hitler's entourage – that he was thinking of expansion in the East and in December the prospect of establishing an independent Ukraine under German vassalage was freely spoken of in Germany.

4. Since then reports indicate that Hitler, encouraged by Ribbentrop, Himmler and others, is considering an attack on the Western Powers as a preliminary to subsequent action in the East. Some of these reports emanate from highly placed Germans of undoubted sincerity who are anxious to prevent this crime; others come from foreigners, hitherto Germanophil, who are in close touch with leading German personalities. They have received some confirmation in the reassurance which Hitler appears to have given to M. Beck [Polish foreign minister] concerning his plans in the East, as well as in the support which Germany has recently given to Italy's claims against France.

5. There is as yet no reason to suppose that Hitler has made up his mind on any particular plan. Our reports show that he may:

(i) Push Italy to advance her claims by force and use his obligations to Italy as a pretext for embarking on war. This course would have the advantage of ensuring the participation of Italy from the outset.

(ii) Begin by launching an attack on Holland. The President will have noticed the recent deterioration of German–Dutch relations and the critical tone adopted towards Holland by the German press. Once in command of Holland and the Dutch coast, Germany would aspire to dictate terms to us and paralyse France. She might at the same time bribe Poland and perhaps other countries with promises of colonial loot; in that event the Dutch East Indies might be allocated to Japan.

(iii) Put forward impossible colonial demands in his speech of January 30 in the form of an ultimatum. This seems the least likely hypothesis.

(iv) Make a sudden air attack without pretext on England and follow up this initial surprise by land and sea operations against the Western Powers. We have received definite information from a highly placed German that preparations for such a coup are now being made. He has, however, no information to show that Hitler has yet made up his mind to execute this plan. . . .

11. In the next few days His Majesty's Government will be considering carefully what further steps they might take to avert or to meet a situation such as they have cause to apprehend, and I will of course keep the President informed of any decision taken.

12. In view of the relations of confidence which exist between our two Governments and the degree to which we have exchanged information hitherto, His Majesty's Government feel bound to state frankly their apprehensions as to the future and to indicate what measures they feel able to take. It would of course be a great help to them if the President had any further suggestions to make.

13. It is impossible as yet for the Prime Minister to decide whether he will himself utter any public warning to Germany before Hitler makes his speech on January 30. The Prime Minister is due to speak at Birmingham on January 28, and, if possible, I would let the President know beforehand what line the Prime Minister would propose to take. If the President were disposed to take an occasion for any public announcement, it might be the more valuable if he were to do so before January 30.

66. Robert Coulondre's optimism on Franco–German relations, 25 January 1939

From Georges Bonnet, Dans la Tourmente, 1938–1948 (Paris, Fayard, 1971), pp. 91–2. Coulondre was French ambassador in Berlin, November 1938–September 1939.

25 January 1939

Dear Minister,

One of the Führer's familiars told me recently that the latter would reaffirm in his speech of 30 January Germany's solidarity towards Italian policy. He added that M. Hitler 'could not do otherwise, but this did not imply formal support for Italian claims against France'. . . . But I am hopeful that your declarations might have the effect of attenuating the expression of this solidarity, of avoiding too firm a position towards Franco–Italian differences, on the one hand by reaffirming our absolute will to resist any compromise on our vital interests, on the other by stressing the happy results that the 6 December accord [Franco–German Declaration of 6 December 1938] has already had for the harmonious development of relations between the two countries. . . .

In any case all the indications that I receive here are rather reassuring as to the 'real' position of the Führer who would like to exercise a moderating influence on M. Mussolini. Also it seems to me essential that a big effort is made in Paris on the French press in order that it does not react too disagreeably against the speech of 30 January. . . .

In a general way dispositions here are good and, apart from Radio-Strasbourg, the tone of our press is approved. The spirit of the 6 December is still living. Let us keep it alive.

67. Daladier's opinions on Britain, Germany and Italy, 6 February 1939

From Orville H. Bullitt (ed.), For the President: Personal and Secret: Correspondence between Franklin D. Roosevelt and William C. Bullitt *(London, Andre Deutsch, 1973), pp. 308–10.*

. . . Daladier lunched with me alone today and we discussed a number of subjects.

. . . after a certain delay Mussolini would make demands which would be totally inacceptable. Indeed so far as France was concerned the answer to any demand whatsoever on the part of Italy would be, 'There is nothing to discuss.' He had every reason to believe that Germany did not desire to go to war with France in support of Italy. Goering not only during their personal conversations at Munich but lately had been communicating with him in a rather surprising manner. Goering had said to him personally and had followed it up: 'Why should France continue to tie herself to a decayed old nation like England – a rouged old maid trying to pretend that she is still young and vigorous and capable of being a satisfactory partner to anyone.' Goering had then proposed that France should join Germany in finishing off England and that the British Empire should be divided between France and Germany.

Daladier said he had replied that this sounded very pleasant but the moment the British Empire was finished France would be the next morsel for Germany and that France could not be detached from England by any such proposal. He said that Goering had continued to talk about the folly of hostilities between France and Germany. Daladier concluded his remarks about Goering by saying that Goering had all the qualities and defects of a Nero but that at the moment he seemed genuinely friendly to France because he knew that the French army was the only real force on the continent of Europe today opposed to Germany. Daladier finally said that he thought he might invite Goering soon to make a visit to Paris.

Daladier said that he had been unable to get any exact information as to what had happened while Chamberlain was in Rome. He had only Bonnet's reports on the subject and he could not trust Bonnet too.

Daladier was of the opinion that Chamberlain in Rome had promised the Italians that he would use his good offices to obtain concessions from France to Italy. He said that the British had denied emphatically that this was the case but that he did not believe the British. He said that he anticipated that if Italy should make demands and France should refuse them, the British would suggest to the Germans that they and the Germans should intervene and settle the matter by a compromise. Daladier said that he fully expected to be betrayed by the British and added that this was the customary fate of allies of the British.

Daladier went on to say that he considered Chamberlain a desiccated stick; the King a moron; and the Queen an excessively ambitious woman who would be ready to sacrifice every other country in the world in order that she might remain Queen Elizabeth of England. He added that he considered Eden a young idiot and did not know for discussion one single Englishman for whose intellectual equipment and character he had respect. He felt that England had become so feeble and senile that the British would give away every possession of their friends rather than stand up to Germany and Italy.

68. Maxim Litvinov distrusts Britain and France, 19 February 1939

From Ministry for Foreign Affairs of the USSR, Soviet Peace Efforts on˗ the Eve of World War II (September 1938–August 1939): Documents and Records, *ed. V. M. Falin et al., part 1 (Moscow, 1973), no. 128. Letter from Litvinov, commissar for foreign affairs, to the Soviet ambassador in London.*

February 19, 1939

. . . Your letter has not convinced me that Hitler and Mussolini may confront Chamberlain with the unavoidability of war already this year. I believe that both Chamberlain and, still more so, the French have decided to avoid war, at least in the coming years, at all costs, and I would even say at any price. It is incorrect to think that the resources of concessions have run out or are running out. Bonnet is himself prepared to go very far towards meeting the Italian demands. François-Poncet has confirmed to our Chargé d'Affaires the fact of Baudouin's talks with the Italians. Concessions in respect of French Somaliland, a free harbour in Jibuti, the railway and the Suez Canal have already been offered by him. With pressure from Chamberlain the concessions could be considerably broadened. As for the German appetites, not to mention the English purse which is ready to open up for Hitler at any minute, there are still the Portuguese, the Dutch, and finally the French colonies whose cession is quite acceptable to Chamberlain. England is likely to cede some of her own possessions if she can convince people that she will thus buy herself out of a war.

So far Hitler has been pretending not to understand the Anglo–French hints about freedom of action in the East, but he may understand them if, in addition to the hints, something else should be offered to him by England and France at their own expense or else if he is promised, in the event of a conflict in the East, not only neutrality or even sympathetic neutrality, but also some active assistance, which I on no account consider to be ruled out. The Polish and Carpatho–Ruthenian direction seems to be closed, for Poland is still dreaming of having her own sphere of influence in the Ukraine. She will, however, be prepared, if necessary, to sacrifice her dreams and to acquiesce in a campaign by Hitler through Rumania. One cannot count too much on resistance by Carol [King of Romania]. Neither would Poland object to a campaign by Hitler through the Baltics and Finland, so that she herself could take action against the Ukraine, synchronizing all this with the policy of Japan.

As you see, Chamberlain still has a fairly vast scope for manoeuvres. But perhaps you fear that Hitler and Mussolini may go too far and present the West with demands which it will be impossible to meet. Let me remind you, however, that both Hitler and Mussolini have enough friends in England and all sorts of reliable sources through which they can be sufficiently well notified in advance about the limits of concessions. During the Czechoslovak episode Hitler advanced his maximal demands, gradually raising them as he obtained information about their acceptability for Chamberlain. At that time he was absolutely sure of his aim and ran almost no risk. The same thing will happen now. Both Mussolini and Hitler, who do not at all relish the prospect of war, will go no further in their demands than the line beyond which, according to the reliable information they have, even Chamberlain's and Bonnet's tractability can come to an end. Of course, I am making no claims that my prognosis is absolutely correct. Any surprises are possible but they must be reduced to a minimum. . . .

Litvinov

69. Stalin's report to the Eighteenth Congress of the Communist Party of the Soviet Union, 10 March 1939

From Soviet Documents on Foreign Policy, *trans. and ed. by Jane Degras, vol. III (Oxford, Royal Institute of International Affairs, 1953), pp. 315–22.*

. . . After the first imperialist war the victor states, primarily Britain, France and the United States, had set up a new régime in the relations between countries, the post-war régime of peace. The main props of this régime were the Nine-Power Pact in the Far East, and the Versailles Treaty and a number of other treaties in Europe. The League of Nations was set up to regulate relations between countries within the framework of this régime; on the basis of a united front of states, of collective defence of the security of states. However, three aggressive states, and the new imperialist war launched by them, have upset the entire system of this post-war peace régime. Japan tore up the Nine-Power Pact, and Germany and Italy the Versailles Treaty. In order to have their hands free, these three states withdrew from the League of Nations.

The new imperialist war became a fact. . . .

It is a distinguishing feature of the new imperialist war that it has not yet become universal, a world war. The war is being waged by aggressor states, who in every way infringe upon the interests of the non-aggressive states, primarily England, France and the United States, while the latter draw back and retreat, making concession after concession to the aggressors.

Thus we are witnessing an open redivision of the world and spheres of influence at the expense of the non-aggressive states, without the least attempt at resistance, and even with a certain amount of connivance, on the part of the latter. . . . The majority of the non-aggressive countries, particularly England and France, have rejected the policy of collective security, the policy of collective resistance to the aggressors, and have taken up a position of non-intervention, a position of 'neutrality'. . . .

Pacifism and disarmament schemes are dead and buried. Feverish arming has taken their place. Everybody is arming, small states and big states, including primarily those which practise the policy of non-intervention. Nobody believes any longer in the unctuous speeches which claim that the Munich concessions to the aggressors and the Munich agreement opened a new era of 'appeasement'. . . . Naturally, the U.S.S.R. could not ignore these ominous events. . . . At the end of 1934 our country joined the League of Nations, considering that despite its weakness the

League might nevertheless serve as a place where aggressors can be exposed, and as a certain instrument of peace, however feeble, that might hinder the outbreak of war. The Soviet Union considers that in alarming times like these even so weak an international organization as the League of Nations should not be ignored. In May 1935 a treaty of mutual assistance against possible attack by aggressors was signed between France and the Soviet Union.

A similar treaty was simultaneously concluded with Czechoslovakia. In March 1936 the Soviet Union concluded a treaty of mutual assistance with the Mongolian People's Republic. In August 1937 the Soviet Union concluded a pact of non-aggression with the Chinese Republic.

It was in such difficult international conditions that the Soviet Union pursued its foreign policy of upholding the cause of peace.

The foreign policy of the Soviet Union is clear and explicit.

1 We stand for peace and the strengthening of business relations with all countries. That is our position; and we shall adhere to this position so long as these countries maintain like relations with the Soviet Union, and so long as they make no attempt to trespass on the interests of our country.

2 We stand for peaceful, close and friendly relations with all the neighbouring countries which have common frontiers with the U.S.S.R. That is our position; and we shall adhere to this position so long as these countries maintain like relations with the Soviet Union, and so long as they make no attempt to trespass directly or indirectly, on the integrity and inviolability of the frontiers of the Soviet state.

3 We stand for the support of nations which are the victims of aggression and are fighting for the independence of their country.

4 We are not afraid of the threats of aggressors, and are ready to deal two blows for every blow delivered by instigators of war who attempt to violate the Soviet borders.

Such is the foreign policy of the Soviet Union.

In its foreign policy the Soviet Union relies upon:

1 Its growing economic, political and cultural might;
2 The moral and political unity of our Soviet society;
3 The mutual friendship of the peoples of our country;
4 Its Red Army and Red Navy;
5 Its policy of peace;
6 The moral support of the working people of all countries, who are vitally concerned in the preservation of peace;
7 The good sense of the countries which for one reason or another have no interest in the violation of peace.

The tasks of the Party in the sphere of foreign policy are:

1 To continue the policy of peace and of strengthening business relations with all countries;
2 To be cautious and not allow our country to be drawn into conflicts by warmongers who are accustomed to have others pull the chestnuts out of the fire for them;
3 To strengthen the might of our Red Army and Red Navy to the utmost;
4 To strengthen the international bonds of friendship with the working people of all countries, who are interested in peace and friendship among nations.

70. Sir Alexander Cadogan on the German annexation of Bohemia and Moravia, 14–16 March 1939

From David Dilks (ed.), The Diaries of Sir Alexander Cadogan, 1938–1945 *(London, Cassell, 1971), pp. 156–7. Cadogan was permanent under secretary of state.*

Tuesday, 14 March
H. back from Sunderland. Told him of my talk with P.M. He inclined to agree that, in case of German 'direct action' O[livcr] S[tanley] shouldn't go to Berlin. All sorts of reports of what Germany is going to do – 'march in' tonight, &c. Probably true. Talk with H., Van, O. S[tanley], Malkin, Sargent [respectively: Halifax, foreign secretary; Sir Robert Vansittart, chief diplomatic adviser; Oliver Stanley, president of the board of trade; Sir Will Malkin, legal adviser to the Foreign Office; Sir Orme Sargent, deputy under secretary]. Nothing to be done to stop Germany. But O.S. shouldn't go. Van wants to withdraw Nevile [Sir Nevile Henderson, ambassador in Berlin]. I against – it's futile. But of course Van doesn't like N. in Berlin. . . . Corbin at 3.15 to pump me. French are thinking – he says – of an 'enquiry' of Berlin. I said there was nothing we could do to *stop* it. Question is one of saving our face. This can be done with least loss of prestige *after* the event, by registering disgust. Rob Hudson [secretary, Department of Overseas Trade] at 4.30 with all sorts of arguments (of course) in favour of O.S. and his going to Berlin. When he'd gone, and before – 2 minutes later – H. went to see P.M., I warned H. to accept Hudson's arguments with a grain of salt. . . . H. rang me up from House with instructions to draft telegrams to Berlin and Paris. The former quite useless – and P.M. realises it, but wants to be 'on the record'. Latter explaining our position about guarantee. 7.15 H. got back and I

and O.S. tried to persuade him that Rob H[udson] must be taken with a grain of salt. O. Stanley came about 7.30 and confirmed that R. Hudson had 'exaggerated'.

Wednesday, 15 March
   Rung up at 6.30 by Resident Clerk, who has been bothered by Miss Layton about refugees in Prague. She wants the Legation to take them all in. Folly! German troops going in at 6.30 this morning. Walked to office with H. We must have statement in both Houses this afternoon. Cabinet, during which I got to work on statement. Went over with it to No. 10 at 12.30, and discussed it with Horace [Sir Horace Wilson, chief industrial adviser], H. and P.M. till 2, when they went off to lunch. I had a sandwich and glass of cider in the Cabinet Room and got statement in order. H. made it at 3. P.M. had to make speech, as there was a debate. Said he would base himself on statement, and did so, but added that he would go on with his 'policy' (? 'appeasement'). Fatal!

Thursday, 16 March
   Picked up H. on way to office. Awful amount of work. Corbin [French ambassador in London] at 12.45 to say his Government wanted us to join in a 'protest'. Czech Chargé [d'affaires] to say German Embassy demanded delivery of his Legation. I said anyhow he and his staff could stay here. Awful day – like last Sept[ember]. . . . Talk with H. about his speech on Monday. Don't know *where* we are. We ought perhaps to take a stand (whatever that may mean) but after P.M.'s speech, can we? He speaking again at Birmingham tomorrow night. Think he's been binged up to be bit firmer.

71. Litvinov on Bonnet, 11 April 1939

From Ministry for Foreign Affairs of the USSR, Soviet Peace Efforts on the Eve of World War II (September 1938–August 1939): Documents and Records, *ed. V. M. Falin et al., part 1 (Moscow, 1973), no. 223.*

April 11, 1939
It appears to us that, like Halifax, Bonnet is talking to you from time to time about the political situation mainly in order to be able to reply to the Opposition that he is 'in contact and in consultation with the USSR.' Bonnet is no more inclined to assist Poland, Rumania or anyone else in Eastern Europe than he was inclined to help Czechoslovakia some time ago, and in talking with us he is also pursuing the aim of securing an opportunity to speak of our unwillingness to participate in assistance. It is therefore necessary to answer him in such a way that he would not be

able, as he was in September, to refer to our replies in justification of his own passivity and his capitulation position. It does not follow from this, however, that we are obliged to respond to his vague hints with any concrete proposals or by disclosing our position. Indeed, in their discussions with us after the episode of the joint declaration, the British and the French have not hinted at any kind of concrete proposal or any kind of treaty with us. If we analyse these discussions, it becomes clear that what they want is to get some kind of binding promise from us without entering into any agreement with us and without undertaking any commitments in respect to us. We are to undertake, before the whole world and more formally in respect of England and France, to assist Poland and Rumania at their first request and in whatever forms they should themselves indicate to us. But why should we undertake such unilateral commitments? We are told that it is in our interests to protect Poland and Rumania against Germany. But we shall always be aware of our own interests and will do whatever they require us to do. Why then should we commit ourselves in advance, without deriving any advantage from those commitments?

All the benefits of the latest Anglo–French fuss have so far gone only to Beck, who can now take stronger stand in negotiations with Hitler and strike a bargain at the expense of Lithuania and the Baltic area. What kind of a struggle with aggression is this, when the predatory appetites of both Germany (the winning back of the Corridor and Danzig) and Poland will be satisfied at one and the same time? What is more, having pledged herself to render assistance to Poland without any reservations, England has in fact concluded a treaty with Poland also against us. True, we do not intend to attack Poland, but nonetheless by strengthening Poland's positions vis-à-vis the USSR, the agreement with England cannot fail to be an inimical act.

Bonnet's statement about his readiness to sign a three-Power declaration with us and England but without Poland is devoid of significance. It is easy for Bonnet to make such generous statements, knowing that England will not accept this, and presuming that the declaration will be unacceptable for us either. . . .

As for the new problems that have arisen in connection with the occupation of Albania, the only thing we know is that contrary to newspaper reports, the British Government has as yet given Greece no guarantees. It has merely stated that it cannot take the attitude of an indifferent onlooker if Corfu and other Greek islands are occupied. According to another version, it has stated that it would consider such occupation to be a hostile act.

François-Poncet is conducting the same tactics from Rome as he had done previously from Berlin. Striving towards an early agreement with Italy, he is trying to intimidate the French Government in his dispatches, definitely overrating the Italian military preparations.

We have information from Turkish sources that Italy has suggested that France should give up her Syria mandate and withdraw so that Syria could then be attached to Italy. France has rejected this proposal. It would be interesting to find out how true this is.

Litvinov

72. Alexis Léger encourages Daladier to stand firm, 15 April 1939

From Archives Edouard Daladier (Fondation Nationale des Sciences Politiques, Paris), 2DA 4/Dr.5. Léger was secretary general of the French foreign ministry.

Paris, 15 April 1939

My dear President,
    Corbin [ambassador in London] wrote to me on the 13th: 'the firmness that the French government has shown in demanding the inclusion of Rumania in the new guarantees offered by the English has made an excellent impression in London circles which complained of seeing the initiative monopolised by Downing Street, generally too slow to understand and to decide. London has been accustomed for so long to see Paris follow the English watch-word that there was complete surprise to see us maintain our point of view in spite of English objections or scruples'.
    I seize this opportunity to let you see a brief note from our Consul in Leipzig on the growing signs of German disaffection towards the Hitler regime.

Your very affectionate and devoted
Alexis Léger

73. Hitler addresses his generals, 23 May 1939

From Documents on German Foreign Policy, 1918–1945, series D, vol. VI (London, HMSO, 1956), no. 433.

After six years the present position is as follows:
    With minor exceptions German national unification has been achieved. Further successes cannot be achieved without bloodshed.
    Poland will always be on the side of our adversaries. Despite the friendship agreement Poland has always intended to exploit every opportunity against us.
    Danzig is not the objective. It is a matter of expanding our living space

in the east, of making our food supplies secure, and of solving the problem of the Baltic states. To provide sufficient food you must have sparsely settled areas. This is fertile soil, whose surpluses will be very much increased by German, thorough management.

No other such possibility can be seen in Europe. . . .

The Polish regime will not resist pressure from Russia. Poland sees danger in a German victory over the West and will try and deprive us of our victory.

There is therefore no question of sparing Poland, and the decision remains *to attack Poland at the first suitable opportunity.*

We cannot expect a repetition of Czechoslovakia. There will be fighting. The task is to isolate Poland. Success in isolating her will be decisive. Therefore, the Führer must reserve to himself the final command to attack. There must be no simultaneous conflict with the West (France and England).

If it is not certain that a German–Polish conflict will not lead to war with the West, then the struggle will be directed in the first instance against England and France.

Basic principle: conflict with Poland, beginning with attack on Poland, will be successful only if the West keeps out. If that is impossible, then it is better to attack the West and finish off Poland at the same time.

It will be the task of dexterous diplomacy [*geschickte Politik*] to isolate Poland. . . .

74. Italy needs peace, 31 May 1939

From Documents on German Foreign Policy, 1918–1945, *series D, vol. VI* (*London, HMSO, 1956*), *no. 459 (enclosure).*

. . . I have entrusted General Cavallero with a confidential document drawn up by the Duce, which is of particular importance for the development of military and economic collaboration between our two countries. The Duce wishes this document to be handed to the Führer, and I would ask you to be kind enough to arrange for it to be transmitted to the exalted recipient. . . .

III

In a memorandum addressed to Herr von Ribbentrop at the time of the meeting in Milan I set out the reasons why Italy requires a period of preparation, which may extend until the end of 1942.

The reasons are as follows:

'The two European Axis Powers require a period of peace of not less than three years. Only from 1943 onwards will an effort by war have the greatest prospects of success.

Italy needs a period of peace for the following reasons:

(a) For the military organization of Libya and Albania, and also for the pacification of Ethiopia, from which latter region an army of half a million men must be formed.

(b) To complete the construction and reconditioning of the six battle-ships, which has already commenced.

(c) For the renewal of the whole of our medium and heavy calibre artillery.

(d) For the further development of plans for autarky, by which any attempt at a blockade by the satiated democracies must be thwarted.

(e) For carrying out the World Exhibition in 1942, which will not only document the twenty years' activity of the Fascist régime but could also bring in reserves of foreign exchange.

(f) For effecting the return home of Italians from France, which constitutes a very serious military and *moral* problem.

(g) For completing the transfer, already begun, of a large number of war industries from the plain of the Po to Southern Italy.

(h) For further intensifying relations not only between the Governments of the Axis Powers but also between both peoples. For this purpose, a *détente* in the relations between the Roman Catholic Church and National Socialism would doubtless be useful, and is also greatly desired by the Vatican.

For all these reasons, Fascist Italy does not wish to hasten a European war, although she is convinced of the inevitability of such a war. It may also be assumed that within three years Japan will have brought her war in China to a conclusion. . . .

75. Daladier refuses to make a new approach to Mussolini, 24 July 1939

From Documents on British Foreign Policy, 1919–1939, *ed. E. L. Woodward and Rohan Butler, 3rd series, vol. VI (London, HMSO, 1953), no. 428.*

PRÉSIDENCE DU CONSEIL, PARIS
24 July 1939

My dear Prime Minister,

I thank you for the friendly confidence that you have shown me in your letter of 13 July. You know the value that I place on these exchanges of personal views. . . .

I consider it also a constant duty for us not to neglect any opportunity

. . . of improving the dispositions of an opposing Power. Thus for a long time I have given thought to all that could be done to bring about a real improvement in relations between France and Italy.

From March on I was concerned to end the press campaign by which Italian opinion was led to believe that France had not replied to Italy's formal and concrete demands. In a broadcast of 29 March . . . I declared that France, still loyal for her part to the engagements signed in 1935, was equally ready to examine all new proposals. . . .

This public request for clarification, which went unanswered, has been renewed through French diplomatic channels.

On 26 April 1939 the French Ambassador in Rome, reminded the Italian Foreign Minister that France had always shown herself ready to examine reasonable suggestions and asked to be apprised of Italian proposals. He could not obtain . . . anything more than a new evocation of very general terms: free port at Djibouti, partial cession of the Franco–Ethiopian railway, admission to the Council of the Suez Canal Company, prolongation of the status of Italians in Tunisia. . . .

Such are the facts which I wanted to specify so as not to leave any doubt in your mind as to the real attitude shown by my government. . . . There was moreover the certain risk of creating a false impression in Italy as to the psychology of the French government, of troubling the good morale of opinion in France itself, and more particularly in the Islamic world of North Africa which, even before the annexation of Albania, had been profoundly shaken by Italian claims in the Mediterranean and in Africa.

I believe then that I have anticipated the suggestion that you wished to make to me. I am not sure though that I entirely share your impression that the Italian government has progressed along the path which we wished to see her take, and that the present moment would be the most opportune to push ahead with my exploratory enterprise. The result of my last sounding could . . . lead me to fear that any new initiative towards the government of Rome . . . might be interpreted by it as an entreaty indicating weakness. . . .

I add a final psychological consideration: if you believe, as I do, that Mussolini committed himself deeply to Axis policy as a result of an initial error on the moral strength of England and France and on their solidarity, you will perhaps share my conviction that the only new element which might truly change his orientation, would be the progressive and spontaneous correction of his own judgement on the determination and solidarity of the Franco–British bloc. In fact all the advances and concessions which could be made to him, by way of conciliation, will add nothing to the weight of his own conclusion, to wit the realistic appreciation of his own interest. . . .

76. A meeting of the military missions of Britain, France and the Soviet Union, Moscow, 14 August 1939

From Ministry for Foreign Affairs of the USSR, Soviet Peace Efforts on the Eve of World War II (September 1938–August 1939): Documents and Records, *ed. V. M. Falin* et al., *part 2 (Moscow, 1973), no. 415.*

Marshal Voroshilov [Soviet commissar for defence]: I want a clear answer to my very clear question concerning the joint action of the Armed Forces of Britain, France and the Soviet Union against the common enemy – the bloc of aggressors, or the main aggressor – should he attack. . . .

Do the French and British General Staffs think that the Soviet land forces will be admitted to Polish territory in order to make direct contact with the enemy in case Poland is attacked? And further:

Do you think that our Armed Forces will be allowed passage across Polish territory, across Galicia, to make contact with the enemy and to fight him in the south of Poland? Yet one more thing:

Is it proposed to allow Soviet troops across Rumanian territory if the aggressor attacks Rumania?

These are the three questions which interest us most. (Admiral Drax confers at length with General Doumenc.)

General Doumenc [head of French mission]: I agree with the Marshal that the concentration of Soviet troops must take place principally in the areas indicated by the Marshal, and the distribution of these troops will be made at your discretion. I think that the weak points of the Polish–Rumanian front are their flanks and point of junction. We shall speak of the left flank when we deal with the question of communications.

Marshal Voroshilov: I want you to reply to my direct question. I said nothing about Soviet troop concentrations. I asked whether the British and French General Staffs envisage passage of our troops towards East Prussia or other points to fight the common enemy.

General Doumenc: I think that Poland and Rumania will implore you, Marshal, to come to their assistance.

Marshal Voroshilov: And perhaps they will not. It is not evident so far. We have a Non-Aggression Pact with the Poles, while France and Poland have a Treaty of Mutual Assistance. This is the reason why the question I raised is not an idle one as far as we are concerned, since we are discussing the plan of joint action against the aggressor. To my mind, France and Britain should have a clear idea about the way we can extend real help or about our participation in the war. (There is a lengthy exchange of opinion between Admiral Drax and General Heywood.)

Admiral Drax [head of British mission]: If Poland and Rumania do not ask for Soviet help they will soon become German provinces, and then the U.S.S.R. will decide how to act. If, on the other hand, the U.S.S.R., France and Britain are in alliance, then the question of whether or not Rumania and Poland ask for help becomes quite clear.

Marshal Voroshilov: I repeat, gentlemen, that this question is a cardinal question for the Soviet Union.

Admiral Drax: I repeat my reply once again. If the U.S.S.R., France and Britain are allies, then in my personal opinion there can be little doubt that Poland and Rumania will ask for help. But that is my personal opinion, and to obtain a precise and satisfactory answer, it is necessary to approach Poland.

Marshal Voroshilov: I regret that the Military Missions of Great Britain and France have not considered this question and have not brought an exact answer.

77. The Obersalzberg speech, 22 August 1939

From Documents on British Foreign Policy, 1919–1939, *ed. E. L. Woodward and Rohan Butler, 3rd series, vol. VII (London, HMSO, 1954), no. 314. For the significance of this speech see H. W. Koch, 'Hitler and the origins of the Second World War: second thoughts on the status of some of the documents', in Esmonde M. Robertson (ed.),* The Origins of the Second World War: Historical Interpretations *(London, Macmillan, 1971), pp. 173–6.*

Decision to attack Poland was arrived at in spring. Originally there was fear that because of the political constellation we would have to strike at the same time against England, France, Russia and Poland. This risk too we should have had to take. Goering had demonstrated to us that his Four-Year Plan is a failure and that we are at the end of our strength, if we do not achieve victory in a coming war.

Since the autumn of 1938 and since I have realized that Japan will not go with us unconditionally and that Mussolini is endangered by that nitwit of a King and the treacherous scoundrel of a Crown Prince, I decided to go with Stalin. After all there are only three great statesmen in the world, Stalin, I and Mussolini. Mussolini is the weakest, for he has been able to break the power neither of the crown nor of the Church. Stalin and I are the only ones who visualize the future. So in a few weeks hence I shall stretch out my hand to Stalin at the common German–Russian frontier and with him undertake to redistribute the world.

Our strength lies in our quickness and in our brutality; Genghis Khan has sent millions of women and children into death knowingly and with a light heart. History sees in him only the great founder of States. As to what the weak western European civilization asserts about me, that is of no account. I have given the command and I shall shoot everyone who utters one word of criticism, for the goal to be obtained in the war is not that of reaching certain lines but of physically demolishing the opponent. And so for the present only in the east I have put my death-head formation in place with the command relentlessly and without compassion to send into death many women and children of Polish origin and language. Only thus we can gain the living space that we need. Who after all is today speaking about the destruction of the Armenians ?

Colonel-General von Brauchitsch [commander in chief of the German army] has promised me to bring the war against Poland to a close within a few weeks. Had he reported to me that he needs two years or even only one year, I should not have given the command to march and should have allied myself temporarily with England instead of Russia for we cannot conduct a long war. To be sure a new situation has arisen. I experienced those poor worms Daladier and Chamberlain in Munich. They will be too cowardly to attack. They won't go beyond a blockade. Against that we have our autarchy and the Russian raw materials.

Poland will be depopulated and settled with Germans. My pact with the Poles was merely conceived of as a gaining of time. As for the rest, gentlemen, the fate of Russia will be exactly the same as I am now going through with in the case of Poland. After Stalin's death – he is a very sick man – we will break the Soviet Union. Then there will begin the dawn of the German rule of the earth.

The little States cannot scare me. After Kemal's death Turkey is governed by 'cretins' and half idiots. Carol of Rumania is through and through the corrupt slave of his sexual instincts. The King of Belgium and the Nordic kings are soft jumping jacks who are dependent upon the good digestions of their over-eating and tired peoples.

We shall have to take into the bargain the defection of Japan. I gave Japan a full year's time. The Emperor is a counterpart to the last Tsar – weak, cowardly, undecided. May he become a victim of the revolution. My going together with Japan never was popular. We shall continue to create disturbances in the Far East and in Arabia. Let us think as 'gentlemen' and let us see in these peoples at best lacquered half maniacs who are anxious to experience the whip.

The opportunity is as favourable as never before. I have but one worry, namely that Chamberlain or some other such pig of a fellow ('Saukerl') will come at the last moment with proposals or with ratting ('Umfall'). He will fly down the stairs, even if I shall personally have to trample on his belly in the eyes of the photographers.

No, it is too late for this. The attack upon and the destruction of Poland begins Saturday, [26 August,] early. I shall let a few companies in Polish uniform attack in Upper Silesia or in the Protectorate. Whether the world believes it is quite indifferent ('Scheissegal'). The world believes only in success.

For you, gentlemen, fame and honour are beginning as they have not since centuries. Be hard, be without mercy, act more quickly and brutally than the others. The citizens of western Europe must tremble with horror. That is the most humane way of conducting a war. For it scares the others off.

The new method of conducting war corresponds to the new drawing of the frontiers. A war extending from Reval, Lublin, Kaschau to the mouth of the Danube. The rest will be given to the Russians. Ribbentrop has orders to make every offer and to accept every demand. In the west I reserve to myself the right to determine the strategically best line. Here one will be able to work with Protectorate regions, such as Holland, Belgium and French Lorraine.

And now, on to the enemy, in Warsaw we will celebrate our reunion.

The speech was received with enthusiasm. Goering jumped on a table, thanked bloodthirstily and made bloodthirsty promises. He danced like a wild man. The few that had misgivings remained quiet.

78. France examines her alliance obligations to Poland, 23 August 1939

From Les Evènements survenus en France de 1933 à 1945: Rapport, vol. II (Paris, Imprimerie Nationale, n.d.), pp. 276–8. Minutes of meeting held at the Ministry of War, 23 August 1939.

MINUTES

of the meeting held at the War Ministry, 23 August 1939, at 6 p.m., under the chairmanship of M. Edouard Daladier.

. . . President Daladier explained that they had to reply to 3 precise questions:

1 Could France remain passive whilst Poland and Rumania, or one of these two powers, disappeared from the map of Europe?
2 What resources had she to prevent this?
3 What measures should now be taken?

First question – Disappearance of Poland and Rumania.

M. Georges Bonnet explained that:

... Considering the situation was it better to be loyal to our commitments and go to war at once, or reconsider our position and profit from the respite obtained by increasing our military power, it being understood, that France ran the risk of being attacked in her turn after a delay of perhaps only a few months.

The reply to the question asked was essentially of a military nature. General Gamelin and Admiral Darlan pointed out that it would be valuable to secure Italy's complete neutrality.

M. Georges Bonnet replied that something might be attempted in this sense.

General Gamelin, questioned on the duration of Polish and Rumanian resistance, explained that he expected Poland to offer an honourable resistance which would prevent the bulk of German forces from turning against us before next spring; by that time England would be at our side. ...

In the course of several exchanges of opinion it was observed that even if we would be stronger in a few months Germany would also be much more so because she would dispose of Polish and Rumanian resources. Consequently France had no choice: *the only solution possible was to keep our engagements towards Poland, engagements moreover which preceded the opening of negotiations with the USSR.*

Second question – State of our resources.

M. Guy la Chambre outlined the state of the air force. ... From the point of view of fighters, we now had modern machines in mass production. ... Our bombers were not yet in mass production, we had to wait for the beginning of 1940. ... In spite of what we knew of German strength ... the state of our air force need no longer weigh on the government's decisions as it had done in 1938. ...

79. Mussolini decides on neutrality and proposes a conference, 31 August 1939

From Malcolm Muggeridge (ed.), Ciano's Diary, 1939–1943, foreword by Sumner Welles (London, Heinemann, 1947), pp. 136–41.

AUGUST 27, 1939. Halifax [British foreign secretary] has informed me [Count Galeazzo Ciano, Italian foreign minister], in a very courteous tone, that the precautionary measures taken in the Mediterranean must not be interpreted as a prelude to hostilities against us. I answer in an equally courteous tone: I am very much interested in keeping in contact with London.

Hitler's answer: He seems still determined to go to war and asks us for three things: not to make known our decision to be neutral until it is absolutely necessary, to continue our military preparations in order to impress the French and British, to send agricultural and industrial workers to Germany. The *Duce* answers that he agrees to do all this and promises a reconsideration of our position after the first phase of the conflict. But when will this first phase end?

This morning he seemed satisfied with his decision 'to stand looking out of the window'. Meanwhile a singular incident takes place. The English communicate to us the text of the German proposals to London, about which there is a great to do but about which *we are entirely in the dark*. Hitler proposes to the English an alliance or something like that. And this was naturally without our knowledge. I was indignant and said so. The *Duce* is indignant too, but does not show it. . . .

In his judgement [*Duce*] the matter of the secret agreement with London is damaging to the Germans. He says that Hitler is acting in this fashion for fear that intervention on the part of the *Duce* will settle the crisis at the last moment, as was done last year at Munich. . . .

For me there is a simpler explanation, namely that the Germans are treacherous and deceitful. Any kind of alliance with them becomes a bad alliance in a little while. . . .

AUGUST 31, 1939 . . . I see the *Duce* again. As a last resort, let us propose to France and Great Britain a conference for September 5, for the purpose of reviewing those clauses of the Treaty of Versailles which disturb Europe. I warmly support the proposal, if for no other reason than because it will widen the distance between us and Hitler, who wants no conferences and has said so many times. François-Poncet [French ambassador] welcomes the proposal with satisfaction but with some scepticism. Percy Lorraine [British ambassador] welcomes it with enthusiasm. Halifax receives it favourably, reserving the right to submit it to Chamberlain. . . .

80. Daladier's reaction to Mussolini's conference proposal, 31 August 1939

From Archives Edouard Daladier (Fondation Nationale des Sciences Politiques, Paris), 2DA 7/Dr.5 Daladier's manuscript notes, 31 August 1939.

To say 'yes' – it's an immediate demoralisation for France. . . .
         – it's the loss of the best trumps of our game: namely our military and moral force.

- we would lose face, for after having said and repeated that the German–Polish conflict should be settled first, we would make a complete *volte face*.
- at the conference we would be asked to accept the dismemberment of Poland and to make concessions to Italy. If we say no we would probably have lost the trump of our moral strength. If we say 'yes': it's the end of our influence in Europe, our moral collapse in the United States without speaking of internal difficulties.

To say 'no' – it's a serious risk of war
         – it's perhaps the resignation of ministers
         – it's perhaps the unleashing of a strong pacifist campaign in France

Solution proposed: don't close all doors: take advantage of the fact that Germany and Poland now accept direct contact and especially that Germany has repeated in its reply to England that the absence of a German–Polish settlement prevents a general settlement.

81. Britain and France disagree on the timing of their ultimatums to Germany, 2 September 1939

From Documents on British Foreign Policy, 1919–1939, *ed. E. L. Woodward and Rohan Butler, 3rd series, vol. VII (London, HMSO, 1954), nos 740, 741. Memoranda of telephone conversations.*

FOREIGN OFFICE, *September 2, 1939, 9.50 p.m.*
The Prime Minister informed M. Daladier that he had received the views of his Government regarding certain questions of procedure, but the situation here was very grave. There had been an angry scene in the House of Commons after he had made his statement in which he had said that we were consulting with the French Government on the question of the time-limit to be allowed to Germany. His colleagues in the Cabinet were also disturbed because at the Cabinet meeting in the afternoon it had been decided that the time-limit was to expire at midnight tonight. But in the absence of French concurrence it had been impossible for him to say that in the House. If the French Government were to insist on a time-limit of forty-eight hours to run from midday tomorrow, it would be impossible for the Government to hold the situation here. The Prime Minister said that he quite realised that it was France who must bear the burden of the German attack, but he was convinced that the situation here was such that some step must be taken this evening. He proposed as

a compromise that we should announce that the Ambassadors had been instructed to present the ultimatum at 8 a.m. tomorrow morning and that if the German Government had not given the required assurance by midday tomorrow we should consider ourselves to be in a state of war as from that hour.

M. Daladier said that the French Cabinet had met after the meeting of the Chamber. They had received during the day from Count Ciano a message in terms similar to those which he understood Count Ciano had addressed to Lord Halifax. In this message Count Ciano had proposed a five-Power conference as a last attempt to maintain the peace. The French Government had said that that could not be contemplated unless Germany first evacuated occupied territory and restored the situation to what it had been before hostilities had been begun. Count Ciano had observed that there was still a hope of German agreement if we could put off our *démarche* until midday tomorrow, and the French Cabinet had endorsed this view. If between now and midday tomorrow the German Government gave a refusal, it would then be possible to address an ultimatum to the German Government. In that case, unless the British bombers were ready to act at once, it would be better for France to delay, if possible, for some hours attacks on the French armies. At this point M. Daladier said that he could not say anything more definite on the telephone. It was agreed to resume the conversation in about a quarter of an hour.

FOREIGN OFFICE, *September 2, 1939, 10.30 p.m.*

The Secretary of State said that he was now in a position to inform M. Bonnet of the position of His Majesty's Government. They had decided that it was essential to make some announcement this evening owing to the difficult position which had arisen in the House of Commons. In that announcement it would be necessary to insert some definite hour after which, if Germany had not given the necessary assurances, we should be in a state of war. That was the first point.

As regards the second point – the time-limit which should be inserted in the ultimatum – the proposal of His Majesty's Government was that the Ambassadors should call upon the Minister for Foreign Affairs at 8 a.m. and inform him that if he could not give a satisfactory reply by midday then after that hour we should be free to take action to fulfil our obligations to Poland.

In view of what M. Daladier had said, it appeared that there would be great difficulty in reaching agreement with the French Government on this time-table. If that were so, what His Majesty's Government would propose would be that they should be free to act on this time-table, that is to say, send separate instructions to His Majesty's Ambassador to act without his French colleague, provided the French Government would give an assurance that they would follow suit within twenty-four hours.

M. Bonnet said it would be far preferable that the two Ambassadors should make a joint *démarche* together, and he again asked whether it would not be possible to wait until midday tomorrow.

The Secretary of State repeated that it seemed very doubtful whether the Government could hold the position here. For his part he did not see any very grave objection to our acting at 8 a.m. and the French Government at midday. In any case it was impossible for His Majesty's Government to wait until the latter hour.

Appendix: The Relative Strengths of the European Powers

Table 1   Land forces (strengths, expressed in divisions, are war strengths)

	January 1938	August 1939
Germany	81[1]	120–30
Italy	73	73
France	63	86
Great Britain	2	4[2]
USSR	125	125
Czechoslovakia	34	—
Poland	40	40

Notes: [1] This figure included twenty-four *Landwehr* divisions which were not fully trained or equipped.
[2] Maximum force immediately available for service overseas.
Sources: Committee of Imperial Defence, 'A comparison of the strength of Great Britain with that of certain other nations as at January 1938', Cabinet Papers (Public Record Office, London), CAB 24/273; *Documents on British Foreign Policy, 1919–1939*, ed. E. L. Woodward and Rohan Butler, 3rd series, vol. VI (London, HMSO, 1953), app. V; General M. G. Gamelin.
Servir, vol. II: *Le Prologue du drame (1930–1939)* (Paris, Plon, 1946), p. 351.

Table 2   Air strengths (for Great Britain, France and Italy metropolitan strengths only are given)

	January 1938	August 1939
Germany	1,820	4,210
Italy	1,301	1,531
France	1,195	1,234
Great Britain	1,053	1,750
USSR	3,050	3,361
Czechoslovakia	600	—
Poland	500	500

Sources: Committee of Imperial Defence, 'A comparison of the strength of Great Britain with that of certain other nations as at January 1938', Cabinet Papers (Public Record Office, London), CAB 24/273; *Documents on British Foreign Policy, 1919–1939*, ed. E. L. Woodward and Rohan Butler, 3rd series, vol. VI (London, HMSO, 1953), app. V; League of Nations, *Armament Year Books*.

Table 3   German air strength, 1934–9

	I	Contemporary British estimates of total Luftwaffe first-line strength			II	Present-day (1973) estimates of actual total production for the Luftwaffe	
July	1934	550	C.I.D.1151B			1934	840
June	1936	920	plus 100% reserves C.I.D.1241B			1936	2,530
January	1937	1,230	C.I.D.1296B				
July	1937	1,548	D.P.(P) paper of 7th July 1937			1937	2,651
November	1937	1,950	'identified aircraft' A.I.Sitrep of 30th November 1937				
August	1938	2,650	A.I.Sitrep of 31st August 1938			1938	3,356
September	1939	4,320	plus 4,900 reserve Air Staff Minute of 20th September 1939			1939	4,783

Note: There was no agreed definition of what constituted first-line strength. Consequently, contemporary and present-day estimates are estimates only and no precise figures can be given. In 1934–6 German strength included converted civil aircraft and other types which, by British standards, were not first-line aircraft. Contrary to what is often asserted, contemporary British estimates did not attribute to the Luftwaffe far more aircraft than it possessed. In fact German strength was slightly underestimated.

Source: Stephen Roskill, *Hankey, Man of Secrets,* Vol. III, *1931–1963* (London, Collins, 1974), appendix B.

Table 4   Naval strengths of the leading powers, August 1939

	Capital ships	Aircraft carriers	Submarines
Germany	5	—	65
Italy	4	—	104
France	7	1	78
Great Britain	15	6	57
USSR	3	—	18
United States	15	5	87
Japan	9	5	60

Source: Jane's Fighting Ships (London, 1939).

A Note on Further Reading

Since this book is intended primarily for those with no French or German only works in English are listed.

The foundation of any study of international history in this period lies in the official collections of documents:

Documents on British Foreign Policy, 1919–1939 (continuing) (1946–   )
Documents diplomatiques français, 1932–1939 (continuing) (1963–   )
Documents on German Foreign Policy, 1918–1945 (1948–   )
Foreign Relations of the United States: Diplomatic Papers (1943–   )
New Documents on the History of Munich (Prague, 1958)
Soviet Peace Efforts on the Eve of World War II: Documents and Records (Moscow, 1973).

Another source of great importance is the private papers, speeches and memoirs of the politicians, diplomats and military leaders:

Britain: L. S. Amery, *My Political Life*, Vol. II (London, 1955); F.T.A. Ashton-Gwatkin, *The British Foreign Office* (London, 1949); The Earl of Avon, *Facing the Dictators* (London, 1962) and *The Reckoning* (London, 1965); Brian Bond (ed.), *Chief of Staff: The Diaries of Lieutenant-General Sir Henry Pownall*, Vol. I, *1933–1940* (London, 1972); Lord Butler, *The Art of the Possible* (London, 1971); Neville Chamberlain, *In Search of Peace* (London, 1939); Winston S. Churchill, *The Gathering Storm* (London, 1948); Hugh Dalton, *The Fateful Years* (London, 1957); David Dilks (ed.), *The Diaries of Sir Alexander Cadogan, 1938–1945* (London, 1971); Lord Gladwyn, *The Memoirs of Lord Gladwyn* (London, 1972); The Earl of Halifax, *Speeches on Foreign Policy* (London, 1940) and *Fulness of Days* (London, 1957); John Harvey (ed.), *The Diplomatic Diaries of Oliver Harvey, 1937–1940* (London, 1970); N. Henderson, *Failure of a Mission* (London, 1940); Lord Ismay, *The Memoirs of General the Lord Ismay* (London, 1960); Robert Rhodes James (ed.), *The Diaries of Sir Henry Channon* (London, 1967); Thomas Jones, *A Diary with Letters, 1931–1950* (London, 1954); Ivone Kirkpatrick, *The Inner Circle: Memoirs* (London, 1959); R. Macleod and D. Kelly (eds), *The Ironside Diaries, 1937–1940* (London, 1962); R. J. Minney (ed.), *The Private Papers of Hore-Belisha* (London, 1960); Nigel Nicolson (ed.), *Harold Nicolson: Diaries and Letters, 1930–1939* (London, 1966); Viscount Norwich (A. Duff Cooper), *Old Men Forget* (London, 1954); John Slessor, *The Central Blue: The Autobiography of Sir John Slessor, Marshal of the RAF* (London, 1956); Lord Strang, *The Foreign Office* (London, 1955) and *Home and Abroad* (London, 1956); Viscount Templewood (Sir Samuel Hoare), *Nine Troubled Years* (London, 1954); Lord Vansittart, *The Mist Procession* (London, 1958).

Czechoslovakia: Edward Benes, *From Munich to New War and New Victory* (London, 1954).

France: General André Beauffre, *1940: The Fall of France* (London, 1967);

Georges Bonnet, *Quai d'Orsay* (Isle of Man, 1965); Paul Reynaud, *In the Thick of the Fight* (London, 1955).

Germany: Norman H. Baynes, *The Speeches of Adolf Hitler*, 2 vols (London, 1942); B. Dahlerus, *The Last Attempt* (London, 1947); H. von Dirksen, *Moscow, Tokyo, London* (London, 1952); U. von Hassell, *The Von Hassell Diaries, 1938–44* (London, 1948); F. von Papen, *Memoirs* (London, 1952); Joachim von Ribbentrop, *Memoirs* (London, 1954); Hjalmar Schacht, *Account Settled* (London, 1949) and *My First Seventy-Six Years* (London, 1955); Paul Schmidt, *Hitler's Interpreter* (London, 1951); Albert Speer, *Inside the Third Reich* (London, 1970) and *Spandau: The Secret Diaries* (London, 1976); F. von Weizsäcker, *Memoirs* (London, 1951).

Italy: Malcolm Muggeridge (ed.), *Ciano's Diary, 1937–38* (London, 1952) and *Ciano's Diary, 1939–43* (London, 1947) and *Ciano's Diplomatic Papers* (London, 1948).

Japan: Nobutaka Ike, *Japan's Decision for War: Records of the 1941 Policy Conferences* (Stanford, Calif., 1967); Joyce C. Lebra (ed.), *Japan's Greater East Asia Co-Prosperity Sphere in World War II* (London, 1975); Ian Nish, *Japanese Foreign Policy, 1869–1942* (London, 1977). In the absence of English translations of private papers and memoirs the documents published in Lebra and Nish are invaluable.

Poland: Jozef Beck, *Final Report* (New York, 1957); Waclaw Jedrzejewicz (ed.), *Diplomat in Berlin, 1933–1939: Papers and Memoirs of Jozef Lipski* (New York, 1968); Waclaw Jedrzejewicz (ed.), *Diplomat in Paris, 1936–1939: Papers and Memoirs of Juliusz Lukasiewicz* (New York, 1970).

Romania: Grigore Gafencu, *The Last Days of Europe* (London, 1947).

Soviet Union: Maxim Litvinov, *Notes for a Journal* (London, 1955); Ivan Maisky, *Who Helped Hitler?* (London, 1964).

United States: John M. Blum (ed.), *From the Morgenthau Diaries*, 2 vols, *Years of Crisis, 1928–1938* (Boston, Mass., 1959) and *Years of Urgency, 1938–1941* (Boston, Mass., 1965); Charles E. Bohlen, *Witness to History, 1929–1969* (London, 1973); Orville H. Bullitt (ed.), *For the President: Personal and Secret: Correspondence between Franklin D. Roosevelt and William C. Bullitt* (London, 1973); Cordell Hull, *The Memoirs of Cordell Hull* (London, 1948); Harold L. Ickes, *The Secret Diary of Harold L. Ickes*, Vol. 2, *The Inside Struggle, 1936–1939* (London, 1955); Nancy Harvison Hooker (ed.), *The Moffat Papers: Selections from the Diplomatic Journals of Jay Pierrepont Moffat* (Cambridge, Mass., 1956); Edgar B. Nixon (ed.), *Franklin D. Roosevelt and Foreign Affairs*, 3 vols (London, 1969); George F. Kennan, *Memoirs*, Vol. 1 (London, 1968); Sumner Welles, *The Time for Decision* (New York, 1944).

For useful selections from public and private papers, see Martin Gilbert, *Britain and Germany between the Wars* (reprint, London, 1976); Ruth B. Henig (ed.), *The League of Nations* (Edinburgh, 1973); J. Noakes and G. Pridham (eds), *Documents on Nazism, 1919–1945* (London, 1974); Joachim Remak, *The Origins of the Second World War* (New Jersey, 1976).

The best general introductions to the subject are R. A. C. Parker, *Europe, 1919–1945* (London, 1969); A. J. P. Taylor, *The Origins of the Second World War* (2nd edn, London, 1963). For detailed discussion of the issues and assessments of the continuing debate, see Keith Eubank, *The Origins of World War II* (New

York, 1969); Joachim Remak, *The Origins of the Second World War* (New Jersey, 1976); Esmonde M. Robertson (ed.), *The Origins of the Second World War: Historical Interpretations* (London, 1971); William R. Rock, *British Appeasement in the 1930s* (London, 1977); and the contribution by D. C. Watt in A. Sked (ed.), *Crisis and Controversy: Essays in Honour of A. J. P. Taylor* (London, 1976).

For the 1920s background, see Sally Marks, *The Illusion of Peace: International Relations in Europe, 1918-1933* (London, 1976); Anne Orde, *Great Britain and International Security, 1920-1926* (London, 1978).

For the international crises of the 1930s, see Christopher Thorne, *The Limits of Foreign Policy: The West, the League and the Far Eastern Crisis of 1931-1933* (London, 1972); Frank Hardie, *The Abyssinian Crisis* (London, 1974); Arthur Marder, 'The Royal Navy and the Ethiopian crisis of 1935-36', *American Historical Review*, Vol. 75 (1970), pp.1327-56; R. A. C. Parker, 'Great Britain, France and the Ethiopian crisis, 1935-36', *English Historical Review*, Vol. 89 (1974), pp. 293-332; James Thomas Emmerson, *The Rhineland Crisis, 7 March 1936* (London, 1977); Dante Puzzo, *Spain and the Great Powers, 1936-1941* (London, 1962); John F. Coverdale, *Italian Intervention in the Spanish Civil War* (Princeton, N. J., 1976); Glen T. Harper, *German Economic Policy in Spain* (The Hague, 1967); J. W. Bruegel, *Czechoslovakia before Munich* (London, 1973); Keith Robbins, *Munich* (London, 1968); Roy Douglas, *In the Year of Munich* (London, 1977); Donald Lammers, 'From Whitehall after Munich: the Foreign Office and the future course of British policy', *Historical Journal*, Vol. 16, No. 4 (1973), pp. 831-56; Paul W. Schroeder, 'Munich and the British tradition', *Historical Journal*, Vol. 19, No. 1 (1976); Sidney Aster, *1939: The Making of the Second World War* (London, 1973); Walther Hofer, *War Premeditated* (London, 1955).

For Britain, see Sidney Aster, *Anthony Eden* (London, 1976); Correlli Barnett, *The Collapse of British Power* (London, 1972); The Earl of Birkenhead, *Halifax! The Life of Lord Halifax* (London, 1965); J. R. M. Butler, *Lord Lothian* (London, 1960); Maurice Cowling, *The Impact of Hitler: British Politics and British Policy, 1933-1940* (London, 1975); J. A. Cross, *Sir Samuel Hoare: A Political Biography* (London, 1977); Keith Feiling, *The Life of Neville Chamberlain* (London, 1946); Martin Gilbert, *The Roots of Appeasement* (London, 1966), *Sir Horace Rumbold* (London, 1973), *Winston S. Churchill*, Vol. 5 (London, 1977) (with companion volume of documents); Paul Hayes, *Modern British Foreign Policy: The Twentieth Century, 1880-1939* (London, 1978); David Marquand, *Ramsay MacDonald* (London, 1977); W. N. Medlicott, *British Foreign Policy since Versailles* (London, 1968); Keith Middlemas and A. J. L. Barnes, *Baldwin: A Biography* (London, 1969); Keith Middlemas, *Diplomacy of Illusion* (London, 1972); Simon Newman, *The British Guarantee to Poland* (London, 1976); Norman Rose, *Vansittart: Study of a Diplomat* (London, 1978); Stephen Roskill, *Hankey, Man of Secrets*, Vol. 3 (London, 1974); Neville Thompson, *The Anti-Appeasers: Conservative Opposition to Appeasement in the 1930s* (London, 1971).

For the Dominions, see Ritchie Ovendale, *'Appeasement' and the English Speaking World: Britain, the United States, the Dominions and the Policy of 'Appeasement', 1937-1939* (Cardiff, 1975).

For British policy and the Far East, see Bradford A. Lee, *Britain and and the Sino-Japanese War, 1937-1939: A Study in the Dilemma of British Decline* (London, 1973); W. Roger Louis, *British Strategy in the Far East, 1919-1939*

(London, 1971); Peter Lowe, *Great Britain and the Origins of the Pacific War* (London, 1977); Stephen E. Pelz, *Race to Pearl Harbor: The Failure of the Second London Naval Conference and the Onset of World War II* (Cambridge, Mass., 1974); Ann Trotter, *Britain and East Asia, 1933-1937* (London, 1975); Stephen Lyon Endicott, *Diplomacy and Enterprise: British China Policy 1933-1937* (Manchester, 1975).

For France, see Anthony Adamthwaite, *France and the Coming of the Second World War, 1936-1939* (London, 1977); Anthony T. Komjathy, *The Crises of France's East Central European Diplomacy, 1933-1938* (Columbia, N.Y., 1977); J. Néré, *The Foreign Policy of France from 1914 to 1945* (London, 1975); Neville Waites (ed.), *Troubled Neighbours: Franco-British Relations in the Twentieth Century* (London, 1971); Geoffrey Warner, *Pierre Laval and the Eclipse of France* (London, 1968); Robert J. Young, *In Command of France: French Foreign Policy and Military Planning, 1933-1940* (London, 1978)

For Germany, see Alan Bullock, *Hitler: A Study in Tyranny* (London, 1964); Rudolph Binion, *Hitler Among the Germans* (London, 1977); William Carr, *Arms, Autarky and Aggression: A Study in German Foreign Policy, 1933-1939* (London, 1972); Gordon A. Craig, *Germany, 1866-1945* (London, 1978); John Hiden, *Germany and Europe, 1919-1939* (London, 1977); Klaus Hildebrand, *The Foreign Policy of the Third Reich* (London, 1973); Andreas Hillgruber, 'England's place in Hitler's plans for world domination', *Journal of Contemporary History*, Vol. 9, No. 1 (1974), pp. 5-22; David Irving, *The War Path* (London, 1978); Meir Michaelis, 'World power status or world dominion?', *The Historical Journal*, Vol. 15, No. 2 (1972), pp. 331-60; Norman Rich, *Hitler's War Aims*, Vol. 1 *Ideology, the Nazi State, and the Course of German Expansion* (London, 1973); Ronald M. Smelser, *The Sudeten Problem, 1933-1938: 'Volkstumspolitik' and the Formulation of Nazi Foreign Policy* (Folkstone, 1975); J. P. Stern, *Hitler: The Führer and the People* (London, 1975); Robert G. L. Waite, *The Psychopathic God, Adolf Hitler* (London, 1977); Gerhard L. Weinberg, *The Foreign Policy of Hitler's Germany: Diplomatic Revolution in Europe, 1933-1936* (Chicago, Ill., 1970).

For Germany and the Soviet Union, see Walter Laquer, *Russia and Germany: A Century of Conflict* (London, 1965); D. C. Watt, 'The initiation of the negotiations leading to the Nazi-Soviet Pact: a historical problem', in C. Abramsky (ed.), *Essays in Honour of E. H. Carr* (London, 1974); Gerhard L. Weinberg, *Germany and the Soviet Union, 1939-1941* (Leiden, 1954).

For Germany, the United States of America and Japan, see James V. Compton, *The Swastika and the Eagle: Hitler, the United States and the Origins of World War II* (New York, 1967); J. M. Meskill, *The Hollow Alliance: Germany and Japan* (New York, 1966); E. L. Presseisen, *Germany and Japan: A Study in Totalitarian Diplomacy* (New York, 1969).

For Italy, see Ivone Kirkpatrick, *Mussolini: Study of a Demagogue* (London, 1964); C. J. Lowe and F. Marzari, *Italian Foreign Policy, 1870-1940* (London, 1975); Esmonde M. Robertson, *Mussolini as Empire-Builder: Europe and Africa, 1932-1936* (London, 1977); Denis Mack Smith, *Mussolini's Roman Empire* (London, 1976); Mario Toscano, *The Origins of the Pact of Steel*, 2nd edn (Baltimore, Md, 1967); Elizabeth Wiskemann, *The Rome-Berlin Axis* (London, 1966).

For Japan, see John Hunter Boyle, *China and Japan at War, 1937-1945*

(Stanford, Calif., 1972); R. J. C. Butow, *Tojo and the Coming of War* (Stanford, Calif., 1961); James William Morley (ed.), *Deterrent Diplomacy: Japan, Germany and the USSR, 1935-1940* (New York, 1976); Ian Nish, *Japanese Foreign Policy, 1869-1942* (London, 1977).

For Poland, see Anna M. Cienciala, *Poland and the Western Powers, 1938-39* (London, 1968)

For the Soviet Union, see Ronald Hingley, *Joseph Stalin: Man and Legend* (London, 1974); John Erikson, *The Soviet High Command, 1918-1941* (London, 1962); B. N. Ponomaryov, A. A. Gromyko and V. M. Kovostov (eds), *History of the Foreign Policy of the USSR*, Vol. 1, *1917-1945* (Moscow, 1966); Adam B. Ulam, *Stalin: The Man and His Era* (London, 1974).

For the United States of America, see Dorothy Borg and Shumpei Okamoto (eds), *Pearl Harbor as History: Japanese-American Relations, 1931-1941* (New York, 1974); James M. Burns, *Roosevelt, the Lion and the Fox* (New York, 1956); Richard Dean Burns and Edward W. Bennett (eds), *Diplomats in Crisis: United States-Chinese-Japanese Relations, 1919-1941* (London, 1974); William L. Langer and S. Everett Gleason, *The Challenge to Isolation, 1937-1940* (New York, 1952); Joseph P. Lash, *Roosevelt and Churchill* (London, 1977); Arnold A. Offner, *The Origins of the Second World War: American Foreign Policy and World Politics, 1917-1941* (New York, 1975); John E. Wiltz, *From Isolation to War* (London, 1968).

For defence policy, see J. R. M. Butler (ed.), *Grand Strategy*, History of the Second World War: United Kingdom Military Series, Vol. 1, *Rearmament Policy* by N. H. Gibbs (London, HMSO, 1976); Peter J. Dennis, *Decision by Default: Peacetime Conscription and British Defence, 1919-1939* (London, 1972); Harold C. Deutsch, *Hitler and His Generals: The Hidden Crisis, January-June 1938* (Minneapolis, 1974); Edward L. Homze, *Arming the Luftwaffe: The Reich Air Ministry and the German Aircraft Industry, 1919-1939* (London, 1976); David Irving, *The Rise and Fall of the Luftwaffe: The Life of Luftwaffe Marshal Erhard Milch* (London, 1973); Michael Howard, *The Continental Commitment: The Dilemma of British Defence Policy in the Era of Two World Wars* (London, 1972); H. Montgomery Hyde, *British Air Policy between the Wars, 1918-1939* (London, 1976); Robert J. O'Neill, *The German Army and the Nazi Party, 1933-1939* (London, 1966); Esmonde M. Robertson, *Hitler's Pre-War Policy and Military Plans, 1933-1939* (London, 1963); Stephen Roskill, *Naval Policy between the Wars* Vol. 2 (London, 1976); D. C. Watt, *Too Serious a Business: European Armed Forces and the Approach to the Second World War* (London, 1975).

For rearmament, the economy and war origins, see Berenice A. Carroll, *Design for Total War: Arms and Economics in the Third Reich* (The Hague, 1968); F. Coghlan, 'Armaments, economic policy and appeasement', *History*, Vol. 57 (1972), pp. 205-16; J. P. D. Dunbabin, 'British rearmament in the 1930s: a chronology and review', *The Historical Journal*, Vol. 18, No. 3 (1975), pp.587-609; B. H. Klein, *Germany's Economic Preparations for War* (Cambridge, Mass., 1959); C. A. MacDonald, 'Economic appeasement and the German "Moderates", 1937-1939: An introductory essay', *Past and Present*, Vol. 56 (1972), pp.105-35; Alan S. Milward, *History of the World Economy in the Twentieth Century*, Vol. 5, *War, Economy and Society, 1939-1945* (London, 1977); R. A. C. Parker, 'Economics, rearmament and foreign policy: the United Kingdom before 1939 –

a preliminary survey', *Journal of Contemporary History*, Vol. 10, No. 4 (1975), pp. 637–48; Robert Paul Shay, *British Rearmament in the Thirties: Politics and Profits* (London, 1977). T. W. Mason, 'Some origins of the Second World War,' in E. M. Robertson (ed.), *The Origins of the Second World War* (London, 1971).

For economic issues generally, see B. W. E. Alford, *Depression and Recovery? British Economic Growth, 1918–1939* (London, 1972); Carol M. Cipolla (ed.), *The Fontana Economic History of Europe*, Vol. 6, *Contemporary Economies*, 2 parts (London, 1977); Ian M. Drummond, *British Economic Policy and the Empire, 1919–1939* (London, 1972); T. Kemp, *The French Economy, 1913–1939* (London, 1972); Charles P. Kindleberger, *History of the World Economy in the Twentieth Century*, Vol. 4, *The World in Depression, 1929–1939* (London, 1973); H. W. Richardson, *Economic Recovery in Britain, 1932–9* (London, 1967); Alice Teichova, *An Economic Background to Munich* (London, 1974).

For the role of Intelligence, see Paul W. Blackstock, *The Secret Road to World War II: Soviet versus Western Intelligence, 1921–1939* (Chicago, Ill., 1969); F. W. Deakin and G. A. Storry, *The Case of Richard Sorge* (London, 1966); David Dilks, 'A question of intelligence', *The Listener*, 12 October 1978, pp.464–5; David Irving, *Breach of Security* (London, 1968); David Kahn, *The Code Breakers* (London, 1967); Ronald Lewin, *Ultra Goes to War* (London, 1978); František Moravec, *Master of Spies: The Memoirs of General František Moravec* (London, 1975); Kenneth Strong, *Intelligence at the Top* (London, 1969); Barton Whaley, *Codeword 'Barbarossa'* (Cambridge, Mass., 1973); Roberta Wohlstetter, *Pearl Harbor: Warning and Decision* (Stanford, Calif., 1962).

For public opinion and the media, see D. Ayerst, *Guardian: Biography of a Newspaper* (London, 1971); D. G. Boyce, 'Public opinion and historians', *History*, Vol. 63, No. 208 (1978), pp. 214–28; Asa Briggs, *The History of Broadcasting in the United Kingdom*, Vol. 3, *The War of Words* (London, 1970); Ernest K. Bramsted, *Goebbels and National Socialist Propaganda, 1925–45* (East Lancing, Mich., 1965); Franklin Reid Gannon, *The British Press and Germany, 1936–1939* (London, 1971); Tom Harrisson and Charles Madge, *Britain by Mass Observation* (London 1939); *The History of The Times*, Vol. 4 (London, 1952); Nicholas Pronay, 'British newsreels in the 1930s', Part 1 *History*, Vol. 56 (1971), pp. 411–18, and Part 2, *History*, Vol. 57 (1972), pp. 63–72; Jerry Kuehl, 'Film as evidence – a review', *History Workshop*, Vol. 2 (1976), pp.135–9; Daniel Waley, *British Public Opinion and the Abyssinian War, 1935–6* (London, 1975); K. W. Watkins, *Britain Divided: The Effect of the Spanish Civil War on British Political Opinion* (Edinburgh, 1963); John Evelyn Wrench, *Geoffrey Dawson and Our Times* (London, 1955).

For the diplomats and the League of Nations, in addition to the memoirs and private papers already cited see Gordon A. Craig and Felix Gilbert (eds), *The Diplomats, 1919–1939* (reprint, London, 1968); Paul Seabury, *The Wilhelmstrasse: A Study of German Diplomats under the Nazi Regime* (Berkeley, Calif., 1954); Gordon Waterfield, *Professional Diplomat: Sir Percy Lorraine* (London, 1973); Ruth B. Henig (ed.), *The League of Nations* (Edinburgh, 1973); F. Walters, *A History of the League of Nations* (London, 1952); J. Barros, *Betrayal from Within* (London, 1969): P. Raffo, *The League of Nations* (London, Historical Association, 1974).

For collections of articles and extracts from writers, see Hans W. Gatzke (ed.), *European Diplomacy between Two Wars, 1919–1939* (Chicago, Ill., 1972);

Esmonde M. Robertson (ed.), *The Origins of the Second World War: Historical Interpretations* (London, 1971); W. Roger Louis (ed.), *The Origins of the Second World War: A. J. P. Taylor and His Critics* (New York, 1972); John L. Snell, *The Origins of the Second World War: Design or Blunder?* (Boston, Mass., 1962).

An indispensable work of reference is J. A. S. Grenville, *The Major International Treaties, 1914–1973: A History and Guide with Texts* (London, 1974).

INDEX